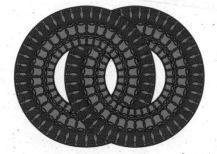

Letters from a Distant Shore

Letters from a Distant Shore

Marie Lawson Fiala

CavanKerry ◊ Press LTD.

CavanKerry Press Ltd.
Fort Lee, New Jersey
www.cavankerrypress.org

Library of Congress Cataloging-in-Publication Data

Fiala, Marie Lawson.
Letters from a distant shore / Marie Lawson Fiala. -- 1st ed.
p. cm.
ISBN-13: 978-1-933880-19-8 (alk. paper)
ISBN-10: 1-933880-19-8
1. Lawson, Jeremy--Health. 2. > Brain--Hemorrhage--Patients--
California--Biography. 3. Mothers and > sons--California--Biography.
I. Lawson, Jeremy.
II. Title.

RC394.H37F53 2010
362.197'4810440092 B--dc22
2010002045

Cover art Nancy Stahl © 2010

First Edition 2010, Printed in the United States of America

Letters from a Distant Shore is the seventh title of CavanKerry's Literature of Illness imprint. LaurelBooks are fine collections of poetry and prose that explore the many poignant issues associated with confronting serious physical and/or psychological illness.

CavanKerry is grateful to the Arnold P.Gold Foundation for the Advancement of Humanism in Medicine for joining us in sponsoring this imprint. Offering LaurelBooks as teaching tools to medical schools is the result of shared concerns--humanism, community, and meeting the needs of the underserved. Together with the Gold Foundation, CavanKerry's two outreach efforts, GiftBooks and Presenting Poetry & Prose, bring complimentary books and readings to the medical community at major hospitals across the United States.

CavanKerry Press is grateful for the support it receives from the New Jersey State Council on the Arts.

Forth may we go to tell all realms thy grace:

Inspired of thee, may we count all but loss,

and stand at last with joy before thy face.

Hymn

from *Toulon, Pseaumes octante trois de David* (1551)

Introduction

THE MOST DIFFICULT LIFE EVENT for a mother is the catastrophic illness of her child. Fortunately, the occurrence is rare for this life changing event, but when one's own child is diagnosed with a potentially fatal illness, the diagnosis dynamically changes the lives of the parents, other children and extended family and friends. All possible strength and support is required for everyone to survive the tragedy.

This book is a remarkable chronicle over several years of such a life event. A mother, writing from her unique perspective, describes her powerless frustration over her child's ruptured but inaccessible artery (arteriovenous malformation or AVM) and consequent neurologic injury. The parents are offered numerous treatment options, many of which are themselves life threatening. They must make difficult choices for their comatose son, Jeremy.

Finally, with Jeremy clinging to life, family and friends seek a miracle and turn to an hour of prayer. Remarkably, this sentinel event marks a turning point for Jeremy, and he proceeds to a long and slow recovery. Rehabilitation and physical therapy grind along bringing additional stress to the entire family. After a year of therapy and clinical improvement, the parents make yet another life threatening decision to proceed with definitive therapy. They choose high dose radiosurgery in an academic center and accept these new struggles. Again, there is slow clinical improvement. After two years, Jeremy's AVM is obliterated and a reasonably normal life can proceed. The capacity of the family, siblings and friends to endure over this long stretch of time is amazing.

Most parents end such an ordeal with divorce; siblings usually develop chronic social issues; adults become dysfunctional. This book's outcome as seen through a mother's eyes is what providers, patients, families and mothers wish could be achieved for all.

—William Wara, M.D.
Chairman, Department of Radiation Oncology (Retired)
University of California, San Francisco Medical Center

Foreword

"NOTHING MARKS the last normal hours of your life as special," writes Marie Lawson Fiala in *Letters from a Distant Shore*. "You awaken one morning to the same mundane details as any other day…Without warning life pivots sharply, and you have left your last, inestimably precious, normal moment far behind."

On an ordinary day in Berkeley, California, a seemingly healthy 13-year-old boy suddenly collapses and loses consciousness, sending his family of five into a tailspin. The cause of Jeremy's coma is a massive cerebral hemorrhage caused by a rare congenital vascular defect. It is a nightmare scenario for any parent: the sense of the world splitting open, the sudden confrontation with the fact that all of one's education, one's preparedness, one's love, are powerless to save a beloved son from pain and suffering. One moment, Fiala's world involves her demanding work as an attorney, birthday parties, grocery shopping, bathing the children—the ordinary and hectic activities of an educated urban family, presided over by parents who have attempted, "through vigilance and determination," to "build secure lives" for their children.

But no amount of vigilance and determination could have prepared Fiala and husband Kristor for the terrible fact of their son's sudden battle with death. Combining beautifully nuanced descriptions with the matter-of-fact language of medicine and the raw energy of emails sent out to family members and friends throughout the harrowing ordeal, Fiala brings the fear and disorientation of this moment and its aftermath into stark relief, so that one almost feels one is there with her at Jeremy's bedside in the ICU as the priest administers Last Rites, and later, as she washes her son's listless body, as he opens his eyes for the first time, sits up, and, finally, miraculously, speaks.

Letters from a Distant Shore is a memoir about parenthood, about the unbreakable bond between a mother and son, a bond that is tested and strengthened by the endless day-to-day challenges of caring for the sick. It is a deeply tender narrative, told with unflinching emotional honesty. It is also a memoir about community, urging us to believe that, in the most difficult times, we need not struggle alone. Above all, it is a memoir of faith, written in a time when faith is so often called into question.

In the last decade, we have seen our world torn asunder by misguided faith. Millions cite faith as an excuse for acts of terrorism, as a rationalization for war, as a mandate for the exclusion of others from basic civil rights. It is a challenging time indeed for matters of faith, and the very mention of the word "faith" is perhaps met today with more skepticism than ever before in American history.

I must admit to bringing my own skepticism to the table when I sat down to read this book. As the mother of a young boy, I was gripped from the outset by the story of a mother's struggle with her son's critical illness. But as a child of the Bible Belt, immersed at an early age in an atmosphere of religious intolerance, I was wary of the theological subtext. It is a testament to the power of Jeremy's story, as well as Fiala's gifts as a storyteller, that my skepticism soon dissolved—"like salt in a water glass," to borrow a simile from the author. I walked away from this memoir with a deeper respect for the power of faith to fortify and to heal. A boy lies in a hospital bed, bruised and speechless, perched precariously between life and death. His desperate parents put out a call for prayer, a call which is heard not only by their friends, family, and church members, but also by strangers around the globe. It is in the immediate aftermath of this prayer vigil that Jeremy suddenly, inexplicably speaks the words that his mother "will carry always: 'Ow, that hurts.'"

Three simple words, childish and mundane and miraculous, three words that mark the end of Jeremy's silence, the beginning of his journey home. This is by no means the end of Jeremy's struggle, but it is a moment that gives hope to the family, and, indeed, to the reader. It is impossible to read this memoir without acknowledging that there are simply some things which defy explanation, things beyond our limited powers of understanding. Herein lies the profound message of this book: hope and faith are not antiquated notions, out of step with the hectic, highly technical machinations of modern life. Hope and faith still matter.

—Michelle Richmond

To my children —

Jeremy Day, wounded angel, on whom
God's hand rests gently,

Annelise Marie, constant and radiant as
the northern star,

and David Gabriel, beloved warrior
and seeker of truth

Once

THREE SILVER-FRAMED PHOTOGRAPHS of my children are grouped on my office desk. Although the images are long outdated, I keep them as a reminder of a different time, a different life from the one I live now. The pictures are set in an old cloister—sepia limestone walls, walkways, balustrades, and steps, cracked, veined with gray. The air shimmers in the early morning light. David Gabriel sits on the paving in the rounded shape of a one-year-old, leaning on a tiny starfish hand, his bare feet and nubbin toes pink curves against the stone. He is an elfin child, hair brilliant platinum, thick and gently curling, his eyes almond-shaped and a startling celestial blue. Annelise Marie, four years old, brave despite her shyness, stands with hands clasped behind her back and one foot tucked behind the other, her hair the color of honey and thick cream, with rounded cheeks and cupid's-bow mouth like a Hummel angel. Her eyes are sea glass, one aquamarine, the other golden-green. And my firstborn, Jeremy Day, six, leans on his elbow on a stone wall. He looks straight and true into the camera. Jeremy is Tuesday's child, full of grace, with bright golden hair, long fine hands, and the promise of high cheekbones beneath translucent skin. His eyes reflect the morning sky in shades of blue and gray. The image captures his essential quality of stillness. Most children his age are photographed in arrested motion. Jeremy seems always to be watching, measuring, poised on the edge of discovery, and wonder.

1

Memory takes me back to that day, to my seat on a cold limestone step, to the trusting smiles, the bursts of laughter, the sound of feet racing up stairways and down corridors, the feeling of a small warm tired body settling on my lap. I was at peace. My children were well loved, and safe. Safety. The chimera I held in my hands, until it melted away between my fingers. Until one ordinary day, seven years later, when one of these children fell to the ground, broken beyond repair. One ordinary day, a day when I fell off the edge of the world.

In centuries past, mapmakers cautioned sailors against crossing into uncharted waters with the legend, "Heere ther be dragouns." I had no reason to think that the edge of the world might be so close, or that dragouns would menace my personal landscape.

My husband, Kristor Lawson, and I had built a comfortable and bounded life for ourselves and our family from inauspicious beginnings. I was an immigrant child of immigrants. Even at an early age I knew that existence was precarious. On his first day after disembarking in New York City, my father, a former Czech army officer who was fluent in five languages, apprenticed himself to a housepainter. He spent the remainder of his working life in the construction trades. The work was not always steady and, when he had a job, the pay was barely adequate to support a family of six. My mother cooked meatless meals, cut down secondhand clothing to fit her four daughters, and wept over the bills at the kitchen table. Money was scarce in our home, but kind words and affection were even scarcer. Children were neither seen nor heard, and children were better off not being seen or heard.

I resolved to make for myself a life different from the one I had grown up in. I was the first person in my family and the only student in my graduating class at a small, rural high school to go to college. I paid my way through Stanford University and Law School with merit scholarships and loans, supplemented by jobs as a fast-food worker, babysitter, store clerk, tutor, secretary, and technical writer, and then dedicated my energy, thought, and many late nights to becoming a partner in a major law firm.

Kris was a preacher's kid from a family with many books but modest means. He had been a professional outdoorsman when we met. I was a passenger on a whitewater rafting trip down the Colorado River through the Grand Canyon, and he was one of the guides. After five years of practicing law, my tightly ordered life had come to feel more empty than peaceful, and I was ready for change. I noticed Kris immediately. He was tall and muscular, with skin the color of teak, long, wavy blond hair, and a golden moustache. His eyes—which I later discovered were bright Nordic blue—were hidden behind black reflecting sunglasses. At the start of the trip I ventured an inane but friendly greeting, and got a curt, monosyllabic response. A brush-off. *What a jerk*, I thought. *Avoid that guy*.

Several days into the trip, I was surprised when he sat down on a rock next to me after dinner, and even more surprised when he asked me about my job as a lawyer, and how I had come to take this river trip. I answered. And he answered. And then we were talking, and finding that we had many things to talk about, from a common interest in neuroscience, which we both had studied as undergraduates, to our similar Catholic (mine) and Episcopalian (his) religious traditions. Eventually I discovered that behind the dark glasses he was just Kristor, who was quiet because he thought deeply about many things, and didn't speak until he was sure he had something meaningful to say. We kept talking for the rest of the trip, and by the time it was over I knew that I never wanted our conversation to end.

Kris had left the rivers and mountains for the city to be with me, and had been adrift in various unsatisfying jobs for years while he educated himself in finance. Eventually he started his own investment advisory firm with three partners; the firm had just turned the corner from scary start-up to success.

We had been married for fifteen years, and lived in a wooded hilly neighborhood in Berkeley, California, in the first home we had owned, a brown-shingled Craftsman house built during World War I. I believed that, through vigilance and determination, we could build secure lives for our children—lives carefully composed of homemade organic baby foods, sturdy car seats, untreated cotton clothing, lead-free painted toys, filtered water, sunscreen, Sesame Street, and small and caring independent schools—and so keep all dragouns from our shores. That illusion crumbled as our child faded into unconsciousness. The life I was living, the future I had imagined for our family, dissolved like salt in a water glass.

A new life took its place. A life of anguish and grace, fear and hope, faith and a few small miracles. A life in a lonely place at once distant, and around every corner.

A place I now call home.

Remembered Tragedy

There is some shape, form, design as of artistry in this universe we are entering that is composed of catastrophes and missing parts. . . . What if, by searching the earth and even the sky for those missing parts, we should find enough of them to see catastrophe change into the shape of remembered tragedy?

—Norman Maclean

NOTHING MARKS the last normal hours of your life as special, nothing that you look back on and say, "There, that was the turning point. If only I had paid attention, I would have known, I would have treasured those hours. If only . . ." You awaken one morning to the same mundane details as any other day: housework, grocery shopping, squabbling children, sticky hands and faces, small irritations, and small pleasures. Without warning life pivots sharply, and you have left your last, inestimably precious, normal moment far behind. Then you would give anything to have it back, but it is lost to you forever.

———

Labor Day weekend is an ambiguous holiday, a turning

point between seasons, the exuberant high notes of summer mingling with the sadder, deeper tones of fall. Warm light slanted through the kitchen windows that Saturday morning, illuminating the blue fruit bowl on the counter, filled with peaches. Amber globes flushed with rose, they glowed against the cold cobalt ceramic. A breeze lifted and stirred the white curtains over the sink. The sunlight still spoke of summer: deep red roses, a pitcher of lemonade on a garden table, and bees going about their work. But the outside air smelled of vineyards ready for harvest, dying leaves, short days and cold nights ahead. Autumn was whispering at the window.

I had made brunch, as I usually did on weekends—scrambled eggs, waffles, sliced strawberries—and set the kitchen table with blue-and-white dishes and fresh flowers from the yard in a terracotta pitcher. This was my favorite meal of the week, and with an extra day before going back to work, my mood was even lighter than usual on a Saturday morning. The day was full of possibilities as Kristor, the children, and I sat around the table eating, laughing, and making plans.

"Hey, guys, how about if we go for a swim later today? You can play 'Let's Get Dad' in the pool," Kris said, laughing, his eyes crinkling with pleasure at his own "dad humor." Kris has a big booming laugh, and loves playing the clown for his children's amusement.

"Yeah, let's *get* Dad," Jeremy said, punching Kris playfully in the shoulder. "And after that, can we have a barbeque and make burgers for dinner?" he asked.

Annelise added, "Yeah, and walk down to College Avenue and get ice cream cones! Can we, Mom?"

"That sounds great, but don't forget that David has a birthday party to go to, and I've got to do some office work. I'll drive him, Kris, if you can finish the dishes."

The doorbell rang. Jeremy had invited a friend over to visit. At thirteen, Jeremy was tall and broad-shouldered, with eyes like a winter sky, and downy golden cheeks. So far, his adolescence had been free of drama. He had a dignified, thoughtful disposition, a kind heart toward others, and an offbeat sense of humor that easily sparked into laughter. He had always done exceptionally well in school, but during the past year Kris and I had worried about his social life. Although he had a few deep friendships, he was not popular and was having trouble adapting to the cynical posturing that seemed normal for teenage boys, posturing for which he was both too young and too old. Too young, in that he was still naïve and sweet, and too old, in that he saw no need to be anyone other than himself. Jeremy and his visitor disappeared into the family room and a fantasy world on the computer screen.

Annelise (whom we also called Lisie), who was eleven, spread an art project out on the living room floor and busied herself with colored pencils, so engrossed that her nose nearly touched her drawing. She had turned out to be gifted artistically as well as a talented singer and actor, and had already set her mind to having a career on the stage. Given her fiercely determined nature and singular focus on whatever she essayed, I didn't doubt that she would succeed.

David, at eight years old, was our very bright and uncomplicated little boy, equally happy playing roughhouse games with his friends or poring over a book of Greek mythology. After brunch I drove him to the birthday party at his school playground, a vast stretch of unsheltered asphalt. While he and his friends waged a running squirt-gun battle and ate too much pizza and cake, I found a bench in a fringe of shade and sat down to work through a heavy briefcase of papers.

I was nearing the end of a three-month-long trial in which I represented one of the nation's largest banks. Billions of dollars were at stake, and I needed to prepare my closing argument. I represent large companies in high-stakes litigation. Often the client's future course or even its continued existence depends on the outcome of the case I'm handling. This can be heady stuff. And fun, in the same way that playing chess is fun—plotting tactics, planning strategy, working through various scenarios and possible outcomes.

There are few professional experiences that can match the intensity of trying a case. The workload is crushing: combing through thousands of documents to select trial exhibits; reading hundreds of pages of deposition testimony, looking for a few nuggets; writing and responding to briefs on evidentiary issues; getting your witnesses ready to testify; preparing cross-examination of the other side's witnesses when you're not sure what they're going to say until they take the stand; and on, and on. Everyone sleepless, red-eyed, burned out, bad-breathed, living on fast food, Diet Coke, and adrenaline; at attention in court all day and working late into the nights in conference rooms junked with stacks of papers, heaps of paper clips tangled with rubber bands, Post-Its, highlighters, document storage boxes, empty coffee cups, and fast-food containers. It is an exhilarating but exhausting ride, and I was very glad that this particular trial was nearly over so that I could return to a life more balanced in favor of my family.

Lord, it's hot. The air weighed against my skin like a heavy woolen blanket. The light was merciless; my head hurt and eyes ached from squinting at black squiggles on blindingly white paper.

Finally the birthday party was over and I collected my dirty little boy for the ride home. Once there, Annelise, the take-charge mother-in-training, volunteered to coach David through a shower in the second-floor master bathroom. "Now squirt some of the shampoo—that's the green stuff—on your head, Davey. Rub it in well. Keep your eyes closed! Now stick your head under the water . . . don't open your eyes! Mom, David got shampoo in his eyes . . . MOM!" I kept an eye on them while folding laundry in the bedroom.

Jeremy's friend had left, and he and Kris were downstairs, quiet.

I heard Kris's slow, heavy tread up the stairs. He stopped in the bedroom doorway, frowning slightly, and said, "I need to talk to you," motioning that I should step out into the hallway.

Now what? Exasperated, I expected to hear that we needed to make one more run to Office Max for school supplies or that Kris was once again having problems with our home computer. *Just what I need, another complication to get in the way of working on my trial argument.*

"There's something wrong with Jeremy; I think he may be having a stroke," Kris said quietly, in such an ordinary voice that I stared at him blankly for several seconds, unable to make sense of his words. "I think Jeremy is having a stroke," Kris repeated deliberately, my rational husband who always thought through all the implications before speaking.

The world roared, and shrank down to a black point like sand sucked through an hourglass.

Jeremy had called out to Kris from the kitchen a few moments earlier. He was losing control of his right side. Kris found him slumped heavily against the door jamb and helped him slide slowly, slowly, down onto the floor.

My heart lurched and accelerated. "Lisie, get David out of the shower and dried off, and STAY HERE," I rapped out and flew down the stairs, swiveled at the landing, leaped down more stairs, and skidded around the corner into the kitchen. "KRIS, CALL 911!" echoed off the stairwell in my wake. Jeremy was lying on his back on the bleached oak floor between the stove and the refrigerator. I fell to my knees next to him. His eyes, usually so luminous, were dark with terror. "Mom, what's wrong, I can't move my right side; what's wrong with me?" he asked, with a child's faith that I could take away his fear. "Help me," he pleaded, "please help me, please . . . please . . ." His words trailed off. And

I, despite my fierce and watchful mother love, my worldly competence, I could do nothing to save him.

———

Even as Kris called 911 and then our pediatrician, my mind refused to accept what was happening. Over the years of parenting, there had been many false alarms. A high fever turned out to be flu, not meningitis; a fall on the playground produced a bump on the head, not a concussion. *Surely there's got to be some other explanation; this can't be as bad as it seems.*

I hunched over Jeremy, stroking his hair with my left hand, gripping his hand tightly with my right, holding him with my eyes, and talking aloud nonstop: "Our Father, who art in heaven, I love you Jeremy, I love you, breathe, Jeremy, breathe, hallowed be thy name, keep breathing, thy kingdom come, I love you, I'm here, thy will be done, oh God, Jeremy keep breathing, breathe in, breathe out, on earth as it is in heaven, I'm here Jeremy, stay with me, breathe . . . breathe . . ."

Jeremy had lost all movement in the right half of his body. One eye was still blue, the other all pupil, a black window on the catastrophe happening in his brain. As he pleaded with me to help him, his speech slurred and slowed into unintelligibility. *He's slipping away; he might be dying.* I was not ready. *This cannot be happening.* There was no time to help him prepare to meet death. My boy. He slid toward unconsciousness too quickly, with fear as his last companion, leaving me behind.

Within minutes a fire truck pulled up, blocking the narrow street outside the kitchen windows, and the room filled with large men in hard boots and turnout gear, and with questions: A fall? Blow to the head? Drugs? I answered mechanically, faintly surprised at my ability to talk normally. My mind seemed to have fractured along horizontal fault lines. The high-level processor was still in charge, calm, rational, refusing to yield to hysteria. The child-mind beneath was curled under the bedclothes, hands over ears and eyes shut tight. At the deepest level, nightmare creatures slithered through subterranean waters, leaving dimly felt ripples in their wake.

With an oxygen mask strapped to his face, Jeremy no longer spoke but still struggled valiantly to lift his head from the floor, to rise above the darkness that engulfed him. An ambulance arrived and spilled more men into the crowded kitchen. The paramedics worked fast. They lifted him onto a gurney and carried him to the street. Somewhere between the door of the house and the sidewalk, his brain shutting down one sector at a time, Jeremy stopped breathing. The paramedics hoisted the gurney into the ambulance, leaving the back doors open, and bent over him.

Standing on the hot asphalt, I felt detached, as if watching a movie, while the paramedics threaded a tube down Jeremy's throat and connected him to a ventilator. "What is happening, what's wrong with him?" I asked. There had to be a reassuring explanation, some life raft to hold onto, if only I could think of the right questions to reach it.

"We need to get to the hospital quickly; the doctors will tell you what's going on," one of the young men answered in a brisk voice. "No, you can't stay with him; you have to ride up front." They clamped the gurney down as I climbed up next to the driver and gave directions to Children's Hospital of Oakland, the regional pediatric trauma center. Kris waited behind to call family members and find someone to stay with Annelise and David.

At the hospital Jeremy was wheeled through the emergency entrance directly into the trauma room, and a half-dozen members of the emergency response team descended on him. I stood outside the closed doors, suspended in a bubble of disbelief, questions churning in my head. *Is he dying? Will they let me see him while he is still alive?* I knew that a trauma team doesn't stop working until after the point of death, that quite likely the doors would open and they would call me in to see his body on a gurney, and I would not have had a chance to say good-bye.

A dark-haired woman appeared at my side and put her arm around me, tried to urge me down the hall. She was the hospital social worker, she said in a gentle voice, we should go somewhere quiet to talk. I shook her off. *What could you possibly say to help me?*

Kris arrived. I pointed wordlessly at the trauma room doors, which just then crashed open. Jeremy was wheeled at a run to the CT scan for imaging. We followed into the dark, chilly control room to watch through the glass as he was rolled into the scanner. Petra, our pediatrician, who had cared for Jeremy for most of his life, was suddenly there in a white summer frock, straight from a Labor Day party. She is a brilliant diagnostician and one of the calmest people I know. I looked at her, hoping for reassurance. Images of Jeremy's brain drowned in an ocean of blood scrolled across six computer screens in black-and-white. "This is very serious," Petra said, her smooth young face pale, her voice strained. "You should prepare yourselves. This is very serious."

———

Jeremy was almost unrecognizable when I finally saw him again late that evening. It had been hours since he entered surgery, hours when we waited to learn whether he would die while the surgeons took such rough measures as they could to save his life.

I was alone. Kris had just gone home see after Annelise and David. Every certainty that made up my life had been smashed to pieces and swept into a howling black whirlwind. There was no up, no down, no past, no future, only the searing present. My mind was a small frightened animal in a dark cage, keening in grief, running from side to side and flinging itself against the wires until it was torn and bleeding, but finding no escape. I paced the linoleum tiles like a labyrinth, praying for Jeremy's life and bargaining desperately with God. *Please, take me instead, let me take his place.* What I meant was, *Please don't let me be the one left behind* . . . My life without Jeremy would be a parched and barren landscape. A lifetime spent mourning my child was beyond my power to endure.

Finally, close to midnight, a cluster of nurses and orderlies appeared at the far end of the hall, pushing a gurney and IV stands and carrying equipment. Jeremy was a motionless form in their midst. He was wheeled into a darkened corner in the intensive care unit, trailing a parade of medical appliances behind him.

Surgeons don't stop to clean up as they operate. Jeremy's head was wrapped in bandages already saturated with blood seeping from holes that had been cut through his skull. The hair at the back of his head was a wet and matted dark red. Plastic tubes draining blood from deep in his brain sprouted from the bandages. His hospital gown and blankets were soaked with blood at the neck and groin, where the flesh above his femoral artery had been cut down for an arterial line. A breathing tube connected to a ventilator ran down his throat, a feeding tube down his nose. IV lines pierced both arms and one leg; a catheter drained urine. There was white tape everywhere—anchoring lines and tubes, attaching sensors to his torso, holding his eyes shut—more tape than skin. Two orderlies lifted him from the gurney and slid him onto the hospital bed, while the nurses connected the lines and tubes to medical equipment and monitors.

To see my child like this, flesh of my flesh, the tender body that I had cared for, so violently desecrated . . . for a moment I recoiled, a coward. I couldn't bear to look at him. Shuddering, I seized hold of myself. *This is no time for fear.* I couldn't leave whatever part of Jeremy was alive in this mutilated body alone.

I took a shaky step toward the bed, and then another, and another, until I was standing close, looking down at him. Hearing, vision, speech were gone, but touch remained. I cautiously reached through the tubes and wires to stroke his cheek with the backs of my fingers and cup my palm under his chin. He was warm. Under my hand his heart still beat. My son still lived.

Words (1)

Faith is one of the forces by which men live.

—William James

Without prayer, I should have been a lunatic long ago.

—Mahatma Gandhi

JEREMY HAD SUFFERED a massive cerebral hemorrhage when the choroidal artery deep in the left side of his brain spontaneously exploded. The hemorrhage was caused by a rare congenital vascular defect called an arteriovenous malformation, or AVM. An AVM is a tangle of abnormal blood vessels that are hybrids between true arteries and veins; it looks like a knot of spaghettini. These blood vessels are exceptionally fragile. The arteries that feed the malformation are swollen and thin-walled. The venous part of the malformation receives blood directly from the artery at a higher pressure than the veins were designed to handle. Over the lifetime of the patient, a rupture is almost certain, although a hemorrhage during childhood is uncommon.

When the artery connected to Jeremy's AVM burst, a torrent of blood flooded the ventricles, which are the open chambers in the center of the brain normally filled with cerebrospinal fluid. The pressure compressed his brain like a sponge. The first evening a neurosurgeon cut through his skull and threaded two tubes into the ventricles to drain the blood from his head. The ruptured blood vessel continued to bleed, but at least the drains relieved the pressure on his brain. Nothing more could be done except to wait, and hope that the bleeding would stop. And pray.

It is not easy to arrange for last rites at a bedside in the ICU. This ritual includes the sacrament known in the Roman Catholic, Eastern Orthodox, and Anglican Churches as the Anointing of the Sick, a blessing with holy oil, and the Viaticum, literally the "provision for the journey," which is the Eucharist administered to those in danger of dying. Although we were members of the congregation at Grace Cathedral in San Francisco, the staff there did not make pastoral visits to Berkeley. Kris's father, Peter, a retired Episcopal priest who lived an hour north of the city, did not feel able to minister to his grandson's spiritual needs at a time when he himself was so deeply submerged in grief. At our request Peter called the pastor of our neighborhood parish, Father Bruce, and asked him for help. We had not known Bruce before he came to the hospital on the second morning after Jeremy's hemorrhage.

Father Bruce was in his mid-thirties, with a lean athletic build, thick, glossy, black hair, bright blue eyes, and a kind gaze. He arrived at the hospital dressed in black, wearing the inverted Roman collar, and carrying a wooden case.

Ah. Even in this dreadful moment, the familiar vestments evoked an echo of comfort. My clenched fingers loosened, and Kris's knotted brows smoothed fractionally.

Standing inside the entrance to Jeremy's ICU cubicle, we softly exchanged introductions and explanations: "Our oldest child . . . the day before yesterday . . . no sign of waking up . . . the doctors can't say . . ."

Bruce set the wooden box on the small bedside table. It

held oil and holy water in tiny crystal bottles, the Host, and the satin stole signifying his spiritual office. He kissed the center of the stole, raised it over his head with both hands and laid it across his shoulders, opened a prayer book, and read the first words of the service. "Peace be to this place, and to all who dwell in it."

Comfort fled. The realization that we were saying this rite for my baby, who had been born and baptized only a short time ago, impaled me like a spear. The pain froze my blood and bones and sinews, until all that I felt was one slow heartbeat after another, sustaining a life I was no longer sure I wanted to live.

Bruce kept reading. The words fell into the air and settled softly on our son's silent form. "He who dwells in the shelter of the Most High, abides under the shadow of the Almighty. He shall cover you with his pinions, and you shall find refuge under his wings . . ."

Bruce blessed the oil and, with his thumb, anointed Jeremy's forehead below the bandages with the sign of the cross, over his bruised and bleeding brain. "Jeremy, I lay my hands upon you in the Name of the Father, and of the Son, and of the Holy Spirit. . . . As you are outwardly anointed with this holy oil, so may our heavenly Father grant you the inward anointing of the Holy Spirit. . . . Of his great mercy, may he forgive you your sins, release you from suffering, and restore you to wholeness and strength. May he deliver you from all evil, preserve you in all goodness, and bring you to everlasting life."

Since Jeremy could not speak or swallow, Kris and I said the confession of sin for him. "Most merciful God, we confess that we have sinned against you in thought, word, and deed, by what we have done, and by what we have left undone. . . . [H]ave mercy on us and forgive us, that we may delight in your will, and walk in your ways . . ." We received the Eucharist on his behalf, the Host as dry as paper on my tongue.

If there be power in words, then it was here, in the liturgy written to comfort those whom all else has failed. The words took on shape and substance. For a few moments, I rested against them. "The Almighty Lord, who is a strong tower to all who put their trust in him, to whom all things in heaven, on earth, and under the earth bow and obey: Be now and evermore your defense . . ."

The brief service over, Bruce carefully folded the stole and repacked his case. We talked quietly for a few moments: "Thank you for coming . . . we'll let you know . . . yes, we'd like that . . . any time, one of us will be here . . ."

Bruce left at exactly the right time. I stood at the entry to Jeremy's cubicle and watched him walk down the long, crowded ward and past the nurses' station. Heads lifted. Visitors, patients' families, and staff registered the somber black jacket and plain black shirtfront. Their eyes caught on the inverted white collar. As he passed, here and there a face rose, eyes sought his, a hand was tentatively raised. He paused and exchanged a few hushed words.

Bruce would visit two to three times a week throughout Jeremy's hospitalization and become our pastor and our friend.

———

This crisis altered my spiritual landscape with the force of a hundred-year flood. Life was distilled to its fundamentals. Only those things that mattered remained: breath, heartbeat, the earth's patient turning from dusk to dawn to dusk again, our family unbroken for one more day. And along with these, faith.

Both my husband and I had grown up in the knowledge and love of God. Kristor's parents met, married, and conceived him while they were students at Yale Divinity School; they named their baby after a famous theologian. "Kristor" means "Christ bearer." As a PK (preacher's kid), Kris grew up in a series of rectories, sharing family space with vestry meetings, pastoral counseling sessions, and parishioners' visits. A typical week included multiple church services at which his father officiated and Kris and his brothers sang in the choir. With such beginnings, I teased him, what choice did he have in choosing his faith? But the truth is that Kristor embraced his Christianity gladly, and to a depth not often explored by laymen. His knowledge of theology rivals that of any seminarian, and if he had not been a boatman, businessman, and husband, he would have been a priest. Or more likely, given his essentially solitary nature, a monk. Kristor continued to sing as an adult with the Grace Cathedral Choir. He has an otherworldly countertenor voice. Even now, listening to him on a Sunday morning breaks my heart open, as much for his transported expression as for the pure soaring melody.

My religious foundations are far more ordinary. I was born into a Czech-Austrian family that had been staunchly Roman Catholic since the tenth century. Like my mother and my grandmothers, as far back as is recorded in parish registers, I was named after the Virgin. My ancestors were poor and simple people. Their faith was carried in their blood, not acquired from books. It sustained them through wars and famine, suffering and grief, death in places I have never seen. Faith is my inheritance, cut and polished from rough stone by people with nothing else to give. The qualities of devotion, taught and learned, live on, deep inside my bones. With such a heritage, I also had little choice in the choosing. And, like my husband, I chose joyfully.

One advantage of a religious upbringing is that talking, and listening, to God is practiced early, and comes as easily as breathing. I do not remember a time when I did not feel God's presence in my life. People have asked me to describe this feeling. My vague and imperfect attempts at an answer sometimes exasperate friends or acquaintances, especially nonbelievers. "But what do you mean?" they ask. "Be more specific." It is difficult. Imagine being asked to describe what it feels like to know your heart is beating. You know that it does; you feel a comfort and surety about its faithful contraction in your chest; you know that it has always been there, and will be there until you feel no more. But to say *how* you know? You know in ways you do not consciously apprehend. Every thought, breath, and movement depend upon it. Every cell in your body testifies. I feel God's presence in the same way. I know it below the level of thought, or breath, or movement. Every cell in my body testifies.

As I grew older and attended college, I constructed a more mature framework around my belief. Although I didn't approach Kristor's depth of theological literacy, I read the seminal Christian writers, and discovered that some of the best minds of the Western pantheon—Paul, Augustine, Thomas Aquinas, Isaac Newton (who is known for science but devoted more time to Scripture), Martin Luther, C. S. Lewis—had successfully reconciled spirit and mind, logic and belief, faith and doubt. But rational validation did not matter to me in any consequential sense, any more than knowing the chemistry of water matters to a thirsting man. What matters is that water is cool and wet and necessary for life.

This is not to say that I have been impervious to drought. Like any deep and long commitment, faith ebbs and flows. Over the course of a twenty-five-year marriage, I have not always felt in love. At times, it has required the decision to love in order to summon the emotion, just as over the course of a lifelong relationship with God, faith has sometimes been a verb, not a noun—something I did, not something I had. Faith has been a gift, but one that has been nourished by prayer and practice.

When my well-regulated world was swept away on an arterial flood, I was left adrift without a compass. The first few days of Jeremy's hospitalization I was tumbled up, down, and around by the unchecked tide of events. If I had tried a thousand times to imagine what it felt like to be one breath away from losing a child, I could not have imagined it. This was alien territory. I groped for any point of reference. There was none. I was drowning in darkness.

The faint unwavering light of faith came gradually into focus, at the very edge of my perception at first, like shape emerging from a suddenly darkened room. Amid the chaos, faith remained. I needed only to be still long enough to notice it. It did not flicker or fade. It lightened my darkness, provided a fixed point around which to orient myself, as mariners on uncharted seas found their bearings by Polaris.

Luke wrote that Christ brings "light to them that sit in darkness, and in the shadow of death." Two thousand years later, no one spoke to me more clearly. I believe it no coincidence that Luke was a physician.

Words (2)

IN THE NEXT DAYS Kris and I alternated between twenty-four-hour shifts at home and in the hospital intensive care unit, where we watched for any sign of Jeremy's awakening. Our families and friends, dispersed around the country and beyond, were frantic for news, but we were hard to reach. The ICU had no bedside telephones. We were not allowed to make calls on a cell phone because the signal interfered with medical equipment, and in 1998 electronic communications such as texting, blogging, and social networking websites did not yet exist. But everyone, however far away, had an e-mail address.

Late into the third night at Jeremy's bedside, I explored the dusty corners of the ICU cubicle on hands and knees and found—Hallelujah!—an unused live telephone jack behind a cabinet. That tiny aperture in the wall became my connection to the world. Sitting next to Jeremy's bedside in the dark, I wrote out an update on his condition on my laptop and e-mailed it to family and a few close friends.

From: Fiala, Marie Lawson
Sent: September 8, 1998 12:48 A.M.
To: Jeremy Network
Subject: Late at Night (I)/Update No. 1

Saturday of Labor Day weekend dawned hot and hazy, what we call earthquake weather in the East Bay hills. I made brunch, read the paper, did some office work, took David to a birthday party, folded laundry, and at 2:50 watched my older son collapse on the kitchen floor and enter unconsciousness. It was a country then new to me, but now excruciatingly familiar.

Jeremy is paralyzed on the entire right half of his body, from his facial muscles to his toes. This may be from injury to the brain resulting from the bleed, or from the irritation of neural tissue caused by contact with the blood, and most likely is some of both. The outcome can't be predicted until much time has gone by. He has reclaimed the use of the left side of his body and, though unconscious, vigorously works at pulling out the many tubes that are keeping him alive and stable. Kristor and I spent most of the day (literally) wrestling him under control. His left wrist is tied fast to the bed, but he is both strong and sneaky and has a talent for contorting himself in a way that allows him access to the bothersome tube or line.

We wait for Jeremy to awaken. Waking from a coma is a long and painful struggle, not the instantaneous recovery seen on TV. His eyes flick open from time to time, but it doesn't seem that he can see us yet.

I have learned many things quickly. Most of all, that I would give the world and all in it to walk again, holding Jeremy's hand. Or to push him in a wheelchair and be able to talk to him. That the faith that for me has always been as natural as breathing is powerful beyond anything I had expected. All day long the force of God's love has rushed through me like a cataract in a canyon and poured out over Jeremy, with plenty to spare. I love you all.

This was the first of many messages. At first I wrote only to pass on news. As time went on, writing the updates became part meditation, part prayer, a way of processing the days' events. The e-mail distribution list grew exponentially as my messages were forwarded on, and on again. Those who read them were moved by Jeremy's courage as he fought to regain his life. Cards, letters, and e-mail messages poured back from hundreds of people who were following Jeremy's story online from across the United States and Canada and as far away as Europe, Africa, and Australia. Their kindness and compassion buoyed me and carried me along.

In the weeks and months that followed I continued to record the story of my family's new life. Late at night, when I was exhausted by the struggles of the day, a key turned in the attic of my mind, a door opened, and sentences marched out whole through my fingers onto the pale-blue computer screen. I could not sleep until that upper room was emptied of words. In writing I found an intuitive, blind salvation, a lifeline that tethered me to solid land. When I wrote I retreated to a sanctuary in my head, high above the dark waters that flooded the lower levels of my dwelling place.

I could not avoid those waters altogether. Too often, waves of feeling buried me in anguish as I witnessed the ruination of my son's mind and body and relinquished all but the barest form of hope. *Does he still breathe? Will he awaken?* But I was able to turn that key from time to time, enter the room upstairs, and find, if not respite from pain, then at least a calm place to take it in and weave it into the structure of who I was and was becoming.

And so, I wrote.

From: Fiala, Marie Lawson
Sent: September 9, 1998 8:03 A.M.
To: Jeremy Network
Subject: From the ICU/Update No. 2

A rocky day for Jeremy Day. Much pain, thrashing, hard to control. His sleep lightened at times; he kept trying to move his right side and was very frustrated that he couldn't. Still no sign of awakening. He cried once, big tears rolling down his cheeks. He is running a 103-degree fever; doctors suspect infection. Must wait 24 hours for test results. Antibiotics will begin. I'm having a hard time coping.

Jeremy is hurt in his thalamic region. Imagine the brain like a tree. The specialized higher centers in the cortex are branches and twigs. All information processed in the cortex channels down to the "trunk" at the base of the brain, and all signals go to the body only through that switching station and then out the spinal cord. That place where all the nerve signals come together and are processed for sending out to the body is the thalamus. So Jeremy's injury may affect any and all aspects of brain function, including cognitive, motor, and emotional processing. Too soon to tell which one or ones.

My horizons have altered dramatically. High school applications a dream receding into distance. Ditto completing eighth grade. Ditto work. I live minute to minute. Just glad when fever goes down, when Jeremy opens his eyes briefly, when I can flex his right foot (which is hyperextended and becoming rigid) up to a 90-degree angle. Grateful for family and friends and many kindnesses large and small.

Asleep

THE ICU AT CHILDREN'S HOSPITAL was a large open ward, with cribs and beds lined up a few feet apart and a busy, congested central nurses' station. Shortly after he arrived, Jeremy was moved to the only private bed in the ICU, in a separate glass-walled room with shades at the windows and a door that could be closed to help keep out the clamor from the larger ward outside. This space was normally reserved for patients with infectious diseases. Jeremy had been isolated because his nervous system was hyper-irritable. A healthy brain masks sensory input—that is, it discriminates between important and unimportant stimuli, and tunes out the latter. Otherwise, we would be constantly assaulted and overwhelmed by a flood of visual, auditory, and tactile information. Jeremy had lost that ability. During his first hours on the open ward, the bright lights and penetrating sounds—a ringing phone at the nurse's station, a crying baby, a clanging instrument— caused his nerves to fire uncontrollably. He convulsed, arching his back, flinging himself against the steel bars at the sides of his bed, and flailing wildly with his good arm. He needed quiet.

Quiet, of course, was a relative term. Jeremy's cubicle saw heavy traffic. Doctors I had never seen before walked in, picked up and frowned over Jeremy's chart, checked his vital signs, lifted his eyelids and shone a flashlight into his eyes, pricked his extremities with pins, asked the same questions as the previous doctor had, and spoke brief, unhelpful sentences: "There's no change yet." "We'll have to wait and see." The nurses repeated the same routines, more frequently. Technicians stuck needles into his arms or legs for blood samples. Aides left the next day's menus, with boxes that would never be checked. Family members and close friends came. Their earnest, helpful expressions collapsed as soon as they entered the cubicle. They stood awkwardly at the foot of Jeremy's bed, shocked at what they saw, not knowing what to say. They hugged me, bending their faces to my shoulder, and cried. My eyes stayed dry; my body remained rigid, refusing to give in to illusory solace. Nothing anyone did could redeem this reality.

The small room was crowded with equipment. Jeremy lay in the middle of a forest of metal poles, an undergrowth of tangled plastic cables. The ventilator pumped mechanically, pushing air into his lungs. Clear plastic tubes sprang out of the bloodstained bandages swathing his head and connected to liter-sized plastic bags suspended from stands on either side of the bed. They siphoned out blood from the artery that was still hemorrhaging at the center of his brain. More poles held bags that dripped glucose into Jeremy's veins and liquid formula down his nose and into his stomach, and collected urine.

Monitors were connected by lines to sensors taped to Jeremy's chest, neck, hands, and feet, with displays that tracked his pulse, blood pressure, respiration, and blood oxygen levels. Their screens glowed blue and green. Bright lines traced in rapid succession across their faces. I had quickly learned to read the digital displays. Certain numbers sent my own pulse racing. Alarms beeped or buzzed when Jeremy's blood pressure dropped dangerously low, or his heart raced to 170, 180, 190 beats per minute, or, despite the ventilator's steady pumping, his blood oxygen fell far below normal levels.

The bedside cabinets were jammed with supplies—

sponges, dressings, bandages, tapes, tubing, waterproof mattress pads, formula, medications—thrown promiscuously together. The clutter contrasted sharply with the calm surroundings Kris and I cherished at home. One of our many shared qualities was a deep thirst for order. Kristor's tools were suspended in neat rows from pegboards in the garage; our linens were squarely folded, stacked, and classified by size and color; medicine cabinets held only the essentials; and there was not a junk drawer anywhere in the house. I pulled out Jeremy's bedside drawer, pawed through the contents, picked up a foil packet of swabs, a tube of ointment, threw them back down, and shoved the drawer closed. Organizing it was hopeless. The steel spring in my chest coiled tighter.

Kris or I had been at Jeremy's bedside constantly in the three days since his collapse. We shuttled back and forth between hospital and house, alternating shifts. At least we didn't have to worry about keeping our jobs. Partners at both our firms had said immediately, "We'll cover for you for as long as necessary; do what you need to do," and they continued saying it for months. Bless them for that. Our around-the-clock presence was both rare—very few other parents stayed in the ICU consistently—and critically necessary, as Jeremy needed minute-to-minute attention, which the staff weren't able to provide because they had too many patients and were burdened with paperwork. Although this was one of the best pediatric hospitals in California, like most other healthcare institutions it was increasingly stressed by limited resources and growing demands on its services, and the nurses grumbled about their workloads.

At home, our two younger children were feeling the aftershocks of Jeremy's trauma. Annelise and David had started the new school year right after Labor Day. Lisie, in sixth grade, had just moved up to the middle school at a different campus, a new and frightening environment. She was tearful and anxious in the mornings before leaving.

"Mommy, how will I know how to find the Spanish class-room?" "Mommy, I don't know how to find my locker." "Mommy, the teacher said we had to find a newspaper clipping by Friday. but she didn't say what kind of clipping, and I don't know what she meant." Her lips trembled; her eyes welled with tears.

I tried to hold and soothe her: "It'll be okay, baby, it'll be okay." She stiffened in resistance, wiped her face, squared her shoulders beneath the new backpack, and climbed resolutely aboard the school bus. *So much like me.*

David, starting second grade, was quiet. Too quiet. I couldn't get him to talk. "Sweetie, are you feeling scared?"

"No."

"How's your new teacher?"

"Okay."

"Do you have friends in your class?"

Silence.

Feeling helpless, I watched his shiny blond head leaning against the window as the school bus pulled away. *My poor little one. I hope this doesn't damage him forever.*

I was not kind to Kris when I walked back into Jeremy's room on the third day. I hadn't seen my husband for more than twenty minutes at a stretch since Jeremy was admitted, but instead of taking a moment to connect, I launched into a sharp cross-examination: "Was the doctor here? What *exactly* did he say?"

Kris thinks and speaks more slowly than I do, and his answers didn't come quickly enough to quell my terror at this out-of-control situation. I snapped at him, "Darn it, I need you to tell me what's going on! I can't be here every minute!"

Silence. After a sleepless night, Kris was too tired for a pointless argument. He gathered up his belongings—a dirty tee-shirt, a book, his toothbrush. "Bye, love," he said quietly, giving me a quick kiss. "Take care of our boy." He bent over Jeremy's bed, kissed him, and made the sign of the cross on his forehead. Then he was gone.

Jeremy was in a coma, but his sleep was not peaceful. He drifted up and down through levels of unconsciousness, agitated and in pain. I watched the monitors, sponged his face, flexed his arms and legs to keep them limber, and carried on a one-sided conversation. "Hey, guy. It's Mommy. You're in the hospital. You had an accident, kind of like a stroke. Your body's trying to heal itself." Perhaps he could hear me through this bloody semblance of sleep.

Jeremy's left side—the side that wasn't paralyzed—was tied tightly to the bed frame with nylon webbing to keep him from tearing the tubes out of his head. For some reason I fixated on the idea that the straps were tied too tightly. Over and over again I untied and reknotted them, checking how much slack there was against Jeremy's skin, measuring how high he could lift his arm when the straps were fully extended to make sure that he couldn't reach his head. He lay motionless.

Suddenly, Jeremy exploded in a frenzied struggle. He strained against the straps, clawing at his head to rip out the tubes. I threw my body across his to hold him down. He was surprisingly strong, and bucked beneath me, his left hand dangerously close to his skull. I screamed out through the open door, "Come quickly, please! Help me! Help me!"

Two nurses ran in. One pinned Jeremy's left arm to the mattress with both hands while the other filled a syringe. "Hold him, hold him still! I'm giving him a shot of morphine!" The effect was almost immediate. Jeremy's muscles relaxed. His left arm fell to the side, his fingers opening like a flower.

In the late afternoon, the director of Children's Hospital's Rehabilitation Center stopped by Jeremy's room for a brief assessment. "Hi, I'm Dr. Joe," he introduced himself. "That's easier for the kids to remember, and less intimidating."

Dr. Joe was one of the people who gave this hospital its outstanding reputation. In his mid-forties, he had fine, thinning, sandy hair, a soft, round face, bright blue eyes behind rectangular glasses, and an ineradicable smile. His tie was loosely and crookedly knotted, and his shirttail was coming untucked. He talked fast, without stopping or slowing for breath, and he told me a lot more than I was ready to know: "We're not sure what's going to happen, of course; there's no way to tell what's going on inside his brain. He could wake up tomorrow, or stay in a coma much longer. And there's also no way to predict how much brain damage he'll have when he wakes up. Based on my experience, I'm certain there will be residual brain damage. You should expect that he'll be in rehab for months before he can go home. He'll have to start from the beginning and relearn everything, from how to chew and swallow food to how to talk."

I slumped beneath the weight of his words. "Oh," I said weakly. "I see." I didn't see. I wasn't prepared for this onslaught of information. It was too much to process, too soon. I pushed Dr. Joe's words away without letting them penetrate, and turned to Jeremy's bed again.

———

In the evening, Kris brought Annelise and David to the hospital for their first visit. Whether to allow them to see Jeremy was one of the many hard decisions we had had to make in the past three days.

Annelise and David had asked generally how Jeremy was, but they didn't seem to want detailed answers. Kris and I walked the sharp edge between reassurance and lies. "Jeremy is very sick, and right now he is asleep, but soon he will wake up and start feeling better." We worried that seeing Jeremy in the hospital would make his condition too real for them. In the ICU they would also see at least a dozen other critically ill or injured children, many of them babies and toddlers—bandaged, bleeding, burned, amputated, intubated, catheterized, crying, moaning, whimpering. In the first few days I avoided looking up from the floor when I walked through the ward. Our adult visitors were unnerved, some in tears, by the time they reached Jeremy's bedside. How hard would it be for Lisie and David to see this much suffering?

The hospital social worker, the same woman who had tried to comfort me in the emergency room, earnestly counseled against a visit: "Seeing your son would be very traumatic for young children. They'll remember him like this for the rest of their lives. Wouldn't it be better to let them remember him as he was?" Kris and I talked it over during our brief shift overlaps, and made the opposite decision. We did not know from hour to hour how long Jeremy would live. Lisie and David should have the chance to see him once again. While it was still possible to be together, we would be together.

We had taken home a Polaroid photograph of Jeremy to help prepare them. To some, the picture might have seemed morbid, even grisly. Jeremy's head was swathed in stained gauze and adhesive. Tubes snaked out from under the bandages and above the neckline of his hospital gown, tubes ran into his nose and mouth. To me, it was beautiful. Jeremy's face was peaceful. His skin was luminous, lit from within. His exceptionally long, dark eyelashes rested gently, like feathers, against his softly curving cheeks. He was still very much alive.

Standing in the entrance to Jeremy's room with Kris's arms around their shoulders, Annelise and David looked small and very frightened. Lisie gathered her courage and walked steadily forward until she saw Jeremy's bandaged face and head above the covers and stalled in her tracks. David hung back behind her, all pained dark-shadowed eyes and pinched gray cheeks. He was too short; he couldn't see Jeremy at all, only the foot of the bed and the poles and screens and tubes and wires. I quickly rose from the chair at the head of Jeremy's bed and went to them, hugged them, and whispered, "Don't be scared, don't be scared, it's just Jeremy, it will be all right."

Crying silently, they took timid steps toward the bed. But as they drew nearer they saw that it was still Jeremy, his own dear self, beneath the tubes and bandages. They moved closer still, and stood next to him. We had told them that Jeremy might be able to hear even through his coma. They gingerly took his hands and spoke. Annelise first: "Hi, Jeremy, it's Annelise. I came to see you. I miss you so much."

David echoed in a low uncertain whisper, "Hi, Jeremy . . . Hi, Jeremy."

Annelise recovered more quickly. She was anxious to tell Jeremy that she had brought in a giant poster made by the students at their middle school. With Kris's help she unrolled it, and told Jeremy what it looked like. "It's really big, and there's cutout pictures glued on the top, and people drew little cartoons, and lots of kids signed their names, and wrote things: 'Get well, Jeremy. We miss you!' 'Hey, dude, sorry you're sick!'" The longer she talked, the better she felt. Her voice became animated and her leftover summer glow returned. Together, she and Kris pinned the poster to the wall alongside Jeremy's bed.

David had a harder time. He leaned into me. "Mom, I don't know what to say." I cupped my hand at the back of his perfectly rounded head, gently stroked down to the soft silvery hairs at his nape, whispered back, "It's okay, sweetheart, you don't have to say anything special. Just let him hear your voice." David tried again. I could see the thoughts moving behind his pale cornflower eyes, searching for a subject, gathering strength. "Hi, Jeremy . . . in my new classroom we have a bunny and two gerbils. The bunny's name is Mr. Flopsy . . . and . . . my teacher has six cats at her house."

I kissed the side of his head, put my arm around his fragile bird-wing shoulders. "You're doing great, sweetie."

"And . . ." A long wait. David's face knotted with his valiant effort. "She said sometime we can visit her house and see them . . ." It was the best he could do.

In fits and starts, the one-sided conversation continued. Kris lowered the bed rail, and Lisie leaned both elbows on the edge of the mattress as she continued her earnest monologue about teachers and classes. Kris and I added news about our own two cats and friends who had stopped by. David sat sideways on my lap next to the bed, resting his head on my shoulder, smiling now and then when Kris made a small joke.

Jeremy lay silently, his chest rising and falling and his eyelashes fluttering occasionally as he slept on.

———

After they left, I reclined the chair close to Jeremy's bed, arranged the thin hospital sheets, blankets, and pillows to make a sleeping place, lay down and shifted into the most comfortable position possible, and stared into the darkness at the bright red, green, and blue pinpoints winking from the monitors. Our portable CD player was turned on at low volume. My mind slowed, faded, floated up and away with the music, Enya's voice weaving in and out of hearing: *"Strange how/my heart beats/to find myself upon your shore./Strange how/I still feel/my loss of comfort gone before."* The sharp edges of thought softened and wavered, images forming and reforming like patterns in the clouds, filling in the pauses between the musical phrases. An island, the middle of the sea. Jeremy's breath sighing like the surf. *"Cool waves wash over/and drift away with dreams of youth."* Dark sky overhead. No sight of mainland, no light but stars. The only sounds my steady heartbeat, your straining breath. *"So time is stolen/I cannot hold you long enough."* I could not hold you long enough, could not hold you strong enough, could not keep you safe. *"And so/this is where I should be now."* This moment, this day, this night, my heartbeat, your breathing, all that was left. *"Days and nights falling by/Days and nights falling by me."* I hold you now, and forever. And sleep.

Beginnings

Eventually, all things merge into one, and a river runs through it. The river was cut by the world's great flood and runs over rocks from the basement of time. On some of the rocks are timeless raindrops. Under the rocks are the words, and some of the words are theirs.

—Norman Maclean

ONCE I IMAGINED that I lived a planned and ordered life. Looking back, I see that the most precious things have come to me by serendipity, or by grace. I lean toward grace as the explanation.

In 1980 I was a young lawyer working toward partnership at my large San Francisco law firm. I spent my days studying dusty precedents and devising legal arguments, mapping pinheads where angels danced. My evenings and weekends played out to a disco soundtrack, in an increasingly disappointing pursuit of fun at one party or another, on one "ohmigosh-it's-only-been-twenty-minutes-I-would-gnaw-my-arm-off-to-escape" date after another.

As the year waned I found it easier to be at home alone than to go out. Home was a tiny garden apartment in San Francisco's Haight-Ashbury district. A wall of

French doors faced the western sun, and opened onto a small deck with steps descending to a pocket-handkerchief lawn and flower beds. In the late afternoons, wisps of Pacific fog transformed the garden into a pale gauze landscape. The wood floors and white-tiled countertops sparkled; sheer curtains blew at the open windows; a vase of flowers splashed red across the kitchen table. My belongings were simple but pleasing. Things stayed where I put them. I brewed small pots of strong dark coffee and basked in the sunlight in a comfortable chair with a book of poetry and my green-eyed cat on my lap.

But solitude came to feel lonely, not just alone. I wanted to look up from my book and say to someone across the room, "Listen to this," and read a passage aloud. I wanted to pour two cups of coffee and bring them to bed on Sunday morning along with the newspaper. I wanted someone else's shoes lined up next to mine in the closet, and a second pair of jeans hanging over the back of a chair. Winter came on, the nights grew long, and I was still alone. The idea that I might always be alone disquieted my dreams and increasingly shadowed my daylight hours.

Late the following spring, the Grand Canyon, slicing through the high desert of northern Arizona, intersected with my very urban life. A friend of a friend of a friend in New York City canceled a long-planned rafting vacation down the Colorado River, leaving a space to be filled if the trip deposit were not to be forfeited. By the time the search for a substitute traveler reached me, three degrees of separation and three thousand miles removed, the trip was only weeks away. I had never gone whitewater rafting before. My outdoor experience was limited to childhood camping trips, which I remembered as mostly miserable, sandy, and cold. But my thirtieth birthday was approaching and I wanted change more than I needed comfort, so I said yes. I left law office and gauzy garden, briefcase and business suits behind me, packed shorts, tee-shirts, swimsuits, flip-flops, and a few toiletries in a duffel bag, and headed out into the desert. I had no idea what I had signed up for.

The Grand Canyon is the most sought-after river trip in the lower forty-eight states. Its rapids are legendary in the whitewater world, with fearsome hydraulics, massive waves and holes, swirling eddies, and enormous whirlpools. Worldwide, whitewater rivers are rated using Roman numerals I to VI according to the International Scale of River Difficulty. The Colorado River is rated on a scale of one to ten, and one of its rapids, Lava Falls, is an eleven.

The river inspires awe and respect in even the most seasoned rafters. I learned why shortly after the put-in, where I had stowed my gear in a waterproof black bag and clambered aboard a fifteen-foot-long Army-surplus rubber raft. Our group consisted of five rafts, each holding three or four passengers and rowed by a guide with a long pair of oars. We pushed off into smooth water, but soon we heard a huge roar downstream, echoing off the canyon walls. "What's that?" I nervously asked our guide, Kim.

Kim, a tall, muscular woman with thick brown hair clipped at the back of her head, a wide face, and wire-rimmed glasses, looked at me impassively: "A rapid."

It was Horn Creek, not the largest but one of the more technically difficult rapids on the river. (Rated an eight, it's big enough.) It was already late afternoon, and the narrow band of sky between the top of the rock escarpments was turning dark. The canyon narrows at that point, and the brooding vertical walls ahead framed a menacing black gorge. Between them ran a smooth, shiny line of water and beyond it . . . empty space, punctuated with an occasional spume of spray spitting skyward. We were approaching the edge of a waterfall.

Is this really happening?

There was no time to worry. Kim shouted quick instructions: "Brace with your feet! If we start to flip, go for the high side! And when we get past the first drop, *bail like mad!*" And then we were over the edge and in it, the raft standing nearly on its head and then bucking up over monster waves, Kim pulling on the oars with all she had to avoid the huge hole at the bottom of the drop, the noise unbelievable, walls of water falling hard on top of us, the raft wallowing under the added weight, a calm moment, *bail! bail! . . . now hang on!*, another wave crashing, and another, and finally we were spinning in the pool below. *Whoo-hoo!* Everyone in the boat was wearing a big crazy smile, and I could feel the same grin stretched across my face.

I didn't speak with Kris for the first three days of the trip, beyond our abortive initial interchange. There were plenty of other things to think about. Meeting the other guides and passengers. Just hanging on and hoping we wouldn't flip on the roller-coaster rides through the rapids—Granite, Hermit, Crystal—each a maelstrom of huge crashing waves. Learning how to set up camp every night in a different unlikely location—rock ledges above the water, a narrow strip of beach, the shore of a tributary stream. And most of all, the canyon itself.

Seen from the river, a vertical mile below the earth's surface, the Grand Canyon is a place unlike any other, an ancient cathedral of rock and water. The canyon walls are a billion years old, black and green and rust, shaped and fired by heat and pressure, cut and carved by the river's motion. Each layer captures thousands of millennia in stone: Vishnu schist, Zoroaster granite, Bright Angel shale. The sky is azure or stormy gray by day, deep-space black by night. The sun rises late in the canyon, the bronze light slowly creeping down the walls, marking off eons of time with every few feet of illumination. At night the diamond moonlight leaches color from the landscape, limning sand and rocks and water in silver, gray, and white. And within and through it all, the river. Flowing green and clear in some places, at others it is churned a creamy café au lait or runs bright red, *colorado*. Shining steel in front of the boat when the light reflects off its unbroken surface, or roiled into twenty-foot high rapids by its violent descent over rocks along its course. Sometimes it sings a soft susurration, sometimes it thunders, always it beats at the heart of the canyon.

Although I didn't talk with Kris, I noticed him—neatly rigging his boat in the morning, effortlessly climbing a scree slope on a hike, chopping vegetables in the camp kitchen before dinner, laughing at a private joke with one of the other guides. He was, as I've said, gorgeous, and I wasn't blind. But he remained aloof with the passengers, and I wasn't interested in pushing past his reserve. I was busy finding my own place in that daunting environment—wearing the same increasingly muddy tee-shirt and shorts day after day, keeping up on a steep and narrow side canyon trail, taking a turn rowing, shaking a scorpion out of my sleeping bag, washing up in a bucket of silty river water.

I loved it. A place so stripped down, so bare, that nothing came between me and knowing who I was. At night I lay under the jet-black sky and felt my heart beating and knew I was alive.

After dinner on the evening of the third day, I walked down to the edge of the river and perched on a rocky shelf, listening to the freight-train rumble of a rapid just downstream. Kris came over and sat down next to me, holding a bottle of tequila. "So, why'd you come on the river?" he asked. I told him. We talked for a long time, and after I went back to my campsite that night—alone—I lay awake, wondering, *Is this really happening?* The next morning, Kris said, "Why don't you ride with me today," and I did—that day, and every other day for the remainder of the trip. I left the river two weeks later in love with the man with whom I would share my life.

The Sweet Cool Passage of Air

WHO KNOWS THE SOURCE of a breath, the impulse that opens diaphragm, ribs, lungs, drawing the sweet air in cool passage down nose and throat? Who notices when the body says, yes, it is time to open again and fill, and then time to close and empty? Who thinks, I have taken a breath; will there be another? And will there be yet another? We take for granted our own respiration. The mind wants to forget, to get on with more needful matters. It leaves the opening and closing to the unconscious brain below, which works faithfully on and on, sending a steady signal to the distant lungs, saying, breathe, breathe, breathe . . . in and out, in and out, in and out.

I now had reason to attend to many things I once took for granted. Breath was among them. Jeremy had been without his own breath for four days. As his brain filled up with blood, Jeremy simply . . . quietly . . . stopped . . . breathing. A large noisy machine took over the job, which it performed with cold efficiency. IN, it said. OUT, it said. The ventilator breathed for Jeremy in relentless rhythm, twenty breaths per minute. Wheeze . . . wheeze . . . wheeze. A line of perfectly formed peaks marched across a monitor screen, each peak representing one machine-made inhalation and exhalation. With each wheeze, each peak, Jeremy's chest rose and fell beneath the thin hospital gown.

Jeremy and the ventilator were at stalemate. Continuing to force pressurized air into his lungs could cause "ventilator-induced lung injury," damaging the fragile alveolar tissue and permanently diminishing his lungs' capacity to absorb oxygen. The solution was to take him off the ventilator. Yet the doctors did not know whether Jeremy would breathe on his own once it was turned off, or whether his brain had been too badly damaged.

The morning of the fourth day after Jeremy's hemorrhage, the ICU's chief resident paused during rounds, trailed by a covey of junior residents and interns, and announced that she had decided to try weaning Jeremy from the ventilator. She was an intimidating figure, impassive as an African queen, a coronet of black braids wound around her head, impeccably dressed in a gray suit, matching heels, and hose. Wearing old sweatpants with tiny holes at the knees and an oversized tee-shirt that I had slept in, I felt especially disheveled by comparison with this woman, who a week ago would have been my peer. The doctor briskly explained the procedure as her entourage stared at my son: "Over a period of hours we'll step down the number of ventilations per minute. As his body craves oxygen, his brain should jump-start the respiratory signal, and he should start breathing on his own."

That was the theory, anyway. She didn't say how likely it was that this strategy would work, or what alternatives we had in case it didn't. I thought of questions. *What if Jeremy can't breathe on his own? Will you try again? How long can he live like this?* I decided not to ask them. I suspected she wouldn't have any answers I liked.

At mid-morning, the day nurse entered the cubicle and made the first adjustment to the ventilator timing. She was a pleasant-faced young woman with red hair and white freckled arms below the sleeves of her blue scrubs. The peaks on the monitor slowed down and spaced farther apart. She stood with her hand on Jeremy's pulse and watched the screen. "How are Mom and Dad holding up?" she asked kindly, her eyes never moving from the displays. "Are you

getting any sleep? You need to keep up your strength."
After ten minutes, she left us alone with the ventilator, and
Jeremy's sleeping form.

Since the two younger children were in school, Kris
and I were both at the hospital. We sat on opposite sides of
Jeremy's bed, stroking his arms or holding his hands, our
eyes fixed on the monitor. We were quiet except for small
murmured observations: "His fever is down." "His eyes are
dry; I'll get some drops." Kristor tends to keep his thoughts
on the inside, and I didn't draw him out, although there
would have been comfort in that connection. I didn't want
comfort. I wanted to stay at the center of my suffering, acutely
aware of the tenuousness of Jeremy's existence from one
inhalation to the next. This was his reality, each questioning
pause bitterly incomprehensible, each answering breath
sweetly hopeful. I wanted to be wholly present in the space
between each question and answer with him.

At intervals the nurse came in and adjusted the
number of ventilations per minute downward, and then
downward again, and then again. We stared intently at
the monitor screen, hoping to see an imperfect tracing,
a short wobbly hillock among the ventilator's tall
symmetrical peaks that would tell us that Jeremy's own
breathing had begun. *Babies are meant to sleep with their
parents*, I remembered, *because they imprint their breathing
after their parents' strong patterns. Perhaps some ancient part
of Jeremy's mind will feel our rhythm, and do the same.* One
hour passed, then two, three . . . I wasn't sure whether
slowly or quickly. Time seemed to be uncoupled from the
world we usually inhabited. I filled a paper cup with water
from the sink, and sat down. Kris went to the window,
peered out at the waning afternoon through the blind, and
sat down. I stroked the back of Jeremy's hand. Kris stood
at the foot of the bed and stretched Jeremy's feet. I went
to the bathroom. Kris leaned his head back and dozed
briefly, then awakened with a start. I unwrapped a granola

bar, broke off half, and passed the other half to Kris. We chewed. I rubbed my eyes. We watched the monitor.

Six hours had passed.

Suddenly a small uncertain peak appeared at the right side of the screen, moved quickly across, and vanished from view at the left edge. Jeremy had taken a breath. A bolt of joy flared in my chest, tempered by doubt. Was it really there? "Kris, did you see anything?"

"I think so. I'm not sure."

We stared at the screen intently. Nothing more at first, just the ventilator's tracings. Then, perhaps ten minutes later, another small peak.

"There! Do you see that?"

"Yes. It was there!"

And, eventually, another. Jeremy's breaths were erratic, so shallow that I could not see his chest move when he inhaled on his own. Yet he kept trying. The stunted irregular peaks continued to appear, each one surprising us with hope.

Over the next several hours Jeremy's own breathing became more assured and regular. The doctor came in to check his vital signs and decided he was stable enough to be removed from the ventilator completely. The nurse turned off the machine. The wheeze was silenced. This was the deciding moment.

"This will be messy," the nurse warned. I closed my eyes as she pulled the long slimy tube out of Jeremy's windpipe, and said a silent prayer: *Please, God, help him remember how* . . . Jeremy gagged and coughed harshly, sending the monitor tracing into paroxysms. Kris and I waited anxiously, eyes on the screen, as the line settled into a new pattern.

Jeremy breathed. His chest lifted and fell on its own. Haltingly, with agonizing intermittent pauses, but enough. Jeremy breathed. He breathed.

Small and Precious Things

JEREMY WAS AN UNPLANNED CHILD. Kristor and I had been together for two years and married only nine months when I discovered I was pregnant. I thought the prospect of starting a family lay comfortably in the future. I had so much to do before I was ready—travel, work advancement, time together as a couple. But nature had no regard for my plans. Or, as I said later, God knew better than I did what I needed.

I did not enjoy having my body hijacked by a small stowaway. I was nauseated for nine months. Imagine a bad night after eating suspect sushi, then multiply that oh-please-make-it-stop feeling by twenty-four hours, seven days a week, for forty weeks. Every simple activity—getting out of bed, showering, dressing, making my way to work—required massive effort. Take three steps, bend forward, hold onto the wall, and breathe deeply. Do not throw up. Do not throw up. Even when I was sitting still at my desk, my head spun and my stomach lurched. Almost everything I tried—dry toast, apricot nectar, peppermint tea, ginger capsules—stopped the nausea. For ten minutes. Nothing worked longer than that. I ate saltines throughout the day to buy short respites, spilling white crackermeal down the front of my clothes. As the baby and I grew larger, I was reduced to wearing garish printed polyester dresses and baggy stockings that pooled at my ankles, I no longer fit into my shoes, and I lost sight of my legs in stages. I was increasingly despondent. No more intimate dinners for two, no more late night parties, no more travel. No more possibilities.

Kris tried hard to be whatever I needed him to be during the pregnancy, but I had no idea what that was.

"You look beautiful."

"No, I don't. I look like a cow."

"Don't be sad. It'll it all work out, you'll see."

"What do you mean, it'll work out? Nothing will ever be the same again."

"Can I get you anything, anything at all?"

Can you get me my life back?

Finally, the end. I started labor after eight months and one week of pregnancy, late at night between the first and second days of an important client's deposition. This also wasn't according to plan. We hadn't finished buying baby clothes and furnishing the nursery; I had a pile of paper on my office desk still to be dealt with; I hadn't even packed a hospital bag. Suddenly, none of it mattered. The baby was coming, *now*, and Kris and I would have to adjust because life was not waiting for us.

The childbirth preparation instructor had promised serene interludes in a warm bath while soothing music flowed from a portable stereo and I visualized peaceful, relaxing images to get past the "discomfort." Instead I got twenty-one hours of pain so immense and merciless that I wanted to die to escape it. Labor felt like the six-foot-high, heavily corrugated tire of a huge earthmover was slowly, slowly running over my abdomen. And then reversing, and doing it again. Forward, back, forward, and back. Again, and again, and again. I didn't care where the hell I was, and if someone had turned on soothing music I would have thrown the stereo across the room.

In Berkeley in the 1980s, childbirth anesthesia was less popular than euthanasia. I was too intimidated by the prevailing politics to ask for serious drugs, and the nurse wouldn't have given them to me if I had. I know this because she refused even my doctor's instruction to administer a dose of Nisentil, a mild analgesic. They had a loud argument about it in the hallway outside my door. "I'm *ordering* this medication. Are you refusing to give it to her?"

"Yes, she's doing fine. *I* don't think she needs it."

I could have killed both of them.

Jeremy was transverse and backward; his head was trapped on one side of my pelvic bone, and he was presenting on his cheek instead of his crown. The doctor tried repeatedly to turn him, reaching his arm up into my uterus at the height of each contraction to pull him straight, without success. (Later he would show me the bruises on his forearm wrought by that six-foot-high corrugated tire.) Jeremy and I labored on and on together, and grew weaker, until his heartbeat dropped sharply and bought me an emergency C-section. A large needle directly into my spine ended the pain, and I was wheeled into surgery. Bright lights blurring overhead and shiny instruments and masked faces and brisk movements and a wide slice deep into my belly and a great deal of pressure and tugging and suddenly—two new people in the room.

My son, red, white, and wet, the doctor's hand firmly gripping the top of his head and his upper palate, wailing in protest at this abrupt entry into the cold and light.

And a mother.

The nurses took the baby to a corner of the operating room, wiped his face, wrapped him in a blanket, and laid him in my arms. He had a thick thatch of black hair, was covered in blood and vernix, and his right cheek bore a circular purple bruise. He looked up at me solemnly with great blue eyes. I rubbed my cheek against his heavy bobbley head and drew in his strong-sweet new baby smell. I was bedazzled. He turned his head toward me, pursed his lips, and nuzzled my breast in search of milk. I fell recklessly, irrevocably, in love.

My borders dissolved, re-formed, took him in. I was

a warm clear lake of emotion. Beneath the surface, darker feelings stirred. A fierce creature awakened from long slumber, stretched and flexed powerful muscles, extended razor claws, raised its head and blinked at the world with dangerous eyes, then roared. Five thousand years of civilization fell away. I was mother, primitive and strong. Let no one touch this child, a steely voice whispered. Let no one touch this child, for he is mine.

———

Before Labor Day weekend of 1998, our life was unexceptional. Kris and I moved from the apartment in San Francisco to Berkeley when I was pregnant with Jeremy because we both knew that we wanted to raise our children in a neighborhood with yards and level sidewalks and overhanging trees. San Francisco offered breathtaking vistas and a vibrant nightlife, but few children rode bicycles up and down its bare concrete hillsides.

Berkeley lies directly east across the Bay from San Francisco. It is a green and flowering town surrounding the University of California campus, built largely before the Great Depression. The streets meander around and over the soft hills that frame its eastern boundaries. Although it has been ravaged by fire at least twice in the past century, the city nonetheless has preserved a vast and motley forest along its sidewalks and in its parks and yards. Tall centuries-old redwoods. Blue-gray eucalyptus, untidy giants with drifts of peeling bark and seed pods about their feet. Graceful pale-green sycamores arching over the broad streets to form the vaulted nave of an outdoor cathedral. The occasional opulent magnolia. Five-fingered maples, fiery in autumn. Delicate sad willows, strangely out of place in the hot bright air. And sturdy California oaks, with their dark-green spiky leaves and gnarled gray trunks that bend to the land in patient perseverance.

A walk through Berkeley in the spring or summer is

intoxicating. Apple, plum, and cherry trees are fountains of cream or blush-pink blossoms. The scent of orange trees ravishes the air. Everywhere wisteria graces weathered brown shingled walls and verandas. Climbing roses twine along arbors and trellises. Star jasmine breathes sweetly along every walkway; rosemary adds an acrid undertone. In the higher hills these scents give way to the dusty-green fragrance of sage.

When Kris and I were looking for a home before Jeremy was born, we settled on a neighborhood that invited walking. A neighborhood with enough relief to make the terrain interesting, but not daunting, at the end of a day's work. A neighborhood with destinations that drew us out of our front door.

If we were low on milk or wanted peppery tomatoes for the dinner salad, we walked to the grocery store three blocks away. For Rick, the owner, the store was as much a vocation as a business. His father had operated the same store since the 1930s, when streetcars ran down the broad avenue outside, taking commuters to the water's edge and the passenger ferries that crossed an unbridged Bay. Rick's father had kept the store open through the Great Depression, extending credit to the local customers who could not pay. His neighbors quietly collected the monies needed to redeem every debt.

For coffee, we walked farther, to the small espresso shop where every morning nattily dressed commuters and spandex-clad bicyclists and unreconstructed hippies and moms with strollers waited in line. Outside, they shared wooden benches and sipped their drinks, while three or four dogs sprawled and panted on the pavement and small children fed muffin crumbs to the resident colony of English sparrows.

Sometimes we just walked along a new street, and admired the restored vintage homes, or commiserated over those that had fallen into disrepair. "Look at that beautiful deep porch! And the leaded glass on the front windows! Too bad, they've really let the roof go," said Kris. Old houses are one of his great passions.

"That house could be beautiful if only someone loved it," I agreed.

As we had envisioned, Kris and I pushed Jeremy's stroller along these quiet pathways. Our footsteps stitched together a quilted map of the neighborhood.

Jeremy was an alert and watchful baby. He sat upright in the stroller, refusing to lean against the angled back. His wide, open face was dominated by enormous solemn eyes that took in every detail of his surroundings. Typically he focused on a single neighborhood object during these walks and pointed it out over and over again with excitement, and sometimes with fear. Over time his attention was riveted on garden hoses, television antennas, cats, and lemons hanging from tree branches. He had a knack for spotting the object of his attention long before Kris or I did: a hose coiled next to a stairway thirty feet from the sidewalk; a lemon tree peeking over a backyard fence; a cat sleeping beneath a parked car. He was never wrong.

Sitting so straight, his soft shapeless hands resting on the protective bar at the front of the stroller, a white sun hat perched over his blond bangs, he was vigilant against all risks. We tried to reassure him. Kris would walk over to the neighbor's stoop, pick up the hose, and wave it around casually. "Look, son, there's nothing to be scared of. It's just a hose, for watering the yard. It's made out of rubber. It can't hurt you." Or I would squat down as the cat walked over and arched its back against my hand. "See, it's a kitty-cat. Just like our kitties at home." We thought that by explaining his world, we could make it safe. We could not know that the greatest risk of all lay dormant, deep behind his deep blue eyes.

Awakening

AFTER SIX DAYS, Jeremy was still asleep. The doctors did not predict when he would awaken. "Give it time," they said. "His brain has suffered a terrible trauma. He won't come back immediately." I wondered late at night, alone in our bed at home, staring into darkness, *What if he doesn't come back at all?*

That Thursday, Annelise and David came to the hospital after school with Kris, as was their new daily routine. They walked into the room easily, no longer afraid of what they would see. Jeremy was just Jeremy, different but still their brother. They stroked his face, held his hands, and took turns telling him about their days. I was surprised at how quickly they had adapted to this changed reality, and proud of their courage.

Annelise went first. She had largely regained her former confident demeanor, although cracks showed once in a while. "Jeremy, Mr. Wilson [the middle school headmaster] asked me how you were doing. He said to tell you that he is coming to visit you, Jeremy, and all the kids still ask me about you all the time." Then, in a quiet aside, "Mom, it's hard to have everybody ask me about Jeremy and to have to talk about it all the time."

I understood so well. "Tell your friends, 'thank you,' dear, and that you don't feel up to talking about Jeremy just now."

David, as always, struggled to muster material for conversation. "Hi, Jeremy, how are you, Jeremy?" Whispered encouragement from me. "Jeremy, our room is really lonely at night without you. I like sharing a room better."

My parents, who had flown down from their home in Washington State the night after Jeremy's bleed and were staying with us, arrived for their evening visit and to provide the respite that allowed us a brief break with the younger children. They were in their seventies. My mother was a petite woman with short silver hair and huge eyes, the blue-violet of pansies, still bright in her deeply lined face. My father was bent from years of hard labor so that when I embraced him I felt the curve of his shoulders and spine leaning toward me like an overhanging bough. He had been a beautiful young man, well muscled, blond, with steely blue eyes and full, sensuous lips. He was still strong, his eyes as piercing as ever. Jeremy looked strikingly like him. Both of my parents spoke with strong accents. My father greeted us, "Allo, everry-von."

"Ent how iss our Cheremy to-day?" my mother asked.

We left Jeremy in my parents' care while Kris, Lisie, David, and I went downstairs to the hospital cafeteria for a hasty, unpalatable dinner. Children's Hospital operated on a shoestring, and the cafeteria choices were limited: steam-table hamburgers, taco casserole, French fries. Iceberg lettuce cut into big chunks. Soggy fruit salad. It didn't matter. The food was only the occasion for a quick family meal, and for that it was good enough. We found seats at one of the least sticky and littered tables, ate fast, and hurried back to Jeremy's room.

When we walked through the door, my parents looked up with joy in their faces. Jeremy was awake; his eyes were open. He turned his head toward the sound of our voices as we entered. He didn't speak. He lay still. Kris and I hurried to the head of the bed and leaned over him. "Jeremy, hello love, hello dear Jeremy," I said softly. My tears dripped in silent splotches onto the sheets. Still he said nothing, but his eyes widened with recognition.

His sister and brother spoke to him tremulously. "Hi, Jeremy, hi. It's me, Annelise. I'm here, Jeremy."

David slipped his short stubby finger inside Jeremy's curled left hand. "Hi, Jeremy, it's me, David. Can you hear me?" Ever so slowly, Jeremy's hand tightened gently around David's finger.

The first wakeful period was brief. Jeremy soon slid under the surface of sleep again, but sleep had loosed its hold on him.

————

Even after the coma lifted, Jeremy's medical condition was desperate. Although his eyes opened and closed, he was not conscious in any everyday sense. He drifted on an ocean of pain and confusion; he could no more muster the intention needed to press the nurse's call button than he could rise from his bed and walk.

The ruptured artery was still bleeding, although more slowly. The tubes in Jeremy's head dripped, dripped, dripped, siphoning new blood from his brain into plastic bags that were changed every few hours. With every bag I watched anxiously to see whether the fluid—the color of burgundy—would lighten. It did not. Day after day the blood dripped, dripped, and there was ever more blood.

In between my hospital shifts, I sat for long hours at our kitchen table, searching the Internet on my laptop, soliciting doctors' names from a wide network of contacts, and calling hospitals and surgeons around the country to describe Jeremy's condition and ask about treatment options. The AVM, the blood vessel abnormality that had caused the hemorrhage, was located in the thalamus, a small, vital structure deep in Jeremy's brain. Unless the AVM was treated in some fashion after the bleeding stopped, it was almost certain to rupture again. Surgery to remove it was the preferred option, but Jeremy had a Grade 6 inoperable AVM, too deep to be removed surgically without causing massive and irreversible brain damage. (Although one prominent neurosurgeon volunteered that he would undertake to operate anyway. As the saying goes, if you're holding a hammer, the whole world looks like a nail—and every surgeon is holding a knife.)

Medical technology had advanced beyond the scalpel, however. The other treatment options were basically of two types. An embolization procedure involved running a guide wire and catheter into Jeremy's femoral artery in his groin, through his heart, up the carotid artery in his neck, and into his brain, all the way to the main blood vessel that was the "trunk" from which the AVM originated. The doctors would then shoot a liquid adhesive called n-butyl cyanoacrylate—popularly known as Super Glue—through the catheter to instantly close off the blood vessels that supplied the AVM. This technique sounded terrifying. Because Super Glue is so fast-acting, the procedure had to be conducted very quickly to avoid devastating consequences—such as, for instance, gluing the catheter to the target blood vessel.

The second option was gamma knife radiosurgery, an intensive irradiation of the AVM blood vessels. Over time, the radiation should cause abnormal cell growth in the lining of the blood vessels that would eventually cause the AVM to wither away. Either procedure might cause permanent loss of blood supply to that portion of Jeremy's brain and therefore permanent brain damage. The gamma knife had some advantages. It could be focused more precisely than embolization could and, because it took effect slowly, allowed time for new blood vessels to grow to serve the stranded parts of the brain as the AVM's blood supply was gradually cut off. If Jeremy lived, we would have to choose between them.

Once the euphoria of Jeremy's awakening receded, the reality that he had not awakened whole set in. His right side remained completely paralyzed, from forehead to toes, with no movement at all and very little sensation when the doctors pricked his arm and leg with pins. The bleed was close to the optic nerve, and his vision was affected; he could not see objects more than a few inches from his eyes. And although he continued to respond to our voices—with faint squeezes of his left hand, a slight nod of the head when I asked, "Are you thirsty?"—still he made no sound.

Dr. Joe, who came by almost every day for a brief visit, said that quite likely the brain injury had permanently affected Jeremy's speech. "It is too early to tell for sure, of course, but the longer he goes without talking, the less likely that his speech will come back," he said, lifting his glasses and kneading his tired eyes. He couldn't say whether Jeremy would recover his motor function either. "We don't know if he'll regain any movement," he said. "We have to wait and see."

I had clung to the mistaken idea that, once Jeremy woke up, the doctors would *do* something to help him recover, and with some medical conditions that certainly would have been true. But although this was a fine hospital, a regional trauma center, the best doctors were helpless to heal an injured brain. They could perform a rudimentary form of carpentry and plumbing—sawing through Jeremy's skull, installing drains to relieve the pressure inside. They could provide stability and life support, IVs for hydration, antibiotics to fight infection. But there were no technologies, no surgeries, no medications that would restore what Jeremy had lost. That he would have to do for himself.

From: Fiala, Marie Lawson
Sent: September 11, 1998 9:45 A.M.
To: Jeremy Network
Subject: Good News/Update No. 3

Jeremy is doing as well as could be expected. Although he is awake, his brain is very confused. After the shutdown, one center after another is booting up. The processing of nerve signals within each center, and between centers, is not yet smooth and synchronized. Try to imagine booting up a mainframe that makes a Cray look like a pocket calculator; it takes time.

Thank you all more than we can say for the many expressions of caring and support. When we're down, we read your cards and e-mail and listen to your messages and are once again buoyed. We have an enormous prayer network working on Jeremy's behalf. We see it working before our eyes. Thanks be to God.

Songs of Silence

OUR HOME WAS THE SPACE that sheltered my marriage and children. It was the place I loved more than anywhere else.

We made its acquaintance on a rainy Sunday late in November, five years into our marriage. Jeremy was nearly four years old, a thoughtful and deliberate child. He was still a worrier who started every car ride by asking, "Daddy, do we have enough gas?" Lisie was a busy-bodied sixteen-month-old toddler, insatiably curious and relentlessly active. Her escapades were already the stuff of family legend, as in the time she lifted the heating register out of the floor and tumbled headfirst down the furnace duct. Kris found her with only the soles of her shoes waving above the floorboards.

Kris and I were still renting, an uncertain state. We never knew whether we would have to move when our lease ran out or if the landlord decided to reoccupy the property. We wanted to stay in our neighborhood, but the homes in the area were large and generally well maintained, and too expensive for our means.

On one of our afternoon outings, we stopped at a "House Open" sign on a leafy, winding street. The house had been built before the Great War in the Craftsman style, anchored to an outcropping of bedrock on a large lot that fell away sharply downhill. In 1910 the country was still young and wide-eyed, and the house was shaped by that outlook. Every window opened onto trees—eucalyptus, oaks, and redwoods—a canopy of leaves and branches, near and at a distance. The house had been poorly tended for many years, but its good strong bones still shone through an accumulation of frippery. Under the plastic chandeliers, stained shag carpeting, and peeling wallpaper lay nine-foot ceilings, oak flooring, and heavy plaster walls. We fell in love with its brave and dignified shabbiness.

Before moving in, we had to make it habitable. My parents drove down from Washington State and spent a month of long days working with us, scraping an inch-thick crust of accreted wallpaper from the walls, repainting every room, refinishing the floors, hacking away overgrown shrubbery, and cleaning twenty years' worth of grease and grime from ceilings, counters, and woodwork. Soon the living room was resplendent with new ivory paint and matching draperies, our deep blue and amber furniture, a jewel-toned Persian rug spread over the hardwood floor, and the original redwood cabinets polished to a soft glow. On a rainy winter day with a banked fire glowing in the tall brick fireplace, there was not a more welcoming room in all the world.

Other rooms took longer to renovate. For the first three winters Kris and I shivered in our bedroom, separated from an open sleeping porch only by a glass door that would not stay closed against the blasts of wind. Eventually the sleeping porch became a master bathroom with wide windows screened by redwoods that had been old when the house was built. In the mornings I showered in a treetop aerie overlooking the hillside garden far below, with its terraced flowerbeds, miniature lawn, and children's climbing structure and sandbox.

In the children's bathroom, we replaced dark wood with cream-painted walls, a stenciled vine twining below the ceiling. Modern Swedish plumbing replaced the Victorian fixtures, but we saved the original six-foot-long bathtub, with its solid brass claw-and-ball feet. That tub held all three of our children at once when they were young, and carried them on voyages to faraway lands of their imaginings.

The kitchen was the center of our family life. Originally it had been decorated in gloomy browns and mustards that soaked up the light like a dirty sponge. With white paint and appliances, glass sconces, and a skylight, it was transformed into a bright and sunny room. The focal point of the kitchen was a long maple table where we ate and gathered to talk, where the children did their homework, where I mixed bowls of cookie batter, on which the children stood to launch toy airplanes, under which I hid them during the 1989 Loma Prieta earthquake. That day the shifting ground rocked the refrigerator back and forth like a boat buffeted by a stormy sea, but the house stood fast. Anchored in bedrock, we lived a safe and ordered life.

On the day Jeremy was taken away, the comfort and warmth of home dropped away like a cloak sliding off my shoulders. That lovely beloved house became only a place where I kept a furnished room to sleep. I spent as much time in the kitchen as was necessary to feed Lisie and David; I ignored the living room's warm invitation; and I showered and dried off in the bathroom without once stopping to look out the window and marvel at the trees.

I lived several miles away, in a small cramped cubicle in a large noisy room in a tall graceless building set by a freeway. My mind never left it completely. Had Jeremy worsened unexpectedly? Had the doctors and nurses missed the first sign of new danger? Had there been a change, however slight, that only I could read? Because I was his mother and he had once lived, whole, inside of me, my body still held a connection to his, vibrated in synchrony with his, like a crystal goblet that resonates with a singer's voice. My son's body sang to me in its silence, and I could hear every note. Who would listen when I was away?

Home, however, still sheltered two children who

were healthy and hurt and frightened. I was their mother, too. That fact moored me to the empty shell that had once contained a whole family.

———

After each twenty-four-hour hospital shift, I returned to the house, dirty and exhausted, carrying an overnight bag full of yesterday's clothes, my grandmother's rosary (stone beads the color of Lisie's golden eye), a few toiletries, my laptop, CDs, cards and gifts from visitors, and a list of things to bring back the next day. It was a small satchel, but very heavy. I carried all the suffering one person could hold inside that black canvas bag, back and forth every day, opening the zipper once in a while to stuff in even more.

My mother and father had quickly packed a small suitcase and again left everything behind to come stay with us when Jeremy was hospitalized. Age had worn down their rigid angles, revealing the softer curves beneath. As grandparents, they more than atoned for their shortcomings as parents. They were tender and loving with our children, and always ready to help us, however limited their means. Jeremy's injury had been nearly as shattering for them as for Kris and me. My father, the stern old army officer, could not talk about his grandson without crying. They would live in our guest room for three months. They shopped for food, ran errands, cleaned house, helped with driving, made two daily hospital visits, and watched Annelise and David when both Kris and I had to be away. Their presence made it possible for us to spend as much time at the hospital as we did.

Still, there was much to do when I returned home every other day: helping Lisie with Spanish translations and science homework, and David with spelling and arithmetic; researching medical options; sorting, reading, and answering the cards and letters from well-wishers that swelled our mail; returning phone calls from family members, friends, and co-workers who wanted to know "how things were going"; paying bills; folding and putting away laundry. Managing the medical bills alone was quickly becoming an enormous task. Most medical providers and procedures were billed separately. Each day's mail brought invoices from the hospital, neurosurgeon, neurologist, anesthesiologist, hematologist, vascular surgeon, pediatrician, MRI and CT scanning departments, pharmacy, and more. We had excellent insurance coverage—we had bought individual policies for each child when they were babies, at a very reasonable cost—and our insurance carrier paid its share of the bills, but a lot of logging, tracking, and faxing was required to stay on top of the tsunami of paper.

It seemed wrong that daily life went on without interruption. It seemed that clocks should have frozen on September 5, that the world should have stopped its spinning, held its breath, and listened along with us for the sound of Jeremy's voice. It didn't. Each day rolled onward into night, and each dawn led to another day. Life did not wait until we were ready to resume living.

Dinner was a vaguely awkward event. There were, as always, five people at our table, but they were not the right five people. Conversation stopped, started, stopped again. "So, how vas skool to-day, Ah-neh-li-seh?" my father would ask.

"Umm . . . okay," she responded.

"Do you vant uss to do tshoppink to-morrow?" my mother asked.

"Sure, Mom. That would be great. I'll make out a list in the morning."

When we talked about Jeremy, I told them small scraps of positive news. "His pain seemed better today," or "He was awake for a few minutes longer than yesterday."

After we cleared the table and washed the dishes, I took Lisie and David upstairs. They were both listless, weighed down by the disruption of their daily lives and events that loomed just outside their understanding. They washed their faces and brushed their teeth at the side-by-side sinks in their stenciled bathroom. David stood on a step stool to reach the taps, and Annelise solicitously loaded his toothbrush as well as her own. After they were finished, I clipped David's fingernails, brushed out the snarls from Lisie's thick, wavy hair, and helped David put on striped cotton jammies while Lisie donned a nightgown and retrieved her favorite stuffed creatures—a faded brown teddy bear, a large gray wolf, and a Raggedy Ann doll made by my mother. The three of us piled pillows at the head of the master bed that was too large without Kris and Jeremy, and curled up together in a tight knot at the center to read a book. We were working our way through the *Narnia* series, the first time for David and the second for Annelise. *The Voyage of the Dawn Treader* had reached the seas beyond World's End, where no ship ever came, and the mountains behind the sun, in Aslan's country.

After we closed the book, Annelise and David climbed into their own beds. I pulled the covers up tight and smooth, said the Lord's Prayer with each one, kissed them good-night, and made the sign of the cross on their foreheads. "Bless and keep thee all the night long, safe in God's arms till morning comes, and joy be thine forever."

———

Annelise and David adopted different survival strategies for getting through the days. Despite her anxieties about school, Annelise soldiered on. Her teacher was warm and kind, and she had both a small number of close friends and a larger cohort of supportive classmates. She became intensely organized, keeping her gear tightly stowed in her backpack, attending to every detail of her homework, fulfilling the assignments with excruciating care. Watching her, I recognized myself. *No, little one,* I wanted to tell her, *no matter how careful you are, how determined you are, you cannot make your world safe.* I did not say it. At eleven, she knew more of this truth than I myself had known only seven days before.

David retreated to silence and solitude. His rich imaginative play life stopped completely: no elaborate blocks-and-Legos military sets, no scenes with jungle animals and dinosaurs sharing a large apartment house, no Tonka dump trucks filled with cargo rolling across the living room floor. David picked one favorite play item, always a Star Wars figure, usually Luke Skywalker, which he carried with him everywhere. This talisman accompanied him to school, into the bathtub, into bed at night. We called it his "object of the day." The four-inch-high warrior-hero kept him safe.

David spent most of his time at home lying on his bed, reading, with his old blue teddy bear, Blueberry, curled in the crook of his arm or snuggled under his cheek. He chose books from the shelves in the room that he and Jeremy shared. *Hatchet*, the story of a thirteen-year-old boy whose plane crash-lands in the Arctic wilderness and who must survive, alone, without tools or food to sustain him. *Mr. Tuckett*, the story of a fourteen-year-old boy who is kidnapped by Indians and who must survive, alone, without language or kindness to sustain him. *The Voyage of the Frog*, the story of a fourteen-year-old boy—named David—who is stranded at sea in a damaged sailboat after a storm and who must survive, alone, without sail or radio to sustain him.

School went badly for David. His second-grade teacher was appropriately sympathetic when she saw me, but she didn't seem to understand David's difficulties. She complained, "David has been so preoccupied, he doesn't listen when I talk to him." Or, "David doesn't follow directions when I tell him that it's time to leave the block corner and go back to reading circle." Or, "Will you look at this!" She querulously showed me David's copybook, in which he was expected to write down small invented stories to build language skills. David had taken a pencil and with heavy, savage strokes that almost sliced through the paper had obliterated every line of text that he had written. Through the dark overlinings I could read parts of the stories that his mind had created and that he couldn't bear to keep: war, death, bombs, death, fire, more death.

His teacher took this as an affront to classroom order. She did not understand that, on the map of David's world, heere ther be dragouns. So many dragouns, so little land, the sea so vast, and his ship so small.

———

After Lisie and David were asleep and my parents had gone to bed as well, I padded around the silent house, compulsively straightening and putting things away: hanging jackets and sweatshirts in closets, lining up the shoes in the front entryway, stacking the day's newspapers in the recycling box. When I had restored as much order as was possible, I, too, went upstairs to bed.

I called Kris at the hospital. He reported on Jeremy's evening, and on the latest news from the doctors. I could hear the weariness under his words. "There's still no change. They want to start physical therapy. Two therapists are coming by in the morning to work with Jeremy's arms and legs . . ."

We made plans for the next day. "I'll be there by eleven . . . do you need a change of clothes? We've got to talk to the insurance company, they need some forms faxed in . . ."

Finally, we said good-night. "I miss you, sweetheart. I love you," Kris said softly.

"I love you too," I answered. "I hope you get some sleep. Give our boy a kiss for me."

———

In the morning, after preparing breakfast and packing school lunches, I drove the children to school. I dropped off Annelise first at the middle school campus. At David's elementary school I parked the car and walked him in. The classrooms were arranged in one long row, with every door opening directly out into the schoolyard. I held David's hand tightly and walked him to his classroom at the very end of the row. Every teacher was standing outside her door, greeting the arriving students and their parents. Every teacher knew me and our family. Most of them had taught Jeremy, and Annelise as well.

As we passed classroom after classroom, each teacher looked up with a morning smile, then recognized me. One after another, their faces fell and crumpled, their eyes overflowed, they reached out to embrace me, we hugged, they cried. I tried to maintain my composure; David was still holding my hand. On we trudged past the next classroom, where the teacher looked up and the greeting was repeated. By the time I reached the door to David's room, the shoulder of my tee-shirt was damp with tears.

David looked stoically ahead, his face blank. I knelt down, put on a smile, and embraced him. "Good-bye, punkin. You'll take the bus home today, okay?" He mumbled, "Yes," then turned away from my arms and trudged into the classroom without looking back.

From: Fiala, Marie Lawson
Sent: September 12, 1998 12:17 A.M.
To: Jeremy Network
Subject: Ebbs and Flows/Update No. 4

I awoke this morning in my own bed, Kris having taken the night shift at the hospital. For a moment it was a normal work day and school day and I was happy. Then I abruptly shifted sideways into the strange parallel universe we now inhabit, and the feeling evaporated. I little knew what I had seven days ago.

When I arrived at the hospital, there were good things. Jeremy was awake again. The ICU nurse allowed us to put tiny bits of Popsicle into his parched mouth. He opened for more; he was able to swallow. After a few tastes the effort exhausted him and he fell asleep.

He is desperate to communicate, but we don't know how. I wrote a few simple words on a large sheet of paper—"I," "want," "feel," "cold," "hot," "hurt," "love," and so on—thinking that perhaps he could point to them to express himself. He looked at the paper so hard; he clearly knew that the markings meant something but he couldn't make the connection. He turned his face away and closed his eyes.

A very hard afternoon. Jeremy's fever soared again to 104. He has no apparent infection. Sometimes the injured brain temporarily loses its ability to regulate temperature. Jeremy was frantic with the irritation caused by the bandages, the IV, the sheet. He writhed and tore at himself, trying to pull the drains out of his head. I held his arm down hard and told him to hit at me with his good left hand; it seemed to release some of his torment. We finally had no choice but to sedate him to give him some peace. The doctors tell us this is a normal part of recovery from a brain injury, but it is so hard to witness.

I end the day at home again. I'm out of steam after the long day and Kris bravely took another night shift. Late at night I miss Jeremy the most. During the day I focus on the many details that must be attended to—his pulse and respiration, blood gas levels, wetting his lips, putting drops in his eyes, moving his inert right leg and arm, sponging his face, reading aloud. I lose perspective; the details become the entire reality. In that world, if Jeremy's vital signs are stable we are doing well. Only when I come home do I know the enormity of our loss.

A line from Isaiah has been circulating in my mind all day. "For He is like a refiner's fire. . . ." We—Kris and Jeremy and I—are being refined down to our very essences. I feel at times as if the flesh will melt from my bones and leave behind nothing but pure spirit focused on the task of healing my son.

Keepsakes

TWO WEEKS BEFORE Jeremy collapsed, we had been on vacation in Hawaii. We had been returning to the same little beachfront condo since he was a toddler. It was an easy trip from the Bay Area. There were daily cheap flights from Oakland nonstop to Maui. We threw shorts, tee-shirts, swimsuits, flip-flops, and a few toiletries into duffel bags, and seven hours after leaving we were on the beach.

I could still see Jeremy there, building elaborate sand castles with Kris and David, jumping the waves, snorkeling, or boogie-boarding alongside Annelise, brown and graceful as a seal, his hair bleached golden by the sun. "Hey, Mom," he said with a huge grin, getting to his feet and pulling up his trunks after a big wave had left him high on the beach. "That was awesome. You want to borrow my board?"

It was awful to see how far Jeremy had regressed. He lay still and silent in the hospital bed, as helpless as an infant. All the gains of his first thirteen years had been washed away. He would travel a hard and lonely path as he struggled to come back. The first time he had learned to speak, to stand, to walk, his progress came easily, a natural maturing of his brain and body. I hoped he would relearn these things. But this time there was no template, no map for him to follow. This time he would have to find his way alone.

My little boy.

When he was very young, I carried him everywhere. He was never so happy as in my arms. On walks I pushed the empty stroller with one hand while I cradled him against me with the other arm. He curled into my chest, laid his head on my shoulder, and breathed small warm puffs of air against my neck as he fell asleep.

Of our three children, he was the one most like me. He was always shy of new things. The first time we went to Hawaii when he was eighteen months old, he was frightened of the waves that roared into shore and dissolved into whispers of white foam. He sat resolutely on the blanket under the umbrella, legs stiff and unbending as he refused to yield his feet to the sand. Eventually he gave in to the pleasures of pail and shovel and became engrossed in pouring golden particles in a hot dry stream from one container to another. Held in my arms, at last he bravely approached the ocean. We stood for a long time in our own small circle, lost in the endlessly shifting blues and greens of the smooth glassy hills rising before us. He would come to delight in the water that he once had feared.

He had always loved language, and books. By twenty months, he had a vocabulary of more than five hundred words, and we stopped counting. His diction was surprisingly adult for a person still so small: "Ac-tu-ally, Mommy . . ." We walked to the neighborhood children's store and bought him an enormous illustrated *Sesame Street Dictionary*. His eyes looked like Christmas morning. He refused to relinquish the book to a shopping bag, and clasping it with baby arms that did not span its width, held it tightly to his chest on the stroller ride home. Remembering, I wondered, *Will he ever read again?*

He loved music, too, from his early days—the louder and more rhythmic, the better. Springsteen's "Born in the U.S.A." was a favorite. Even before he could stand, he rocked back and forth on all fours, his round diapered bottom keeping time to the swirl of sound surging from the speakers. Later, he held onto the stereo cabinet with one hand, the drums, guitar, and saxophone lifting him off the ground to the tiptoes of his boneless rounded feet. This capacity for hearing the movement captured within the notes and the spaces between them, for allowing the sound to transport him beyond gravity, this, too, he had from his mother.

Not all the memories were happy. I reproached myself with my failings as a new parent. His early nights were difficult. In my well-intentioned ignorance, I believed that he needed to sleep in his own room, alone in his crib. He knew that he belonged with Kris and me, where he could pattern his nighttime breathing after ours, where he could draw on our body heat for warmth, where he could satisfy his small and frequent hungers as often as they awakened him. He cried and cried for me at night. I lay in my own bed unable to sleep, fighting my natural urge to pick him up and comfort him on the absurd assumption that this mutual torment was somehow best for him. I should have thrown out the baby books and listened to his intuitive wisdom, and mine.

I was wiser now. I had learned to hear and heed the choices encoded in my genes, the lessons of survival handed down through great distances of time. First among these was that I must not leave my child. He would not face the night alone.

From: Fiala, Marie Lawson
Sent: September 15, 1998 11:25 P.M.
To: Jeremy Network
Subject: Sanguine Thoughts/Update No. 5

The past three days have been a blur of comings and goings between home and hospital, of packings and unpackings, of hasty showers and little sleep, of being torn between our needy healthy children and our even needier sick one. I catch crumbs of sleep, often with my head on the edge of Jeremy's bed, holding his hand.

We've had some setbacks. Last night Jeremy started having seizures, violent uncontrollable spasms of his up-till-now healthy left side and face. His jaw opens and closes rapidly, endangering his tongue. His left arm and leg shake violently. He also has lost much alertness and responsiveness when awake. Most of today he was simply inert. I want a medication or procedure to make this go away, but there is none.

So far the doctors have no explanation, other than that brain injury causes strange things to happen. He had another CT scan; it showed that there is still lots of blood in his brain. The blood increasingly irritates the neural tissue, causing bad things to happen. So much blood already has drained out. How can there be so much still left? The doctors supply no answers. There are no answers. They tell us to wait.

I've been undone by this development. I thought I had come to understand the parameters of what we were dealing

71

with. I understood the injury and the treatment options, and believed we would move in a linear fashion from here to recovery. Just a different form of the illusion that one can create a place of safety by understanding and controlling all the inputs well enough. Apparently I hadn't learned that lesson yet, as I've been smacked across the head with it again. There is no control, bad things happen, and suffering enough is no proof against further suffering. All we can control is how we play out the hand we're dealt.

Letters

BY TEN IN THE EVENING the ICU quieted. The nursing shift change was over, televisions were turned off, and some of the children had fallen asleep. Jeremy, too, had drifted into dreaming, his sleep fractured by small moans and cries and restless shiftings. This was the first calm moment of my day. The torrent of events, questions, conversations, demands, and decisions that had bombarded me from early morning had ended, and I had time to think.

I was done in, but my mind was not quiet enough to sleep. Jeremy's cubicle was dark. In his hypersensitive state, turning on lights would have awakened him. Working mostly by feel, I groped for my overnight bag, unzipped it, found my laptop, powered it up, and plugged it into the phone jack. Sitting in the plastic chair squeezed between Jeremy's bed and the supply cabinet, I logged in and checked the e-mail folder. The room suddenly expanded, with thirty to forty e-mail messages from widely dispersed people who had written about Jeremy. Some of them were friends or family members. Others were acquaintances from work or school. Still others were strangers who knew about us through a chain of connections from one of our personal contacts. Warm words shimmered on the cool blue screen.

From: Sandra, Dallas
To: Fiala, Marie Lawson

Jeremy's name is on my network of prayer lists throughout

the country from Dallas to New York. As the minister in Archbold, Ohio, said in his sermon this morning, the love of God is like a childhood quilt that wraps us, warms us, and protects us. Your faith shines through your messages. I am so thankful you have it while you travel this path.

From: Jennifer, Indianapolis
To: Fiala, Marie Lawson

At church on Sunday, I asked for prayers for all of you. Harriet Crockett, one of the sweetest, purest, oldest women I know, called me up terribly distressed about Jeremy. Now, I know, God hears all of our prayers, but I suspect God truly revels in Harriet's prayers. . . . As a matter of fact, I secretly think God might go to Harriet from time to time for advice. You're in all our thoughts and prayers, and you have Harriet Crockett working for you too.

From: Grace, Philadelphia
To: Fiala, Marie Lawson

I am just one of countless people who have been praying for Jeremy, and keeping your family in my thoughts. All of us who are parents are struck to the heart by what you are going through, particularly because it seems so random and unfair. It could happen to any of us, to any of our children. . . . Remember that the professionals don't always know what they're talking about. They can offer you their best technology and medications and expertise. But in the end, they don't truly know. Keep your hope that things will get better. At times that may be all you have to hold on to. And know that while you are sitting there feeling lost and isolated, there are hundreds of us out here thinking of you. Since the prayer chains seem to cover the country, I would wager you could count on perpetual prayer going on.

From: Jack, San Rafael
To: Fiala, Marie Lawson

I have been reading your e-mails as they come in through Dave. I am so moved by what you are going through. I go home at night and hold our boys, give them extra hugs, and tell them I love them. Your words put life back into perspective, and make each moment so precious. I appreciate so much that you have shared these trials with us. You write with such depth. I know in my heart that Jeremy, his true self, is indestructible. The suffering that his body and thoughts are going though right now is very painful, but also impermanent. I pray for his full recovery, and the cessation of his, yours, and all our suffering. I send you all unconditional love, and the hope that Jeremy finds his way through this rapid, to the calmer waters ahead.

Along with comfort, these letters told of the writers' own griefs and losses: a miscarriage, a crippled child, the passing away of a spouse or a parent, a son or a daughter who died young. As I opened each message in turn and read it slowly, I wept for them, for us, for all the sadness focused on this small screen.

Blinking through tears, I wrote at least a brief note to every correspondent: "Thank you. We feel your compassion and presence with us. Please keep praying. Thank you."

After reading and answering each message, I composed an update describing developments of the past one or two days. I wrote these dispatches quickly, usually very late at night. Almost always a few experiences had been circling in my head, bumping against the walls, waiting to be released into words. The writing cleared my mind of the painful and troubling so that I could finally fall asleep.

Trying to summarize the day's ups and downs in a short message was difficult. Trying to say just enough, to smooth over the hardest parts, was even harder. I felt I could not reveal my true despair because it was important to keep hope alive in these messages, to give people a reason to continue reading, and praying. I could not say, *He is sinking. The doctors have run out of options. I am so terribly afraid.*

When I finished writing I pulled up the e-mail distribution list, which had grown long. Every day more people wrote, asking to be added. I clicked on the "send" icon, touched the world with a fingertip.

I wrote for many reasons. For the satisfaction of being able to shape one small thing in the way I wanted it. To control what I could control. To transform raw and ugly experience into something calm and contained. To remind myself of the possibility of beauty, even if only in words. To witness, so that if our son died, we would have this to remember. And if he lived, so that we would not forget.

Jeremy overall is less alert, less responsive. In addition to the major battles, we fight small brush fires constantly. He has infections in both eyes, for which we apply antibiotic ointment. Just today, an opportunistic fungal infection, encouraged by the IV antibiotics that Jeremy has been given, raced across his feet and through his mouth. He becomes dehydrated, his veins collapse, and it becomes almost impossible to insert new IVs or to draw blood. The fevers rise and fall, with no apparent reason.

Outwardly, little is left of the rich relationship we had with Jeremy two weeks ago. He can't speak at all, and can't see more than a few inches from his face. It has become increasingly hard for him even to lift his eyes, so today he can't meet our gaze. And yet, he is still there behind his frozen face. His reactions show in small movements and moans and facial expressions that I can read with ease. I am still with my son in every important sense.

David has been deeply thoughtful and quiet through all this. Two days ago he suddenly said, "You know, Mom, sometimes God makes mistakes." Short pause. "Sometimes, when God makes mistakes, He makes them with a permanent marker." And sometimes, we are also granted a measure of grace to live with the permanent marker mistakes.

I plan to put this aside and focus solely on Jeremy's next

24 hours. Fed him first solid food—3 ounces of chocolate pudding—today; his eyes widened with pleasure. He gave a first smile with half his mouth at the reading of a Dave Barry story. He looked out of the window at the sky for the first time. Muscles in his right upper thigh twitched. So grateful to have these moments with Jeremy. These are good things to hang onto.

Colors

FOR TWO WEEKS Jeremy's condition had been measured through the clear plastic tubes that drained blood from his brain. Liquid beads emerged one after another from beneath the bandages that swathed his head, rolled slowly down through the tubes, and dripped into the liter-sized bags suspended on either side of the bed. I sat for hours watching drop after crimson drop roll through its plastic tunnel, hang poised at the lower end, and then release its hold to fall into the pool below. I studied every drop, assessed every nuance of color, hoping to see a gradual lightening to the pale straw shade of healthy cerebrospinal fluid. These tiny envoys from inside Jeremy's brain stubbornly remained ruby red, claret red, blood red.

But the fluid refused to clear, signaling that Jeremy was still bleeding, and the doctors increasingly worried about the drains. Blood is sticky. Its proteins clung to the inner walls of the tubes in his head, gradually slowing the drainage. It clotted, as it is designed to do, to close off what Jeremy's brain could only interpret as—what, in fact, were—two massive wounds opening to the outside. The flows slowed, stopped, started again.

Even more worrisome, the liquid dripping from the two sides of Jeremy's brain was no longer the same color on each side. The right, uninjured, side drained almost clear, while the left side, site of the hemorrhage, remained dark red. Normally the ventricles, the large chambers at the center of the brain, are connected, and fluid flows freely from one side to the other. It should have been the same color on both sides. Evidently a blockage had formed between the right side and the left, leaving the left drain as the only escape route for the blood that must leave Jeremy's brain.

On this particularly bad day I was at the hospital, and neither Kris nor I had seen a neurosurgeon for forty-eight hours. I was terrified. Jeremy had been having seizures off and on for several days, his body going rigid and then shaking uncontrollably, his eyes rolling up, his jaw clamping shut convulsively. With each seizure, fear struck me like an earthquake. *What is going on? Is this the end? Why don't they do something to make it stop?*

The neurosurgeon, Dr. Klein, made rounds very early in the morning. I had left instructions with the night nurse to wake me so that I could talk to him. But he had decided that there was nothing to talk about, and told the nurse to let me sleep. When I awoke in the reclining chair in Jeremy's room, the doctor was gone, but my questions were not.

Now it was late morning. Jeremy's left drain, the critical drain, had completely stopped flowing hours ago; the right side was running perfectly clear. There was no escape route for the blood in his brain. Pacing back and forth alongside Jeremy's bed, looking at one bag and then the other, I imagined the blood building up in his brain, destroying the vulnerable nerve cells that Jeremy needed to move, to speak, to see.

What was worse, there was new seepage through the bandages over the place where the right drain entered Jeremy's skull. I bent over him, examined the bandage closely, taking care not to touch it, to avoid contamination that might spread infection into Jeremy's brain. Yes, the bandage was definitely wet. The formerly dark brown patches on its surface were turning lighter rust, yellow, and spreading. The right drain had backed up; fluid was leaking directly out of Jeremy's skull.

Normally I strive to appear outwardly calm, even at times of stress. It is a skill that serves me well in my professional life. No matter how frustrated or worried I feel, I carefully meter out my emotions, keeping them at the cool blue-green end of the spectrum. Now, however, I was redlining, frightened and angry because there was nothing I could do myself to help Jeremy. I was totally dependent on the skills and schedule of a stranger who did not love my son.

I reached the thinnest end of my strand of patience and asked a nurse to page Dr. Klein and tell him that I wanted to talk to him. Dr. Klein was in surgery and did not respond to the page for a long time. I continued to pace. Fear buzzed in my head, a white noise that blocked out everything else. *Where is that damn doctor?* Twenty minutes, forty minutes, more than an hour went by. Finally Dr. Klein made an appearance—a tall, corpulent man in his sixties with a heavy jowled face. He was still wearing surgical scrubs, with a too-small green tartan surgical cap perched on unruly white hair. "What is it you wanted?" he asked with an air of tired irritability.

"Jeremy's left drain is not working. It hasn't been flowing since sometime yesterday evening," I pointed out. My tenor was even. I did not want to use my lawyer persona in this conversation. Alienating this doctor would not serve Jeremy's interests.

"We'll take it out," he responded.

"And replace it?" I queried, still in a reasonable voice.

"No need for that," he said dismissively. "The right drain is sufficient. He'll be fine with just one drain." He turned to go.

"Dr. Klein," I said to his back, "I am not comfortable with that solution, I don't believe the right and left ventricles are communicating with each other."

He turned ponderously, looked down at me as if a cockroach beneath his shoe had suddenly spoken. "There's no need for two drains," he repeated with mounting ill-humor. "We do this all the time. Don't worry yourself about it. We know what we're doing."

Talking down to me lit a match to a very short fuse.

"Doctor," I said, my voice rising, "I may not be medically trained but I'm not stupid. I have been sitting here watching these drains every minute of every hour day after day, and you have not, and I can see that the right drain has been running clear for days and the left has continued to be bloody, and I can see that the drains have been leaking through the bandages as well, so don't come in here and spend thirty seconds telling me that one drain is enough and that I don't need to worry about it because this is MY SON AND I DO WORRY ABOUT HIM, AND TAKING OUT THE LEFT DRAIN WITHOUT DOING ANYTHING MORE IS NOT A GOOD-ENOUGH ANSWER."

By the last words, my voice had risen to a shockingly uncivil level. An acute silence followed. The nurse, standing at the back of the cubicle, looked surprised. Her lips and cheek muscles twitched. Dr. Klein's face purpled beneath the jaunty green tartan. He was probably not accustomed to having his judgment questioned. At the same time, the patient's mother was acting unstable. Perhaps he should humor her, calm her down.

"Well," he said after a profound pause, "let's take a look at that right drain and see how it's doing." He stepped over to the bed and touched Jeremy for the first time, turning Jeremy's head and peeling back an edge of the bandage over the supposedly good drain. A stream of fluid that had backed up and pooled under the adhesive gushed out and ran down the side of Jeremy's face onto his pillow, staining his white pillowcase with a spreading splotch of red-ocher-brown.

For the first time, Dr. Klein looked concerned. "I think we need to get him into surgery," he said. "We're going to have to put in new drains. Tonight."

From: Fiala, Marie Lawson
Sent: September 18, 1998 9:46 P.M.
To: Jeremy Network
Subject: Keeping Vigil/Update No. 8

It is Friday evening and I'm sitting next to Jeremy, waiting to go to surgery. In this quiet time while he sleeps I've been studying the UCSF interventional radiologist's report. Some things a parent perhaps shouldn't read. Jeremy's AVM is located in the middle of an important vascular pathway. The report explains that the embolization (glue) procedure would immediately cure the AVM but also immediately cut off the blood supply to vital "downstream" parts of the brain. Jeremy would permanently lose function in his right arm and leg and likely also his vision. The alternative, the "gamma knife" radiation, would not be effective for 2–3 years after treatment. That means living with a time bomb inside Jeremy's head for all that time. UCSF wants to wait 6–8 weeks to see whether his "dense hemiparesis (paralysis) and visual field loss" persists. If yes, then they'll go ahead with the embolization because Jeremy won't have much to lose. But if he regains some functions, rather than risking whatever mobility and vision he has left, they recommend the gamma knife, with its risk of a rebleed.

Most of the time I feel partly asleep. When I awake it seems inconceivable that these are our choices, this is our future. Hard to know what to do with this information. I opt for a miracle, instead.

———

Jeremy is now in the hands of the surgeons and anesthesiologists. We waited with him up to the door of the operating room. He was scared. Before leaving him we said the prayers for the sick from the Book of Common Prayer, we told stories about his babyhood, we talked about our next trip to Hawaii and feeling the warm small waves wash over his feet as he stands on the edge of sand and sea. We both kissed him and gave him our blessing and sent him off, small and alone. Then we cried.

Folding Together

World as it is,
what's strong and separate falters. All I do
at piling stone on stone apart from you
is roofless around nothing . . .

—John Ciardi

RIS AND I WAITED in Jeremy's room until a neurosurgeon and operating room became available for the surgery to replace Jeremy's drains. Sitting across the bed from me, Kris looked spent. Although his blue Oxford cloth shirt was, as always, neatly pressed, his shoulders sagged, his thick chestnut hair was dull and unwashed, his face was stubbly, and he had deep purple splotches under his eyes. He was quiet, as was his way.

I had felt further apart from Kris each day since Jeremy's collapse. We had had very little time together— one of us was always at the hospital, the other outside— and our conversations mostly focused on medical issues and logistics. I had always thought my marriage to Kris was unshakeable, as solid as the canyon walls above the river where we had met. Now we were each entombed with our own pain, blanketed and bound with it, too alone to speak to one another, too distant to hear each other's voices.

I thought, briefly, *I should reach out to him, say something encouraging.* But I couldn't even find comforting lies to tell myself anymore. And the part of me that had feelings about anything, other than willing that Jeremy should live, was hiding in a closet in the back of my head somewhere. Making Kris feel better was just one more thing I was no longer able to do. *This is why couples break up when they have a family crisis*, I thought. *They have no strength left to hold onto one another.*

Jeremy was closer to coma than consciousness, but he was awake enough to understand that something important was about to happen, and that we were frightened. We took turns talking to him quietly: "You're going to have another operation on your head. You'll be asleep, you won't feel anything. It will be all right. We're with you. You're safe." It was hard to know how much Jeremy took in, but his eyes were wide and anxious and he held tightly to my hand.

"Let's say a prayer, Jeremy," Kris said. He picked up and leafed through the *Book of Common Prayer* that he had brought to the hospital on the first day. "Almighty God our heavenly Father, graciously comfort your servant Jeremy in his suffering, and bless the means made use of for his cure. Fill his heart with confidence that, though at times he may be afraid, he yet may put his trust in you. . . ."

In the early evening the neurosurgeon came in for a pre-op examination. This was not Dr. Klein but one of his partners, a younger doctor with a gentle demeanor and sad brown eyes. He explained the procedure. Two new holes would be cut through Jeremy's skull, and long plastic tubes would be threaded through the soft tissue until they reached the open spaces at the center of the brain. And the risks: coma, infection, further hemorrhage. Death.

The evening moved slowly. At 10:00 P.M. a nurse came

in to start yet another IV. Just seeing her wheel in the supply cart twisted my stomach. Jeremy's veins had never been prominent. Now that he was lying flat and his blood pressure was low, a "good" vein was impossible to find. Every IV took three, four, or more needle sticks before a connection was made. The nurses had an almost superstitious attitude toward this process. It takes conviction to pierce skin, flesh, blood vessel wall with a sharp steel skewer. They lost confidence if they couldn't find a vein by the second or third try.

Tonight, when Jeremy heard that a new IV was needed, he cried silently, tears spilling from the outer corners of his eyes and running down his cheeks. "Oh, sweet guy," said Kris, tears starting from his eyes as well. The nurse tried, missed, grimaced, bit her lip, tried again, missed again. Jeremy held still but moaned softly with each new needle stick. She gave up and called in another nurse to try. Finally, success.

Because it was late and the operating theater was empty and the staff had come to know us, Kris and I were allowed to accompany Jeremy into the pre-op area. While we waited for the anesthesiologist to arrive we each held one of Jeremy's hands and bent over the gurney, talking steadily: "The cats have taken to sleeping on your bed at home; they miss you. The weather's turned hot. These are good doctors. You're going to be fine." The anesthesiologist came in, looking remote and shielded in blue scrubs, hat and mask, and plastic goggles. He injected a syringe of liquid into Jeremy's IV line. Before we had counted to three, Jeremy was deeply asleep. We both kissed him and stroked his forehead before he was wheeled away, and then we were alone.

I wanted someone to hold me, give me a moment of remembered grace, say words to make me briefly forget what was real. I imagined that Kris wanted the same. But all we had was each other, two people near to breaking apart with grief and worry, still trying to look steady on the outside, to find useful sentences to say to the doctors, to prove they could be trusted to stay with their son to the last possible moment before the next great uncertainty.

I remembered part of a poem that Kris and I had read before we were married. We had wanted to engrave the opening line inside our wedding rings, but it was too long: "Most like an arch this marriage . . . two weaknesses that lean / Into a strength. Two fallings become firm."

What we shared was our single-minded focus on keeping the son we had created together alive. *Jeremy bridges the space between us*, I thought. *Maybe it's enough to connect us, for now.*

Kris and I walked back to the ICU to wait in Jeremy's cubicle. The operating room nurse promised to call as soon as he was out of surgery. We sat close together and held hands. Every once in a while a sentence bubbled up through the dense silence.

"What time is it?"

"How long has it been now?"

"When do you think they'll be done?"

It was nearly midnight. At last the ICU nurse looked in to tell us that the operating room had called. The surgery was finished; Jeremy would be in recovery in a few minutes.

The recovery room was large and empty, with space for many gurneys to line up next to each other. We had it to ourselves; Jeremy was the only patient still in surgery at this late hour. We sat on the edges of two mismatched plastic chairs. I couldn't stop shivering.

Finally they wheeled him in. He looked even worse than I had expected. Unconscious. Fresh bandages on his head, already soaked through with bright blood. His face so white it was almost blue. Although heated blankets had been heaped high on his small form, he shook convulsively. Incongruously, someone had put a smiling teddy bear wearing green surgical scrubs next to him on the gurney.

Kris and I rose from our seats, swooped down on the gurney quickly from either side. In unison we stepped close, each laid a hand on Jeremy's form, bent down toward him, gently folded toward him, closed over him on either side like wings.

From: Fiala, Marie Lawson
Sent: September 21, 1998 1:00 P.M.
To: Jeremy Network
Subject: New Horizons/Update No. 9

Jeremy slept peacefully much of the weekend. We saw improvement after Friday night's surgery. He is more alert and responsive. His color, which Friday evening was nearly the gray of his hospital bedding, has been restored to its fading summer tan. We believe that the old drains had not been working effectively and that the resulting buildup had put pressure on his brain, causing last week's decline.

Beyond that we continue to learn to wait. Jeremy's motor/speech/visual deficits remain largely unchanged. The fluid from his head is increasingly lighter red and we pray continuously for it to clear. Jeremy seems to understand everything we say to him, although he can only respond by nodding and shaking his head. We have refined the asking of yes-and-no questions. "Are you cold?" Shake. "Do you want the music on?" Shake. "Are you thirsty?" Nod. "Do you want some Popsicle?" Vigorous nod.

We try to keep our horizons close, but occasionally we have to lift our eyes to longer-term issues. We meet with the UCSF team this Wednesday, which should bring more information about the AVM treatment. These are hard questions to hold in the mind for long. We quickly return to the here-and-now.

Stasis

HUMAN BEINGS SEEMINGLY HAVE an irrepressible tendency to construct a normal life out of whatever wreckage surrounds them. You see the newspaper pictures after every war or natural disaster: Amid the devastation of a ruined city or a refugee camp, families set up homes in tents or bombed-out dwellings, prepare meals, lay a table, make up sleeping places, arrange salvaged belongings on whatever surfaces still exist to hold them. Order takes shape out of a larger chaos. So I, two weeks into an evolving catastrophe, built a new routine from the ruins of a former life.

Morning began early after a night of broken sleep. The neurosurgeon made rounds at 6:00 A.M., and I made it a point to be awake to ask the accumulated questions of the last twenty-four hours. The doctor on call, an older man, very experienced, shone a flashlight into Jeremy's eyes, tested his reflexes with a rubber mallet, and poked him with pins in various places. Still no right-side movement, still no speech. The doctor was carefully noncommittal, but this was clearly not a course toward recovery.

Between 7:00 and 8:00 A.M. was shift change. The night and day nursing staff overlapped, relayed information, handed off responsibilities. Jeremy and I, who had fallen back to sleep after the neurosurgeon's visit, were awakened again for vital signs and more questions. This matter of sleep deprivation loomed huge in the hospital. Jeremy was awakened at one- to two-hour intervals all night for neurological checks. The bags draining his brain filled up and were replaced. His bed became wet and needed to be changed. Other children called out, cried, screamed sporadically. Fluorescent lights were always on; monitors beeped and buzzed; alarms shrieked insistently. Sleep came in tiny increments, not enough, not nearly enough. *How can anyone heal,* I wondered, *under these conditions?*

There was no breakfast tray. Jeremy still couldn't eat, except for occasional spoonfuls of semi-liquid food, and parents don't get trays. Leaving him alone so that I could go to the cafeteria was not an option; he was terrified without me and incapable of grasping the simple idea, "I'll be right back." If I left the room even momentarily, he panicked, wept and flailed and thrashed, and could not be calmed by the hospital staff.

I went hungry unless a visitor brought me something to eat. Often Father Bruce came early in the day with a cup of coffee for me, to say hello, see how Jeremy was doing, and pray together. I was grateful for the prayers. Sometimes I was even more grateful for the coffee. To me, sleepless, unwashed, in stale clothes, coffee was a priceless comfort. It was a small piece of the familiar world, the only ritual that still tethered me to a life that included the morning newspaper read over a cup of coffee, the midday walk from my office to the corner espresso shop, a latte with a friend. Only the coffee was left.

Today, my mother and father were the first to arrive. They peered around the curtain, shyly offering a large steaming paper cup and a pastry bag. With my parents at Jeremy's bedside in case he woke up—he always awakened confused and afraid—I took a few minutes to clean up for the day. This meant carrying my towel, washcloth, and toiletries down the hall to the public women's restroom to wash my face and brush my teeth.

The restroom was open around the clock. Its condition

in the morning, after a night's use by hospital visitors and refugees from the neighboring West Oakland streets, was vile. Pools of urine or vomit, soiled toilet tissue, even used condoms spotted the floor. Toilets were clogged and backed up. Everything that could be stolen had been stolen. The stoop-shouldered day-shift janitor shook his graying head as he pushed a wheeled metal washbucket filled with dirty water and a string mop down the hall. "What kinda person steal soap?" he asked out loud. "These people ain't usin' that soap, you be sure of that."

I took care not to touch anything inside the restroom with my bare hands as I opened the taps and splashed water on my face. Most mornings the floor was so bad that I used my own towel to stand on and blotted my face dry with paper towels—if the dispenser was not empty. If it was, my tee-shirt served the purpose. As I washed, anxiety was a tightness growing in my chest, squeezing the air out of my lungs. *What if he woke up and my parents weren't able to calm him? What if a doctor came by and I wasn't there to hear any bits of news? Hurry, hurry, hurry . . .*

Changing clothes was tricky. I balanced on one foot on the tiny towel while pulling off one shoe and then one pants leg, making sure that the pants never touched the floor, then repeated the process for the other leg. I set the shoes down on a paper towel, folded the pants into a tight bundle on top of the shoes, quickly slipped into fresh underwear and a clean shirt, put the pants and shoes back on while again balancing on each foot in turn, and sealed everything I had used in a plastic bag. Done.

In another life I had taken an hour in the morning to shower, blow-dry my hair, apply makeup, and dress in business clothing. My new routine took between five and six minutes. The woman staring at me out of the restroom mirror looked like a refugee from a homeless encampment: wearing a baggy tee-shirt and jeans, she had stringy un-washed hair, dark undereye circles, and pale rabbity features without eyebrow pencil or mascara. *You look like hell. Good thing you don't need to impress anyone.* I shrugged. Turning away from the mirror, I used the hem of my shirt to open the door, and trotted down the hall back to Jeremy's bedside.

———

Once Jeremy was awake I assembled supplies for his bed bath. We had learned quickly that clean linens were in perpetual short supply. Soviet-style stockpiling was the only solution. I made an early morning run to the linen cart to make sure that Jeremy would have clean bedding, and Kris or I would have a blanket to sleep under that night. Pillows, sheets, waterproof mattress pads, towels, gown, washcloths, soap, basin. I was ready.

I began with his face. There was still considerable crusted blood around his ears and at the edge of the bandages that crossed his forehead. With each bathing I eroded away a bit more of the dark brown sediment. His hair was hopeless. The front half of his head had been shaved to the scalp, but the hair had been left intact on the back half. It was dark and matted with dried blood, sweat, and grease. I tried to wipe Jeremy's hair with the washcloth, but since I couldn't lift his head, I made little progress. Because he had drains in his head, Jeremy had to lie scrupulously flat. Raising his head higher than the end of the tubing would have had the same effect as siphoning gas from a car, except in this case it would have been all of Jeremy's cerebrospinal fluid spilling out, leaving him dead.

My poor, fastidious son. From his infancy Jeremy could not tolerate dirt or messes. During feedings, when a spoonful of pureed food landed on his clothes, hands, or the high-chair tray, Jeremy would point to it, saying, "Uuhh, uuhh, uuhh," and refuse to continue eating until we had cleaned it up. He hated fingerpainting because it meant dipping his hands in sticky goop. And working in clay was nearly impossible. Jeremy brought home sculptures from school that he had obviously poked at with a fingertip as little as possible. Now he was filthy; he smelled of illness and decay. How he would hate this if he knew.

I uncovered a small area of Jeremy's body at a time, dipped a washcloth in the basin, lathered and rinsed, patted dry. I worked around the bandages holding the IV needles to his arms and legs, washing the bruised flesh from many prior punctures. The colored splotches ranged from deep purple-black to a pale yellowish-green, depending on the age of the wound.

Jeremy's trunk was next, a mass of sensors held on by adhesive pads. When the adhesive lost its stickiness, every day or so, the pads were replaced by new pads in new places. Jeremy's chest and abdomen were covered with patches of old adhesive that had turned dark gray and solidified. They were impervious to soap and water.

The poignancy of these simple actions was almost unbearable. By now, I knew every inch of Jeremy's skin as well as I knew my own. Washing another human body is an ancient and archetypal act. We have always washed our infants, washed our elderly, washed our dead. Jesus washed his disciples' feet. For the first time I understood why. Washing the body of another person is an intimate privilege, a profound and loving act. It takes away the space that separates the washer and the washed. The ritual takes on sacramental meaning, connects the two in ways too deep for words.

One of the nurses, Marcus, came in at the end and rolled Jeremy onto his side and held him there so I could wash his back. Marcus's dreadlocks framed the face of a Renaissance angel. A father to three children of his own, he was unfailingly tender with my son. Best of all, he was strong.

After the sponge bath Marcus and I changed the bed, a physically grueling process of layering linens and waterproof pads under Jeremy's body as we rolled him side to side. I often repeated this process three or four times a day, as the sheets became soiled with medication, blood, or urine. My lower back, always weak, throbbed relentlessly.

When Jeremy was clean, it was time for a long list of meds. The worst was dilantin, the anti-seizure medicine. Even the nurses hated giving it. Caustic and unstable, it ate through syringes, tubing, and blood vessels. Marcus and I removed Jeremy's various bandages, checking to see which IVs were flowing and which needed to be restarted. The IV used for dilantin needed to be replaced daily, as the medicine dissolved the vein into a puddle of tissue and a purple bruise.

Jeremy was in pain—he had four big holes in his skull— but pain management was difficult because he couldn't tell anyone how he felt. Marcus gave him a megadose of liquid Tylenol, causing me to worry about liver damage in addition to everything else. It was not enough. He twisted and writhed until morphine bought him a few hours of respite.

The physical therapists came, and we worked on pulls and stretches to keep Jeremy's paralyzed arm and leg from contracting into permanent knots. The speech therapist brought in a picture board, and asked Jeremy to point to symbols representing "drink," "sleep," "music," or "TV." Jeremy stared at the pictures but did not seem to register their meanings.

Between therapies I tried to soothe Jeremy by playing music, reading aloud, or just talking to him. Simple rhythms worked best. Gregorian chant, classical piano. *The Narnia Chronicles*, reread many times, so familiar that the words flowed over him like cool water.

The endless day wore on. Fatigue ground me down. I moved more and more slowly.

Kris came in the late afternoon, and we conducted our own shift change.

"The teacher called. Annelise started crying in school today . . ."

"Jeremy's had his bath . . . a bad day, a lot of pain . . . The doctor didn't say much; just wait and see what happens."

I leaned into Kris's chest. We wrapped our arms around each other and stood, feeling each other breathing. "Good-bye, sweetheart," I said at last.

Tired as I was, leaving was harder than staying. The outside world was an alien landscape bathed in brassy sunlight, too bright, too noisy, too alive to be tolerable. I hurried home to shelter until I saw Jeremy again.

From: Fiala, Marie Lawson
Sent: September 23, 1998 5:25 P.M.
To: Jeremy Network
Subject: Circling the Eddy/Update No. 10

Today we made it through another rough patch. We had been scheduled to drive to UCSF to meet with the AVM treatment team. When I walked into the ICU mid-morning to meet Kris, Jeremy's drains were leaking again, the neurosurgeon had arrived to take them out a second time right then, and Jeremy was being prepped for yet another surgery, which at that particular moment meant multiple needle sticks into his poor depleted veins to start another IV. We cancelled the UCSF appointment.

Now the drains are out and we wait for Jeremy's cerebrospinal fluid (CSF) to begin circulating or not, for pressure to build or not, for any sign that something is going wrong in the unseen country inside Jeremy's head. Two hours after the surgery I noticed that Jeremy's right pupil was much larger than the left, usually a very bad sign neurologically. The attending ICU physician recommended an emergency trip to the CT scan; the neurosurgeon, when reached on the phone, decided to wait for the scan until tomorrow. As Jeremy's CSF normalizes, small glitches are to be expected, he says. It doesn't become an emergency until Jeremy shows signs of losing consciousness or other gross neurological manifestations.

To me now, fragile as I have become, every shift from one level of stability to another feels like an emergency.

There is comfort in being intimately familiar with whatever plateau I currently inhabit, even if the plateau itself is far from normal. Every movement to another level feels like climbing without a rope.

Jeremy has circled back to his baby self. We named him Jeremy Day because he would lie peacefully in the arms of his exhausted father or mother at daybreak and stare out the window at the sunrise over our shoulders. Now when I turn his face to the window side of the room his big eyes gaze out at the sky with the same gravity. His shaven head bobs and weaves without enough strength in his neck to support it. I take care of his bodily comforts. He cannot speak but communicates all I need to know with his eyes. "I love you," his eyes speak. "Thank you," they say. I love him with the same desperate immediacy that I felt for my infant son.

A Prayer for Jamal

I HAD NEVER SEEN A DEATH before our time in the ICU. The first was Jamal's.

I guessed that Jamal was two months old, but he may have been born small due to drugs or malnutrition. He might have been older. That was not an unreasonable supposition, as many of the infants in the ICU came from the surrounding Oakland neighborhoods and had been born to crack- or heroin-addicted mothers.

Jamal had been lying in the steel crib next to Jeremy's cubicle in the ICU since we had first arrived. His arms and legs were too thin for a baby; his skin was like charcoal ashes. His broad face was surrounded by a nimbus of curly black hair. I do not know how long he had lain there.

Jamal had no visitors. Kris and I lived in the ICU twenty-four hours a day, and no one except the medical staff ever came to Jamal's bedside. He cried constantly, high, shrill, penetrating shrieks. Most of the time, no one answered. No one connected by blood and love was with him, and the nurses in the ICU were often too busy to soothe a crying infant. The metal bars, the hospital sheet and blanket, the sensors taped to his tiny torso, the needles, the medical instruments, were all he knew of the world.

I wish it were true that I thought of Jamal only with love and charity during his last weeks, but I was not that good; I was sleep-deprived, unraveling, fighting to hold onto myself and avoid an emotional meltdown. Jamal's constant crying was a nearly unbearable irritant. He never stopped. He gave out wail after wail, an unnatural sound, high-pitched, jagged, with a nerve-jangling metal-on-metal quality. The cry a baby makes after learning that no one hears it. *Ohmigosh, if only he would stop, if only he would just BE STILL.* I played out mental scenarios in which I marched over and snatched him out of his crib, held him close, rocked my body back and forth cooing, "There, there, baby; there, there," until he quieted. But I never did. Touching a stranger's critically ill child in the ICU was out of the question.

On the afternoon after Jeremy's drains were removed for the second time, Kris and I sat at his bedside, wracked with fear. Jeremy was barely conscious. I rocked back and forth in my seat in an agony of tension. Kris sat forward with his elbows on his knees, bowed his head, and ran his hands through his hair over and over. We expected at any moment to see a sign that Jeremy was failing, even as we knew that nothing more could be done to keep him alive.

Suddenly Jamal's bedside alarms shrieked. Kris shot upright in his chair. "What was *that*?" he said. Jamal was in crisis. He had "coded"—his heart had stopped. In an emergency like this, surgery was performed on the spot in the ICU. There was no time to get Jamal into an operating room. Eight to ten doctors and nurses rushed to his crib and hurriedly gloved up. Equipment was rolled in; drapes were hung; the ICU was closed to visitors. Rather than have us walk past Jamal's bed to leave, contaminating the operating field, they told us to stay where we were.

Even Jeremy knew from the noise and activity that something was happening. He opened his eyes wide, looking terrified. "It's okay, honey," I said, stroking his forehead. "Jamal's sick. The doctors are taking care of him."

The medical team worked fast, with great focus. Brisk orders were given in clipped voices; instruments passed from hand to hand. Mostly we saw many blue-gowned backs surrounding the crib, bowed heads, hands reaching to other hands. Later we realized Jamal's chest had been opened up for heart surgery. The team worked on and on, ten minutes, twenty, thirty. Kris and I held Jeremy's hands, bowed our heads, and prayed for Jamal: "O God, the strength of the weak and the comfort of sufferers: Mercifully accept our prayers, and grant to your servant Jamal the help of your power, that his sickness may be turned into health . . ."

Perhaps forty minutes later the crisis abruptly ended. Nothing more could be done. The medical team immediately dissolved away. Jamal was revealed, still and ashen, limbs sprawled loosely, the sheet beneath him a bright wet red. He was alone again. No one stroked his hair, straightened his arms and legs, kissed his soft baby cheek in parting, or covered him against the cold.

Kris turned the pages of the prayer book: "Receive, oh Lord, your child, Jamal, for he returns to you. May he gaze upon you, Lord, face to face, and grant him the blessing of perfect rest."

Jamal's mother came and went briefly. A sullen, heavy young woman in her early twenties, she arrived in the ICU twenty minutes after his death, surrounded by a group of family and friends, gave a perfunctory wail, "Oh, mah *baby*, mah *baby*," and left again. Even then she did not pick him up. A cleanup crew descended in her wake, and Jamal, the bloodied sheets, the surgical drapes, and the equipment were all whisked away in moments. The freshly made-up steel crib waited for its next occupant. No sign remained that only an hour before a human child had lived and suffered and cried there. Died there.

Against the immensity of what I already felt, my sadness for Jamal was scarcely perceptible. Like rain falling on the Pacific, it did not make the ocean deeper. Mostly I felt dull anger that this child had been created and then allowed to live and die, alone. I told myself I should exonerate Jamal's mother and all the other mothers who left their children in the hospital like rubbish. *They're poor. They don't have much education. They come from tough neighborhoods.* But I knew these were lies. A fierce mother-heart has been part of the human heritage since before time was recorded. It does not depend on schooling, wealth, or comfort; it warms every mud-walled barrio and barbed-wire camp, places far worse than urban Oakland. I would not concede less than full humanity to another woman by exempting her from this sacred obligation. Nor would I deny her child this birthright.

In the end, beneath my sadness and anger, I felt huge, selfish gratitude that my son still lived, even as I knew that his life was no more worthy, no more earned, than Jamal's. But he was my son, and my tiger mother's heart burned fiercely, brightly, and would not let him go.

The Darkest Hours

If you are going through hell, keep going.

—Sir Winston Churchill

THE SIMPLEST ACTS, we take for granted, like breathing, or talking, or sitting up. We don't think about how hard it is to do those things until we—or someone we love—can't do them. Until we have to struggle, and hope, and risk to regain them.

I learned that lesson over and over again. Once was on the day after the tubes were removed from Jeremy's brain, when we lifted him into a sitting position for the first time in almost four weeks. This simple action quickly spiraled us into disaster again.

Now that the drains had been removed, the doctors were anxious to get Jeremy upright. The human body is not made only to lie down. Our organs and systems are designed to work in opposition to gravity from a vertical position. Vital functions—circulation, digestion, elimination—become sluggish and inefficient after prolonged bed rest. Jeremy's skin, too, was breaking down, with angry red abrasions that would soon become bedsores, although we were meticulous about turning him regularly and cushioning pressure points at his elbows, hips, knees, and heels with pillows and padding.

Sitting Jeremy up for four minutes took four people and an hour to accomplish. First, a nurse and I wrapped both his legs tightly in Ace bandages from toes to hips. After lying flat for so long, Jeremy's circulation was sluggish, and the pressure of the bandages was meant to keep the blood from pooling in his feet. I kept up a flowing monologue, not sure how much he was taking in.

"Guess what, Jeremy, you're going to sit up today! Isn't that exciting?" The nurse attached a monitor to his upper arm to provide a continuous blood pressure readout. We scooted him until he was lying crosswise on the bed. I climbed up on the bed and sat behind him, two physical therapists sat on either side of him, and the nurse stood in front.

"We're going to help you. Just relax and we'll lift you up." Gradually, we inched him upright. We paused frequently and waited as he turned chalk-white, his blood pressure dropped sharply, and his heart raced to keep up with the unaccustomed demand of pumping blood uphill.

Finally Jeremy was sitting on the edge of the bed with his legs hanging over the side. "There we go. You're sitting up all the way!" His head lolled. His muscles could not support his body because his right side was still completely paralyzed and his left side weakened from disuse. We held him steady as he wobbled and swayed helplessly. His blood pressure dropped to eighty-five, then eighty, then seventy, then sixty; his heart beat more than one hundred and eighty times a minute; he turned blue-gray and started to fade from consciousness, then recovered, then faded, then recovered.

"Hold on, son, hold on. We've got you. Breathe deeply. Breathe. Breathe."

Thirty seconds, forty-five, sixty, ninety, a hundred, one hundred and fifty, one hundred and eighty, two hundred, two hundred and forty long seconds we held him in place, and then gently eased him back down again.

"I'm proud of you. You did great, son." His eyes closed, Jeremy did not react.

Sweat ran down my back and my muscles shook from the strain of supporting his shifting weight. And I was happy. *We're out of the doldrums now, and moving ahead*, I thought. This was the first step toward Jeremy's eventual physical rehabilitation, toward being able to get him into a wheelchair, toward mobility. I could imagine a life outside the hospital again.

That afternoon Jeremy was moved to a bed in a quieter section of the ICU with patients who were less acutely in need of care. I packed up and moved our accumulated belongings—cards, family pictures, CDs and CD player, books, stuffed animals, toiletries, spare socks, Vaseline swabs, drinking straws, extra blankets I had swiped from the linen cart, little sealed plastic cups of fruit juice that I had hoarded from meal trays—and set up our new cubicle. Then I sat with Jeremy into the evening, carrying on a one-sided conversation, reading aloud, feeding him bits of Popsicle. He was awake and alert. At one point he clearly wanted to communicate something. He stared hard into my eyes, his lips trying to form words, but no sound came out. He shook his head in frustration.

"Would you like to try to write something, sweetheart?" He nodded eagerly, yes.

"Here you go." I handed him a large tablet and a felt-tip marker.

We had experimented with writing before, but Jeremy had been unable even to form letters, making only shapeless marks that straggled off the page. This time he worked carefully and slowly, pausing between pen strokes to rest. I sat quietly and waited until he had something he wanted to show me. Ten minutes later he handed me the tablet. Diagonally across the top of the page he had written in wobbly but discernable letters his first words since he came out of his coma,

I LOVE YOU.

My heart swelled and my eyes brimmed with tears. Nothing else mattered. Not his broken body, not the unknown future. Just those words, enough to fill the world.

————

That evening a new resident examined Jeremy. She was the first doctor to see him all day. I didn't catch her name, but she was unremarkable, slightly built, with short drab-brown hair and glasses. Because she was fresh out of medical school, she was painstakingly thorough, hitting all the points on her checklist: Vital signs; pupil dilation; ears, nose, and throat; heart and lungs; abdominal palpitation; arms and legs.

Jeremy had been examined so many times by so many doctors that I didn't pay much attention until she lifted the sheet and frowned and I noticed for the first time that Jeremy's right leg was swollen and purple. She paged the attending physician to the ward. Together they scrutinized Jeremy's leg, pressing gently here and there, both of them frowning. They walked over to the nurses' station to talk privately, and then the attending doctor came back to say that she was ordering an immediate ultrasound scan, although without explaining why.

I was still focused on the day's accomplishments, and I was worried but not frantic as I walked next to Jeremy's gurney down to the imaging department. Jeremy had been through two brain surgeries so far. This was only a swollen leg. It was probably something localized, maybe an infection, something they would be able to treat.

The ultrasound technician squirted gel onto Jeremy's foot and ran the wand over it. He stopped, adjusted the controls, then went over the same area again. The he went over it a third time. Now he was frowning too. I didn't know what he was looking at. All I could see on the screen were wavy black-and-white images that looked vaguely like geologic strata. The tech moved the wand slowly up Jeremy's calf, thigh, hip, and then belly. He was taking a long time, covering each area multiple times. Click, click, click, click: he repeatedly recorded images as he moved up Jeremy's body. *What is he doing?* I couldn't make any sense of the swirls on the screen.

"What do you see?" I asked.

"You really should wait to talk to a doctor."

"Please. Tell me. Please."

"There's no blood flow."

"What do you mean?"

"There's a clot."

"Where? In his foot?"

"All the way up. The vena cava, the main vein draining blood from the lower half of the body, is clotted closed all the way from his toes to his kidneys. There's no blood return from his leg at all."

Suddenly I was in free-fall, plummeting from a place of safety into an abyss. I knew about blood clots. Two years earlier, a friend's college-age daughter had developed a small clot in her leg, perhaps as a result of taking birth control pills. The clot broke loose, causing a pulmonary embolism. She died. An embolism shuts off the blood supply to the victim's lungs. The bronchial passages and pulmonary vessels lock in spasms, the heart struggling violently to pump blood through the obstruction. The victim slowly suffocates until his or her heart gives out.

Jeremy's clot was at least a hundred times larger. If a piece of this monstrous clot broke loose, his bloodstream would carry it to his heart, lungs, or brain. He would die quickly and horribly.

"Let's get him back to his room," the tech said. I want

to scream, *For God's sake don't move him, do something, do something*, but there was nothing that could be done here in the ultrasound room. An orderly wheeled Jeremy's gurney through the halls, up the elevator, and back to the ICU. I was agonizingly aware that every jolt and jostle might shake a piece of clot loose, that he was as close to death as he ever had been. And there was absolutely nothing I could do to prevent it, except to pray with all the intensity I had ever mustered. *Merciful God, let the clot hold, let the clot hold.*

Back on the ward, the attending physician was talking intently into the telephone at the nurse's station, her eyes narrowed. I held Jeremy's hand and tried to keep a normal face for him as my heart pounded and fear spread like poison through my veins. The doctor was on the phone for a long time. Eventually she hung up and motioned me aside.

"I've talked to the neurosurgeon and three other specialists, here and in San Francisco. Normally we'd start him on heparin, a blood-thinning medication, right away to dissolve the clot. But for your son . . . that's impossible. Heparin would also dissolve the clot that has stopped the bleeding in his brain. He'd have a rebleed."

"But what does that mean? What can you do?"

"We're going to have to try something experimental. For adults in a situation like this, we can implant a metal filter in the chest to strain the blood and capture any embolism before it can reach a vital organ. But I don't know that it's ever been done in a child. And there's no surgeon in the East Bay trained to perform the procedure. We're arranging a transport tonight to take you to the University of California in San Francisco. They're a big teaching and research hospital, and they have a doctor who is willing to try to perform this operation."

I left Jeremy alone for a few minutes and walked to the pay phone in the hallway to call home. "Kris, you need to come right away." I explained what had happened. I could hear Kris taking deep quaking breaths. Finally he said, "I'll be there as soon as I can get the kids settled." He paused. "Tell Jeremy I love him."

I sat next to Jeremy's bed, holding his hand and shaking as though the room were freezing. An hour later, Kris pushed open the door to the ICU. He looked awful; his cheeks were sunken and his normally ruddy skin had a greenish cast, but his voice was calm and strong as he greeted Jeremy.

"Hi, big guy. How're you doing?" Kris kissed Jeremy on the forehead and clasped his other hand.

At eleven o'clock at night, Kris and I were still waiting for the transport team to assemble. This would be no ordinary hospital transfer. Moving Jeremy might cause an embolism, so he would travel with a team that could try to resuscitate him if he went into cardiac arrest or pulmonary failure: an ICU physician, two EMTs, an emergency room nurse, and a respiratory therapist. Finally the EMTs strolled onto the ward, pushing a high-tech hydraulic gurney that looked like something off a spaceship. *Hurry, hurry, we must get my son to UCSF, we've got to DO something,* I thought, but they moved carefully and deliberately, lifting Jeremy onto the gurney and then piling all his connected monitors and cables alongside him. My mind circled endlessly around a single thought loop: *Let the clot hold, let the clot hold, let the clot hold.*

I heaped extra blankets on top of Jeremy and all the equipment, for the weather was cold and damp. We floated slowly through the corridors, down the elevator, out the door, and into the night as in a dream. Jeremy shivered violently. The paramedics lifted him into the ambulance. *Be careful, be gentle,* I thought. They painstakingly hooked up his monitors and tubes to the ambulance's built-in life support equipment. *Oh, please, be quick.* The doctor, nurse, therapist, and paramedics climbed in and took their seats. There was room in the ambulance for one more person as well.

"You take it," Kris said. "I'll follow behind in our car." I would not have been capable of this generosity, but Kris knew me, knew that I would not want to go on living if Jeremy died in the ambulance and I was not there with him. A man of enormous heart, he took care of me in the only way he could.

The ambulance eased out onto city streets and then onto the freeway. Through the rear ambulance window I saw the familiar headlights of our car directly behind us. Kris was following closely. At midnight we crossed the Bay Bridge on our way to San Francisco.

————

UCSF was huge, clean, well equipped, and efficient, everything Children's Hospital was not. UCSF also did not allow parents to sleep in their child's room, no matter how ill, how confused, how fragile the child.

Given those two choices, I would have picked Children's Hospital a thousand times out of a thousand—except that now we had no choice.

I was so tired I was almost delirious. This was my second night without sleep. *My son is at risk of dying at any moment; why the hell can't I sleep in his room for a few hours?* "No, sorry, that's the policy, no exceptions," said the clean, well-rested, and efficient nurse. I was banished.

"Go lie down somewhere," Kris said. "I'll come get you if anything happens." The nurse pointed me toward an unused waiting room on the floor below the ICU, now a storage space for dusty furniture. Thankfully, it was carpeted with a stained mud-colored shag that was soft and warm under my tired shoulders as I curled up on the floor, pulled my jacket up as a cover, and immediately fell deeply asleep.

Jeremy was still alive at six o'clock in the morning when I returned to his room. I had never seen Kris so exhausted. He had forced himself to remain upright in a chair throughout the long night because, if he had dozed, the nurse would have made him leave. He went off to get some rest, and I took his place next to Jeremy's bed.

Although Jeremy was awake, the fatigue of the transport and the stress of these new surroundings had set him back, and he was no more mindful than an infant. He did not understand where he was, why he was there, or what was about to happen to him. All he knew was touch and the sight of a familiar face.

I answered an endless stream of questions from an endless stream of new physicians who all came separately to examine Jeremy: the residents, the attending physician, the neurosurgeon, the vascular surgeon, the interventional radiologist. Although we'd brought Jeremy's medical file with us, it was twelve inches thick by now, too much material for these new doctors to read quickly so that they could make immediate treatment decisions. So I told Jeremy's story over and over again with the upper part of my mind, dispassionately, in technical detail, while my deeper brain resumed its work of keeping Jeremy alive. *Let the clot hold, let the clot hold, oh, please, let the clot hold.*

When Jeremy was taken away for an emergency CT scan, I met with the doctor who would perform the surgery. Dr. Frazer was short, stocky, and middle-aged, with piercing blue eyes, wiry gray hair, and a Scottish accent.

"We'll put in a Greenfield filter," he said. He picked up something that resembled a furled steel umbrella frame roughly half the size of my fist, and held it out to me. The device had been invented in 1970 by a young Oklahoma surgeon named Lazar Greenfield, who had lost a patient to a pulmonary embolism caused by clots that had started in the patient's legs and lodged in his lungs. He wanted to create an implantable filter for trapping blood clots. I later learned that his design was inspired by the cone-shaped filter used to remove sludge and debris from oil pipelines.

"We'll go in through a large vein in Jeremy's upper

chest, thread the filter down all the way into the vena cava, and open it," said Dr. Frazer. "See these tiny hooks on the 'legs'? They'll catch and hold onto the inside walls of the blood vessel, like fishhooks. The filter should catch any parts of the clot that break loose below the level of the heart and lungs before it can do any damage."

"Have you ever done this operation on a child before?"

"No. We usually use this to treat elderly people. We have no idea what it will do if it's left in the body over an entire lifetime."

"*Over a lifetime?* Won't you take it out after the clot is gone?"

"Once it's in place, it's not possible to take the filter out."

Jeremy would carry this cold metal spider close to his heart for the rest of his life, however long that might be.

By noon, Kris had returned. Friends who lived close to the hospital had kindly offered their apartment, and Kris had slept in a real bed. Badly. He looked like a hospital patient who had wandered away from his room. *Good Lord, is that what I look like?*

Jeremy's operation had been shoehorned into a full surgery schedule at one of the busiest hospitals in the world. In the middle of the afternoon an operating room opened up, and Kris and I once again walked Jeremy down to a surgery center, met with an anesthesiologist, listened to risk disclosures, and signed consent forms. Then, once again, we waited.

From: Fiala, Marie Lawson
Sent: September 27, 1998 10:24 A.M.
To: Jeremy Network
Subject: Goings and Comings/Update No. 12

We are back at Children's Hospital in Oakland. Jeremy survived Friday's surgery to implant the Greenfield filter, and now the filter should be protecting him from a possible embolism. The UCSF doctors had him transported back to Children's immediately after he came out of the recovery room. They wanted him to recuperate here, in the care of the medical team that had treated his neurological condition from the beginning. It felt good to be back.

Friday night brought more complications. I noticed at 2:00 A.M. that Jeremy's blood oxygen saturation levels had fallen far below the low end of the normal range and were still dropping. He had turned dead-white. I had to convince the night nurse that she should immediately start him on oxygen ("He's probably just breathing shallowly as he falls asleep," she said) and then to call the attending physician, who thankfully took it seriously. A hurried chest X-ray showed that the lower halves of both of Jeremy's lungs had collapsed. The air sacs in the lungs are like little balloons; when they deflate, they lose the ability to transfer oxygen from the air into the bloodstream. The doctor started him on aggressive respiratory therapy, putting a large flexible hose into his mouth that shoots staccato bursts of pressurized air down his windpipe to reinflate his lungs. The treatment is repeated every hour, and I do chest percussion on him in between.

The normal treatment for collapsed lungs would include keeping Jeremy in a sitting position to get him off his back, but this is not possible due to the clotting in his leg. Because he has almost no venous capacity to return blood from his right leg, it is hugely swollen and painful. Sitting him up would cause more blood to flow into the leg, with no way for it to leave. The doctor said to me briskly, "You're between a rock and a hard place." Yes, we are.

It is Sunday night. The time between Thursday morning and now has passed seamlessly. I have lost track of the days and the normal pattern of life. The only sensation is of endless travel with no known destination. I recall a phrase from one of my favorite Psalms, "The Lord shall watch over your going out and your coming in. . . ." And so we continue on. Every new turn in the road shocks and frightens me, but the only choice is to follow it to the end. Baby steps, I keep telling myself, baby steps. No one step is more than I can take. Thank you, family and friends, for staying with us on this odyssey.

The Candle Vigil

Faith is the substance of things hoped for,
the evidence of things not seen.

—Hebrews 11:1

O N A SUNDAY EVENING four weeks after his hemorrhage, Jeremy lay paralyzed, mute, and nearly blind in the intensive care unit. His condition suggested permanent brain damage. His prognosis was bleak. The doctors could not say whether he would ever recover any speech, sight, or right-side motor function, and they had no therapies to suggest other than the passage of time.

Kris and I were desperate for answers. As a last-ditch resort, a true Hail Mary pass, Kristor's father, Peter, proposed the idea of using the Internet to organize a healing prayer vigil among all the people who had been reading my e-mail messages. The Jeremy Network was vast by now, both in numbers and geographic reach. Most of the readers were strangers, connected to us only by the power of e-mail forwarding. I had received hundreds of e-mails from people across the United States and Canada, and from Europe, Africa, and Australia as well: a retired fireman from Toronto, schoolteachers from Rome and Johannesburg, a minister from Adelaide. All of them asked how they could help.

"Let's harness all that energy," Peter proposed. "Just give me the word, and I'll organize it. For you. For Jeremy."

Even before this crisis I was aware that an enormous body of scientific evidence had demonstrated the healing effects of prayer, although no one could explain how or why prayer had this effect. Scientists had long recognized prayer's power to preserve and restore health. One of the first experimenters in the field, Sir Francis Galton, a prominent English scientist, concluded in 1872 that people who believe in prayer are helped by "the undoubted fact, that there exists a solidarity between themselves and what surrounds them . . . that they are descended from an endless past, that they have a brotherhood with all that is. . . . This great idea . . . is quite powerful."

Dr. Alexis Carrel, a French researcher who won the Nobel Prize for Medicine in 1912 for his early work on vascular surgery and organ transplantation, expressed this discovery particularly beautifully:

> Prayer is the most powerful form of energy one can generate. It is a force as real as terrestrial gravity. As a physician, I have seen men, after all other therapy has failed, lifted out of disease and melancholy by the serene effort of prayer. . . . Prayer like radium is a source of luminous, self-generating energy. In prayer, human beings seek to augment their finite energy by addressing themselves to the Infinite source of all energy. When we pray, we link ourselves with the inexhaustible motive power that spins the universe. We pray that a part of this power be apportioned to our needs . . .

Prayer positively influences high blood pressure, wounds, heart attacks, headaches, enzyme activity, cell growth, the size of tumors, the firing rate of the heart's pacemaker cells, the time required to awaken from anesthesia, and blood oxygen levels. Prayer affects not only humans but also animals, plants, fungi, yeast, bacteria, and even the germination and growth rates of various seeds. The results of prayer do not depend on whether the praying person is in the presence of the one prayed for or far away; healing takes place even at a distance. Prayer works whether or not the person prayed for is even aware that someone is praying on his or her behalf. Nothing seems capable of blocking or stopping prayer's effects. Many modern hospitals have instituted programs to study and use prayer as an interventional therapy for their patients.

In 1995, when AIDS was still inevitably fatal, researchers enrolled twenty patients with advanced AIDS in a pilot study at UCSF. All of the patients received the best available medical care, but healers were recruited to pray for the ten patients in the experimental group, which had been selected using a randomized, double-blinded protocol. The healers lived great distances from the patients, and none of the patients knew whether or not they were being prayed for. No one prayed systematically for the control group.

Four patients died during the six-month study. When the data were unblinded, it was revealed that the patients who had died were in the control group.

All ten who had been prayed for were still alive.

During the study, one of the patients developed brain cancer. Amazingly, this patient did not die and eventually made a full recovery. As it turned out, he had been prayed for.

A year later, the same UCSF research team began a larger study that is acknowledged as one of the most scientifically rigorous attempts to assess the effect of prayer on healing. This time, the trial measured the occurrence of twenty-three AIDS-related illnesses in forty test subjects. Each participant was matched by computer with a statistical twin—a counterpart of the same age, with a similar immunological profile, viral load, and number of prior AIDS-related illnesses. One member of each pair was randomly assigned to a control group and the other to a treatment group. All of the study participants were allowed to pray for themselves and to ask others to pray for them as well. What differentiated the experimental group from the control group was that the experimental subjects would receive additional prayers according to a strict protocol.

Photographs of those in the treatment group were sent to forty healing practitioners from a wide range of spiritual traditions. The healers never met the patients in person. They prayed for their assigned patients one hour a day, for six consecutive days, and then rotated on to another patient in the treatment group. In the meantime, the photographs of the patients in the control group were kept under lock and key in the researchers' offices.

When the data were unblinded six months later, the research results showed that the subjects who had not been prayed for were far sicker. They spent 600 percent more days in the hospital. They contracted 300 percent as many AIDS-related illnesses.

And consider this. There was no placebo effect. For the patients, believing they were in the experimental group that was being prayed for didn't correlate in the least with better health. More than half of the control-group patients believed they were being prayed for, and they were no healthier than the other control-group members. The only factor that made a difference was prayer itself.

Even more recently, researchers at Columbia University reported that women at an in vitro fertilization clinic had a higher pregnancy rate when total strangers were asked to pray for their success. The well-designed and carefully blinded study involved two hundred women, half of whom were randomly assigned to a prayer group and the other half to a nonprayer group. None of the women undergoing the IVF procedures knew about the project. The people praying lived on different continents from the study subjects and were incapable of identifying or contacting them. Which women were in which group was not disclosed until after the pregnancy data were reported at the conclusion of the study. The women who were prayed for became pregnant more than twice as often as those who did not have people praying for them.

In publishing their results, the researchers expressed surprise at these findings.

My rational mind can formulate hypotheses explaining how prayer works. Modern physics has established the interconnection among particles in the universe no matter how far apart they are in space-time—what Einstein called "spooky action at a distance." Perhaps through ritual and connection with God, we may make manifest at a quantum level the possibilities of order versus chaos in a probabilistic universe. That is one possible explanation. But prayer may not be comprehensible with reason. It is a mystery. I believed that it worked. Prayer seemed as likely to give me back my son as anything medicine could offer.

Even so, I was deeply reluctant to say yes to Peter's offer, to ask friends and strangers to pray for Jeremy. Although I had a lifelong practice of private prayer, there was something . . . *unseemly* . . . about making it a public, participatory event. It felt like a revival show. What would people think, especially our irreligious Berkeley neighbors and the super-rational lawyers with whom I worked? I could imagine their reactions: "That poor family. They've really gone off the deep end. I guess people will believe any kind of hocus-pocus if they're desperate enough." And it seemed presumptuous to ask hundreds of people to focus their time and attention on just our child. Why should they? Everyone had his or her own troubles to bear. If nothing resulted, as was likely, what would I say to all those people? I would be seen as naïve at best, a gullible fool at worst.

And even more, I was afraid to test my faith. *What if nothing happens? How can I bear even one more disappointment? I've lost so much already.* Of course, faith doesn't follow

Newton's Law; for every action there isn't a proportional reaction. You don't put your money in God's vending machine and pull out a candy bar every time. Faith means ceding control or, more accurately, realizing that control didn't exist in the first place and that you have always been at the mercy of a power larger than yourself. Yet despite the hard lessons of the past weeks, it was still difficult to admit my fundamental powerlessness, to give myself—and Jeremy—over to God.

But we had run out of options. I set aside my worries. They were only about myself. Jeremy deserved this chance.

From: Lawson, Rev. Peter
To: Jeremy Network

This is a request for a special prayer ritual for healing Jeremy Day Lawson. Last week Kris spoke to me about what he had heard about Immersion Prayer for healing. Since the process involves a large number of people gathering in the patient's room, we thought that the ICU was not the place to have that happen. Since Jeremy may be in the ICU for the next couple of weeks, we brainstormed ways to emulate an intense prayer time for Jeremy.

Here's how we'd like your help to intensify the healing prayer energy. On this coming Sunday evening at 8:00 P.M. (in the time zone in which you live, or find yourself), please light a candle and say a prayer for Jeremy and let it burn until 9:00 P.M. Each time the candlelight comes to your attention, simply recall Jeremy. In that way we hope that there will be a coordinated, almost worldwide, period of prayer for Jeremy's healing. If you have engaged others in prayer for Jeremy, please forward this request on to them.

All of us in Jeremy's extended family are immeasurably supported by your love and concern. We feel bound together with all of you in an inexpressible fellowship of holy power.

It enables us to prevail and keep hope when things look so bad, and rejoice when things take a turn for the better.

May God always be praised in you.

Jeremy, who was no longer in critical condition but not recovering, had been shunted to a dreary windowless corner of the ward, far from the nurses' station. This was a storage area of sorts. Excess medical equipment was stacked against the wall on either side of his bed. Large plastic tubs of supplies were piled on metal carts. When a nurse needed a new pack of needles or plastic tubing or a catheter or a liter of glucose, she came back to this corner and rooted through the bins next to Jeremy's bed.

A stained and faded green curtain suspended from a curved metal rod around the bed was intended to provide some privacy, but most of the connecting rings at the top were missing or broken and the fabric draggled on the floor. The narrow space above the head of the bed was fully taken up with the dials, ports, plugs, and hoses that accessed life-support systems. There was not enough wall space to tape up even a small family picture. The only personal element was the wooden cross that had always hung over Jeremy's bed at home. Kris had brought it in and, when he could find no available wall space, pinned it to the inside of the curtain at an awkward tilted angle. I was touched by his care for this small detail. Dear Kris, who always kept his boat so taut and trim.

Eight o'clock drew close on the evening of the prayer vigil. Two visitors had come and gone: the head of Jeremy's elementary school, who had known Jeremy most of his life and could not look at him without weeping; and our neighbor, who had arrived moments after Jeremy's collapse and taken care of Lisie and David while Kris and I went to the hospital. Jeremy recognized them. He tried to communicate but could only nod or shake his head in response to questions. He lifted his good left arm and let it drop to the bed in a gesture of despair. He had no voice.

Kris and I had told all three children that a group of people would be praying tonight for Jeremy's recovery, keeping the explanation simple to avoid raising their expectations. Annelise and David would light their candles at home with Kris.

As for Jeremy, it was impossible to know how much he understood about what was about to happen. He nodded his head vigorously when I told him about the prayer vigil, but information was slippery and didn't seem to catch hold in his mind.

I am not expecting anything, I told myself. *We're doing this for Jeremy, and to give people a chance to feel that they're helping. That's important even if nothing else happens.*

A few minutes before eight o'clock, the Reverend Mary Moore, an Episcopal priest and family friend, joined me in Jeremy's shabby cubicle. Mary was in her late fifties, with thick, wavy black hair dramatically streaked with gray, blue eyes at once kind and piercing, and a resonant voice. Tonight she was wearing a clerical collar under a plain shirt-front, a blazer and skirt, and a heavy cross suspended on a chain around her neck.

There was no candle at Jeremy's bedside. He was wearing an oxygen mask, and an open flame could cause an explosive fire. We simply formed a small circle and held hands. As the clock's minute hand reached its zenith, Mary opened *The Book of Common Prayer* and began: "Oh God, the strength of the weak and the comfort of sufferers: Mercifully accept our prayers, and grant to your servant Jeremy the help of your power, that his sickness may be turned into health, and our sorrow into joy . . ."

Jeremy listened closely. He seemed caught up in the words of the service. For the first time in many hours, he was peaceful. His monstrously swollen right leg had been causing him great pain. The skin was stretched tight and was colored a glassy violet; the flesh underneath was rigid. All day long he had been moaning and thrashing, unable to find a comfortable position, nodding yes frantically whenever morphine was offered. Now he lay still, his wistful slate eyes above the clear plastic mask alternately fixed on Mary and on me. I held tightly to his right hand.

Mary administered unction, anointing with oil. "I lay my hands upon you in the Name of the Father, and of the Son, and of the Holy Spirit, beseeching our Lord Jesus Christ to sustain you with his presence, to drive away all sickness of body and spirit, and to give you that victory of life and peace which will enable you to serve him both now and evermore." Time in our small corner of the universe slowed, compressed by the weight of the ceremony. Words fell into the silence like stones into a still pool:

> *The heavens declare the glory of God,*
> *and the firmament shows his handiwork.*
> *One day tells its tale to another,*
> *and one night imparts knowledge to another.*
> *Although they have no words or language,*
> *and their voices are not heard,*
> *Their sound has gone out into all lands,*
> *and their message to the ends of the world.*

I experienced a heightened awareness of being in the presence of something much greater than myself. The air felt denser. My heart and respiration accelerated. God's love ran like a current through my body, Jeremy's body, the room itself. It took my breath away. I placed my hand on Jeremy's head, focused whatever grace flowed through me toward the healing of his brain, and prayed silently. *Have mercy on us, most merciful Father. Endow Jeremy's caregivers with wisdom. If it be your will, restore him to health, so that he may love and serve you all the days of his life. Grant Kris and me serenity in the face of bad news, and the strength to continue, whatever tomorrow brings.*

Then the hour was over. Mary kissed Jeremy and me good-bye, and left. I sagged with anticlimax. Despite my caveats and misgivings, I had fixed on this evening as a reason for hope, however tenuous. But nothing had changed. The return to ordinary time was jarring.

I called home to say good night to Kris and the younger children. "Hi, Kris . . . Yes, Mary just left . . . It was good. How about you?"

"Hi, sweetheart. I'm glad you were with him . . . We lit a candle on the kitchen table. I read from the Psalms . . . Do you want to talk to the kids?"

"Hi, Mummy," said Lisie. "Is Jeremy better?"

"He's about the same on the outside, dear. I think the prayers made him feel better on the inside."

"Do you want to talk to Davey? Here he is."

"Mommy, when are you coming home?" David asked.

"Tomorrow, sweetie. I'll see you after school."

I held the phone to Jeremy's ear. "Daddy and Annelise and David want to say good night to you. "

"Good night, Jeremy."

"We love you."

"I'll see you tomorrow, son. Sleep tight."

I settled Jeremy for the night—helped him relieve himself, arranged his pillows, and smoothed his sheets and blankets with quick and practiced motions. I told myself I was too rational to be disappointed. But underneath, a tiny part of me had remembered the old Bible stories and had hoped for my son to walk, to see, to speak. Had hoped for a miracle.

————

I was not ready to sleep yet. I hadn't checked e-mail since midafternoon, and I probably had ten or twelve new messages by now. After Jeremy fell asleep, I plugged in my laptop and booted up. As soon as I went online, the computer started chiming. *Ping. Ping. Ping. Ping. Ping.*

I had more than fifty new messages.

From: Ruth, Philadelphia
To: Fiala, Marie Lawson

You named your son Jeremy Day, but in my mind he's always been Jeremy Sunday, because he's your first son, his was a sunny personality, and he is so bright. Also, now, Sunday, the day of resurrection power, the day of victory over death, the day of the Lord. May Jeremy Sunday be lifted from the depression of discouragement and raised in power to hope and believe and work for strength and healing. May Jeremy Sunday turn his face toward the sun and be warmed by its light.

From: Rev. R., Scotland
To: Fiala, Marie Lawson

The Jerusalem Candle has been lit in my Chapel of St. Andrew since we last messaged—and will burn for at least the week—hopefully less time when we get the good news. The prayer circle is now extended to the Abbey at Iona; to Dunkeld Cathedral; to St. Leonard's at St. Andrews; to Inchbroach, Montrose; to St. Lawrence, Kincarding and to St. Mary's and Craigiebank All Saints, Dundee; and to East Anglia in England. Beannachd Dhia Let.

New messages kept arriving as I read, announced by the soft regular chiming. *Ping. Ping. Ping.*

From: Jennifer, Indianapolis
To: Fiala, Marie Lawson

Jeremy is held tenderly in the hearts of all of the Presbyterians at Fairview. Many talked to me after church. I told them of the healing prayer and candle. Many strangers to you have lit the candle and said prayers. You have built a large, faithful congregation in cyberspace. All of you are always in our thoughts and prayers.

From: Nancy, San Francisco
To: Fiala, Marie Lawson

Tonight we all prayed for Jeremy and then took our candles upstairs for some quiet time. I feel such sadness for all of you who are going through this. As I watched the candle burn, the refrain that kept running through my head was, "Lord I'm one, Lord I'm two, Lord I'm three, Lord I'm four, Lord I'm five hundred miles away from home." How long ago it must seem that you were sitting in the kitchen with him at home and everything was fine. How many more miles to travel. You'll all remain in my prayers for the length of this journey—you aren't alone on it.

I opened and read each message, then wrote a short reply. "Thank you. We feel your presence. It is good to know we aren't alone." It took a long time to get through all of them. With each message, I felt lighter.

From: Kathy, Annapolis
To: Fiala, Marie Lawson

Many, many candles were lit. I will keep praying and the prayer chain at St. Anne's is still active. Miracles do happen, I truly believe that. It is hard to have faith sometimes when things seem so desperate. "Fear not" appears in the Bible 365 times. . . . Isn't that interesting, one "Fear not" for each day?

By the time I finished it was after midnight. I powered down the computer and put it away, lay down on the reclining chair next to Jeremy's bed, pulled a blanket over my shoulders, and gazed at the dim ward light filtering through the sad green curtain and the red and blue stars blinking from the monitors in the darkened room. I had awakened that morning with sorrow, but kindness sat beside me as I fell asleep.

From: Fiala, Marie Lawson
Sent: September 29, 1998 3:32 A.M.
To: Jeremy Network
Subject: Something Incredible/Update No. 13

I was at home tonight, Monday evening, twenty-four hours after the prayer vigil for Jeremy's healing circled the globe. When the bedside phone rang sometime after 11:00 P.M., I threw myself across the bed and grabbed for the receiver, my heart racing, preparing myself for yet another emergency. "Hi, Mom. This is Jeremy. I am sorry to wake you up. I love you." A voice I hadn't heard for a month, and had begun to believe I might not hear again in this world. I laughed and sobbed into the telephone. "My God, Jeremy, is that you? You spoke, oh my God it's a miracle, oh, thank you, God, thank you."

My heart flies on the wings of the morning.

Jubilations

Then the eyes of the blind shall be opened, and the ears of the deaf unstopped; then the lame shall leap like a deer, and the tongue of the speechless sing for joy.

—Isaiah 35:6

THE NIGHT AFTER THE PRAYER VIGIL, Kris was back at the hospital. He hadn't said much about the ritual during our midday handoff. His is a more imperturbable disposition than mine, less susceptible to either depression or elation. "I didn't expect anything to change," he said matter of factly. "This is just the next day."

Kris spoon-fed Jeremy his pureed dinner, washed his face and brushed his teeth, and remade the bed. Around 10:30 P.M., the attending and resident physicians made their rounds and once again examined Jeremy, with the same conclusions. He still had no movement, no speech, and limited vision. His paralysis was so profound that he could not even move his tongue or the right half of his mouth. Yet as one of the doctors stuck another pin into Jeremy's right foot, Jeremy suddenly said loudly and clearly, "Ow—that—hurts!"

I will carry those words with me always: "Ow, that hurts."

Every person in the room froze, stunned by what they had heard. Kris said that the hair rose on his arms and at the back of his neck. The silence in the room thickened, became almost tangible. The floor seemed to tilt beneath him, as if revealing its relation to a gravity stronger than earth's.

At last Kris asked, "Jeremy, what did you say?"

"That—hurts!" Jeremy repeated.

"Jeremy, my God, you talked, you talked!" Kris exclaimed.

Jeremy answered, "I—know. I—can't—believe—it. Thank—you—God."

Kris and the doctors were first incredulous, then jubilant. They laughed and laughed and laughed as Jeremy continued to speak, slowly and haltingly, with a split-second hesitation before each word as though hidden gears and levers were turning over to push the words from his mouth. He spoke in small, sometimes disconnected fragments:

"My—name—is— Jeremy—Day—Lawson."

"Yes, yes, it is, son."

"I—go—to—Prospect—Sierra—School."

"Yes, you do, sweetheart."

"Where—is—Mom?"

"She's at home tonight, son."

"Can—I—call—her?"

———————

After Jeremy finished talking to me, Kris called his father.

"Dad?"

"What's up?" asked Peter, in a half-awakened, terrified voice.

"Jeremy wants to talk to you. Is that okay?"

"What? Of course, yes!"

"Hi—Grampa. I—can—talk."

"Jeremy! You can talk! I'm so excited, I can hardly believe it!"

"Yes—I'm—happy—I—can—talk—again."

"I'm very happy too, very, very happy!"

"Thank—you—for—praying. Good—night—Grampa."

"Good night, Jeremy. God bless and keep you all night long. Amen."

From: Lawson, Rev. Peter
To: Jeremy Network

Just like that, out of the blue comes a lost voice that brings joy and hope to all of us. I am so grateful to all of you everywhere, from Finland to Hawaii, who lit a candle for Jeremy last night and who keep him in your prayers. I said to a few of you that Jeremy did not rise and walk last night, but we were patient knowing that miracles take just a bit longer now than when Jesus stretched out His hand and said, "Rise and walk." And now at least a part of the miracle for which we pray came about just a day later when the voiceless boy speaks again and we say, "God is in the midst of us and we are not forsaken. His healing power embedded in us has been unleashed and our hearts are full with the joy of thanksgiving." With our deepest thanks, and our prayers for you all.

Back at home, although it was very late, I was no longer tired. My heart raced with exhilaration. Jeremy was talking, Jeremy was talking! That thought was too big for my mind to hold anything else.

It was too late to rouse the household. I would tell them the glad news in the morning. I reached for my computer. For now, I would tell the rest of the world.

Maybe a Miracle

*Everything that can be counted doesn't necessarily count;
everything that counts can't necessarily be counted.*

—Albert Einstein

I RUSIIED TO THE HOSPITAL the next morning but
hesitated outside of the ICU. What if he had stopped
talking; what if it had all evaporated since last night? I took
deep calming breaths and opened the door to the noisy
ward. Jeremy lay in bed, same as always. He looked up
when I entered his cubicle and said haltingly but clearly,
"Hi—Mommy!"

Mommy. What a beautiful word. I sat down on the edge
of the bed, leaned over and put my arms around Jeremy,
and hugged him hard, for a long time. Tears mingled on our
pressed-together cheeks. "I love you, Jeremy."

"I—love—you—Mommy."

Jeremy's speech still faltered. His mind was not working well enough to form complex thoughts into sentences.
But it was enough. He could speak! He had been living in a
voiceless prison, his pain and fear echoing off the walls of
his mind. At last he had been released through the powerful
magic of words.

News that Jeremy's speech had returned spread quickly among the hospital staff, and his room took on something of a carnival atmosphere, with a constant flow of exuberant visitors wanting to see for themselves. Dr. Joe came by first. He was effervescent over Jeremy's restored speech, bouncing up and down on his toes, his tie askew as always, his bright blue eyes sparking with delight behind his glasses. He talked on and on animatedly, explaining the lack of a medical explanation. "I've never seen such a dramatic recovery of speech before. Never. It's completely unpredicted. Sometimes it takes a while for an injured brain to settle down. The brain really is an amazing thing. It constantly surprises us . . ."

When he paused momentarily, I said, "Dr. Joe, we held a prayer vigil for Jeremy on Sunday night. We know that prayer can have healing benefits, and we think maybe that's the reason that Jeremy started talking the next day."

Dr. Joe hesitated and gave me a quick sideways glance. He opened his mouth but no words came out. I could almost hear the thoughts moving through his head. *They seem like such rational people, so normal, and educated. What is this all about?*

He made a nondescript sound, "umm," then continued talking. "This is great, we'll have to get Jeremy working with the speech therapist right away; maybe we'll see more progress, but don't be surprised if there are setbacks." It was as if I had not spoken. I ducked my head and flushed with embarrassment.

Over the course of the day the neurosurgeon, neurologist, hematologist, attending physician, residents, speech therapist, physical therapists, occupational therapist, and all the nurses on the ward came by to see Jeremy and tell us how amazed and happy they were at his recovered speech. I diffidently mentioned the prayer vigil one or two more times and was met with the same slightly embarrassed reaction as Dr. Joe's. I was surprised. Of course I knew that medical personnel had been resistant to alternative healing in the past, but surely not now, not here. The Bay Area medical community was as diverse and open as any in the country. Doctors took seriously many alternatives to allopathic medicine: herbs, acupuncture, Asian therapies, bodywork of various sorts, nutritional regimens. Holistic medicine was the name of the game. Holistic, yes, it seemed; holy, no.

Like Jeremy's doctors, I, too, am a rational person, trained in the Western analytical tradition. My belief in prayer does not mean that I experience a different reality, only that I experience reality differently. What is music, for example, but black marks made on white paper, representing a collection of sounds of different pitches and intensities? A scientist can describe each note precisely in terms of wavelength, amplitude, and frequency, but can science explain Beethoven's Ninth Symphony? Can physics explain the triumph and tragedy captured in the composition? Not everything that is real can be measured.

After the parade of visitors ended and Jeremy was settled for the night, I pulled my laptop out of my overnight satchel and logged in once again. The silver-blue glow from the screen was the only light in the room. Bending over the computer balanced on my lap, I saw that my inbox was flooded with hundreds of messages from people who had lighted candles on Sunday evening.

From: Whitney, San Carlos
To: Fiala, Marie Lawson

How can we keep trusting when it seems for all the world like God has slipped with his permanent marker, like God Himself is messing up? "Peter," I said [to Jeremy's grandfather], "How should we pray?" "Pray for his complete restoration," came my friend's sure reply, and then a few days later came an idea: a prayer vigil for Jeremy. True, they couldn't bring Jeremy's extended prayer family into the Intensive Care Unit, but they might try the alternative. So the word went out to the e-mail network which now stretched around the globe: from 8:00 to 9:00 P.M. on the coming Sunday evening, in whatever time zone we happened to find ourselves, we were invited to light a candle and to pray for Jeremy whenever we chanced to notice its light. Now I had a problem. I was going to be in Connecticut at a conference. Chances were good we'd be in the middle of a meeting at 8:00 o'clock. Sure enough, as 8:00 approached, we were all gathered in the well-appointed living room of the impressive conference center. Our host was still welcoming us to the event, explaining his hopes for our time together and speaking in a way that did not especially invite interruption or distraction. And there sat my candle on the hearth of the massive fireplace. When 8:00 came I hesitated; I really don't like calling attention to myself, especially with folks I don't know. But for some reason I felt compelled to go ahead and so, hoping God would make me invisible, I slipped out of my chair and over to the candle. When I struck the match, of course, everything stopped and the host looked at me, puzzled. (So much for invisibility.) So I explained to the group about Jeremy and the vigil. Our host proved most gracious and insisted we should all pray, which we did. A few minutes later we went into the chapel to say compline together and Jeremy's candle went with us. The next morning and in subsequent services, someone always prayed aloud for Jeremy and so a day later when I was able to check my e-mail, I shared Peter's update with the whole conference group.

Messages arrived from the rational lawyers at my office and at other firms, our irreligious Berkeley neighbors, outdoorsmen who had worked with Kris in the Grand Canyon and hadn't been heard from in decades, our families, friends, friends of family, students, and strangers. Many of them believed they had witnessed a miracle.

From: Dave, Tiburon
To: Fiala, Marie Lawson

Kristor and I were Grand Canyon boatmen together. We had some great adventures and saw some extraordinary places. But this was the first miracle I have ever participated in. I know for me, this changed everything. I have heard of miracles, but never experienced one. Doing so is less mystical than I would have imagined. More, it just confirms something I already knew but didn't know how to tap. It wasn't much. Light a candle and think. Do it with others. Time and space are one. Coincidence is part of it, but perhaps not as random as the name implies. I hope the doctors can experience, not just observe, meaningful miracles in their own time. Our thoughts and prayers continue to be with your son. His family is vast.

Was it a miracle? I can't say. I am a lawyer, trained to assess evidence and arrive at answers, but analysis supplies no answer to this question. I can tell you that these events happened, exactly as I have described them. Jeremy found his voice again after long silence, and shortly after an intense prayer event. Was it coincidence? Improbable, but possible. Extraordinary, unexpected, rare? All those things, yes. A miracle? Maybe. I don't claim to know God's mind, and if I did, I do not think others would take my word for His intentions. Those who doubt will find reasons to doubt. Those who believe will find reasons for belief. It is enough, for me, to say that it was a great and glorious gift. And, *thank you.*

From: Fiala, Marie Lawson
Sent: September 29, 1998 11:17 P.M.
To: Jeremy Network
Subject: An Extraordinary Story/Update No. 14

Jeremy has spontaneously regained his capacity to speak after having been mute for more than three weeks. Father Bruce and a member of the congregation gifted in healing came in today to pray over Jeremy. When they left, Jeremy said, "They are extraordinary people." Kris told him that he was extraordinary too, to which Jeremy answered, "I'm not extraordinary. I'm just an ordinary person with an extraordinary story." Jeremy made jokes; he talked about the book we are reading to him; he told me again and again how much he loved me.

Jeremy's speech therapist came in for the first time since the prayer vigil and heard him speaking. She said it gave her chills. She had never seen a complete spontaneous recovery of speech like this before. It always comes back progressively and slowly, if at all. The reaction from Jeremy's neurosurgeon and pediatrician was the same—amazement.

As we talked, Jeremy suddenly announced, "I can move my right foot." And he did; he moved it from side to side. "And I can move my arm, too." He then lifted his entire right arm half an inch off the pillow on which it rested. He was able to repeat that movement about five times before tiring.

You can't imagine how remarkable this is unless you had been standing at Jeremy's bedside day and night for nearly a month, washing and massaging his right arm and leg, carefully moving them, bending the fingers and toes, hoping in vain for even the faintest twitch of movement in response to your touch. Not so much as a fingertip had curled previously. The doctors told us two weeks ago that Jeremy's prolonged and total immobility made his ultimate motor recovery doubtful. Then this morning, out of nowhere, intentional movement.

I have been privileged to witness firsthand an inexplicable event, a one-in-a-kazillion coincidence. We all choose how to understand it in terms we can live with. Dr. Joe needs to believe in coincidence. I choose to believe in joy, and in the love of God for my child, and in the power of the many voices who asked for healing.

The Other Side of the World

Sweet sleep, that knits up the ravel'd sleave of care.

—William Shakespeare

WE HAD A NEW HOME. Because Jeremy's medical condition had stabilized, he had been moved from the ICU to the rehab ward, next door to the burn unit. Each room housed two children between a few months and eighteen years old. Each patient had suffered a loss of neurological function caused by illness or injury. Here the focus would be on helping Jeremy to regain such abilities as might come back, and on teaching us how to live without those that did not. I expected we would be here a long time.

Jeremy's new room was small and crowded. Fragments of pictures and cards—images of birthday balloons, flowers cut out of magazines, a wide-eyed kitten—had been left taped or pinned to the walls by previous patients. The dusty closet was crammed with unused medical equipment and other children's toys and clothing. There was no shelf space for books, a radio, a pitcher of water, CDs, or tapes. For the moment I piled our belongings on the floor. The room had a five-foot-long narrow window seat covered with a plastic cushion, where one adult could sleep. The blinds that covered the windows were missing half their slats so that, as I soon learned, it was impossible to block out the street lights that shone on a sleeper's face at night.

I was shocked and made queasy by the amount of stuff in the common areas of the ward. Canes, crutches, walkers, shower gurneys, shower chairs, portable commodes, and everywhere wheelchairs, wheelchairs, wheelchairs—the outward and visible signs that we had entered the land of disability, a world of broken bodies and useless limbs and distorted faces and empty stares. Like most people, I had had little experience with the disabled beyond passing the occasional wheelchair-bound person on the street, and smiling while being careful not to look too closely. Now I lived here, and our son may have been granted permanent residency.

My stomach churning, I tried to reestablish some normalcy by searching for fresh bedding. The linen cart was next door, in the burn ward. If rehab was bad, the burn unit was worse. Some of the children there barely resembled human beings. I kept my head down, but from the corners of my eyes I saw things I dared not look at closely. Gauze-swathed forms, the stubby remnants of fingers and toes, faces like shiny purple Halloween masks. They were only children, badly hurt children, but I could not look up, smile, or say good morning. *What a coward I am. Such a coward.*

Jeremy's blanket was a miserable affair, an ancient cotton thermal weave washed thin and stiff. The room was cold; the air conditioning vent was right over Jeremy's bed, and was apparently stuck on the full Arctic setting. Jeremy's internal thermostat still was malfunctioning, and he was deeply chilled. I made another trip to the linen cart and piled three, four, five of the wretched hospital blankets on top of him but could not get him warm. I climbed up on the bed next to him and held him close. He trembled against me.

That afternoon, a friend from work called, and I told her,

"He's so cold. We're going to have to bring in blankets from home, or maybe go out and buy some, I don't know when." Within hours, two thick fleece blankets were delivered, courtesy of my office friends. Polar fleece is a wonderful material: warm, unpretentious, comforting. One's perspective changes with travel. In these cold new latitudes, the fleece blankets were my most cherished possessions. I layered them over Jeremy and tucked them in snugly. For the first time he stopped shivering.

———

Jeremy's roommate the first night in rehab was Joseph, who was eight years old, just David's age. He was a small, thin boy, with transparent milky skin and light brown hair that hadn't been cut or combed in a long time. Joseph had nearly drowned. His brain was starved for oxygen. His body returned to life but not much of his brain function came back with it. His arms and legs were permanently twisted and drawn up into unnatural positions. His back was arched, his head thrown back; his eyes moved but did not see. He could not talk, and gave no sign of understanding speech. He repeatedly bit his lips and tongue. Blood ran from the corners of his mouth and blossomed brightly on his sheets and pillow.

I found it almost as hard to look at Joseph as at the burn victims next door. I drew closed the curtain that separated his bed from Jeremy's, and tried to pretend that he wasn't there. *God, please forgive me. I can't cope with even one more hard thing. I just can't.* So long as Joseph was silent, I could ignore him. But that didn't last.

Our first night was brutal. Because Jeremy was the most at-risk patient on the ward, he had been assigned this room immediately outside the nurse's station, where five or six staff members congregated at all times, laughing, telling jokes, complaining, eating, and talking on the telephone. The noise level was fierce.

Added to that was Joseph's wailing. A piercing inhuman sound, an empty cry in an empty body. The high ululation went on and on. Jeremy had been sleep-deprived for weeks now. His injured brain still fired wildly when overstimulated. Joseph wailed and wailed in the next bed. "Stop," Jeremy pleaded. "Please, stop!" Joseph's keening rose, dropped, rose again. "STOP!" Jeremy was screaming now. "STOP!" Jeremy tried to say the Lord's Prayer out loud, but he couldn't remember the words. "Our Father . . . oh, God, please; make him stop, please make him stop . . . PLEASE STOP, PLEASE STOP, PLEASE STOP."

The nurses generally didn't care whether a patient slept or not. They didn't hesitate to enter the room at any hour of the night, turn on the lights, and carry on a loud conversation with the patient in the next bed or another staff member. But Jeremy's distress was extreme. He continued screaming. Now there were two high-pitched cries filling our room.

Eventually the night nursing supervisor came in, her tightened lips showing her aggravation at having to deal with this disruption. "I guess we could move you into the room next door," she grudgingly allowed. Joseph's thin wails followed us through the wall.

The next day, one of the nurses told me that Joseph's parents, either unwilling or unable to face living with his severe impairments, had abandoned him to the hospital. He had been here for months. The hospital could do nothing further to help him medically, but his parents refused to come for him. The nurses muttered fiercely under their breaths. "All he needs is to go home," they said. "Why don't they just take him home?"

Much later, when Jeremy was discharged from rehab, Joseph was still there. We came upstairs occasionally to visit him when Jeremy returned to the hospital for outpatient physical therapy. I was getting more sleep by then, and no longer felt on the cusp of collapse. I could see Joseph not as a problem but as a tragic little boy who, no matter how damaged he was, deserved his parents' care. At last Joseph, too, was discharged, not to his family, but to a foster home. I hoped that his new family was able to love him, and that his reasons for crying ended.

Jeremy's new roommate was Imari, who was about fifteen months old. She had espresso skin and thick black hair in many tiny plaits and eyes like dark wild plums. Her soft round cheeks framed a wide, luminous smile. Imari had cancer of the spine that had left her left side paralyzed. But she still smiled and gurgled, played with the toes on her good foot, and cuddled her single stuffed animal.

Like Jamal, Imari lived in a steel crib next to Jeremy's bed. No one came to see her except the nurses and doctors. Imari recognized in me exactly what she needed—a mother. When Kris was on duty she was quiet. But when I was in the room Imari called out to me: "Mamma, mamma, mamma . . ." She called and cooed all night, knowing that I was there on the other side of the curtain separating her bed from Jeremy's. "Mamma, mamma, mamma . . ." When I didn't respond, because it was 2:00 A.M. and I was on the ragged edge of breakdown, she whimpered softly, then cried with sad intensity.

God, help me. I can't give her what she needs. At night, a primal craving for sleep pulled me below the surface with great toothy jaws. Only by the greatest resolve could I drive myself from the narrow window bed every hour to turn Jeremy, give him sips of water, help him urinate, and change his soiled gown or bedding. I had no strength to care for this child who shared my room but not my blood.

When Imari called out to me, I turned away and pulled the blankets high and hoped that she would stop.

Living in extreme circumstances teaches you many things about yourself. Some of those things I would rather not have known.

———

The rehab unit had its own geography and customs. All the patient rooms were arrayed down the outside wall of a long corridor. The sickest children were closest to the nurses' station; the most independent children were farthest away.

At 7:00 A.M. the nurses woke the patients and took vital signs. The breakfast trays were brought up from the cafeteria. Children who could feed themselves ate in their rooms. Children who were too young or infirm to do so were strapped into their wheelchairs, lined up in the hall next to the nurses' station, and fed by the staff.

Most of the patients on the ward spent their days, apart from appointments in the rehab clinic, sitting in wheelchairs at the nurses' station. Here the staff could keep them in view, and they "benefited" from stimulation in the form of hallway noise and traffic. This was another of the sad realities for children who were hospitalized without care from family members. The professional staff could not give each child the individualized attention he or she needed. In some ways it was like caring for children in an orphanage. Things got done efficiently, but that efficiency was frequently at odds with what those children needed most. Quiet time in their own rooms. Someone to brush their hair, dress them, read to them. Someone to notice when they were tired, thirsty, or hungry. Someone to love them.

Fortunately, we were able to take care of Jeremy ourselves, thanks to our employers' compassionate leave policies. Jeremy could not yet aim a spoon at his mouth or hold a cup without spilling, but Kris or I were there to help him at mealtimes. He was on a liquid diet. This meant that whatever foods we picked from the hospital menu—scrambled eggs or a cheeseburger and fries, for example—were thrown into a blender and liquefied into a thick beige-gray paste, which we spooned into his mouth.

After breakfast I washed Jeremy's face and brushed his teeth, changed his sheets, tucked in the blankets, and fluffed the six or seven pillows that kept him positioned properly. Then he underwent physical or occupational therapy. Rehab patients typically see therapists twice a day, morning and afternoon. Usually the patients were taken downstairs to the rehab clinic for therapy sessions. Jeremy was still too weak to leave his room and his movements were restricted because of the blood clot, so for the time being the therapists came to him. The physical therapist worked to stretch and stimulate his paralyzed right leg. The occupational therapist did the same for his right arm and hand.

Between the therapy appointments Jeremy tried to sleep. Not only was he exhausted from the constant nighttime sleep deprivation, but his injured brain needed sleep to recover. Without stimulation from the outside world, the brain can forego much of its normal processing activity and redirect the energy toward healing. And when he slept, I could sleep too. Unfortunately, our naps were also constantly interrupted by intrusions from janitors, nurses, the dietician, aides, and visits from well-meaning friends. Lord, what I wouldn't have given for an hour's uninterrupted sleep.

Taking care of Jeremy was grueling. He needed to be turned from side to side every hour to minimize bedsores. Each shift of position took ten to fifteen minutes and a fair amount of engineering. I untucked his bottom sheet, gripped it tightly at one edge, bent over and pulled as hard as I could to shift him over to the side of the bed. I rolled him onto his other side and braced him there with rolled up towels and blankets tucked behind his back. Then I put pillows under his top arm and top leg, made his head comfortable, untangled the monitor lines and remade the bed. My back was one constant, fiery ache. With each circuit I moved more and more slowly from one side of the bed to the other, on legs that were made of concrete.

In the late afternoons the doctors made their rounds, examined patients, prescribed medications, and noted progress in charts. Jeremy saw at least six doctors each day. He was assigned to the head of the rehab unit, Dr. Joe, and usually saw a rehab attending doctor and a resident physician as well. His neurosurgeon checked his incisions and tested neurological functioning. A hematologist monitored his blood clot. Our pediatrician, Petra, came almost every day to see how Jeremy was doing, chat with us, and discuss her research into the further therapies that would be needed to treat Jeremy's AVM.

Finally dinner: another tray of pureed food. Afterward a sponge bath, a few more chapters of reading aloud, or a movie on the VCR. At 10:00 P.M. the television sets and lights were turned off. I tucked Jeremy in, gave him a good night kiss and a blessing, and sat next to his bed until he fell asleep. In the rooms around us quiet gradually descended. A few of the younger children cried. Mostly they clutched their blankets and stared at the walls until sleep overtook them. Joseph's wails started, stopped, started again.

I lay on the narrow window seat, shivering under the cold downdrafts from the ceiling vents, listening to the forlorn sounds of a world of lost children settling down for the night. I was lost too, drifting in the dark on an ocean of pain and yearning, keeping company only with the glittering stars outside the cold black window. I promised myself that when we finally left this place, I would tell these children's stories, give words to their grief and longing.

From: Fiala, Marie Lawson
Sent: October 2, 1998 12:22 A.M.
To: Jeremy Network
Subject: Late at Night (II)/Update No. 16

Our fourth week of living in the hospital draws to a close. It is lonely here late at night, with only my thoughts for company and the computer for a lifeline. I have not much armor against the darkness that daylight and the companionship of others help keep at bay.

Medical news continues in shades of gray. I met with the interventional radiologist at UCSF today. He is a compassionate, kind, super-bright man, generous with his time and words. I feel reassured that we are in good hands. After hearing about Jeremy's recent progress, he strongly recommends using the gamma knife to treat the AVM. The deformed blood vessels are in such a very small and densely important area of the brain that a millimeter, or less, in area targeted by the treatment will make the difference in whether or not Jeremy permanently loses right side movement and vision. The radiation can be aimed fairly precisely at the affected area. Treatment is still at least a month off. We must wait until all the edema (swelling) of the brain subsides in order to get the clearest possible picture of the target area.

Jeremy also continues to have clotting problems. The clot has now advanced up into the inferior vena cava, the main vein draining the lower half of the body, all the way to the Greenfield filter that was implanted a week ago. Jeremy has had a battery of blood tests and been evaluated by a hematologist. As yet they can't tell us why the clotting continues or what impact the fact that the clot has reached the filter will have. And in any event the normal treatment options are nonexistent because giving Jeremy a blood thinner to dissolve the clot would risk rebleeding at the AVM.

As for the rest, Jeremy more than holds his own. His speech is sometimes articulate and sometimes confused, but still there. Now that he can talk we have insight into the working of his mind. He overflows with gratitude and love for the people helping him in so many ways—us, medical personnel, visitors, the many friends who call or send cards and messages. I don't think there's a person who has come to see him this week who has not felt the abundance of Jeremy's love. It pours out of him in a great tide, without complaint or anger. It's as if this awful injury and his return to the world burned away his imperfections for the moment, leaving only his pure clean spirit shining behind his eyes and skin. I hope more than I can say that we return to the life of petty sibling squabbles and bickerings. But for right now it is a privilege to be in his immaculate company.

Mirror, Mirror

"MOM, DO YOU HAVE A MIRROR," Jeremy asked, lying flat on his back in his hospital bed.

"Why, sweetie?"

"I want to see what I look like."

I felt first surprise, then a sharp stab of realization. *Of course, he's been lying in bed for a month while things were being done to him. He has no idea what he looks like after all that.*

Because I had been so focused on simply keeping him alive, I had hardly noticed the changes in Jeremy's physical appearance until now. Before his injury, Jeremy, like many thirteen-year-olds, was hovering on the edge of adolescence but had not yet made the transition from boyhood into manhood. He was above-average in height, and his contours were still soft and rounded. He had a thick thatch of perfectly straight bright blond hair, widely spaced blue-gray-green eyes, heavy black eyelashes, golden skin with a pale patina of fine hair, the faintest sprinkle of nutmeg freckles across his nose, and a generous mouth that framed small straight white teeth. He was awkward and not entirely comfortable in his body anymore, but his broad shoulders and long smooth arms and legs sang the promise of a beautiful man's form someday. Now he was barely recognizable as the same boy who had eaten waffles and wanted to go swimming on Labor Day weekend.

I coaxed him into a few days' delay. "Jeremy, your hair needs cutting," I said. "The front is short and the back is long. Let's wait until I can find a pair of electric hair clippers and even out your haircut."

"Oh, okay. I always wanted a buzz cut." He smiled and agreed easily, in no hurry to face himself.

The front half of Jeremy's head had been shaved to the scalp during each of his brain surgeries, and the hair was just beginning to grow back. The back half was long, lank and lifeless. I felt a wild desire to preserve it, as I had once put off cutting Jeremy's baby hair in order to hang on to a tangible remnant of a time gone by, but I knew that it must be cut. I asked around the hospital, but no one had hair clippers or any idea how to find them, despite the fact that patients were routinely shaved for surgery. Kristor bought a pair of clippers on one of his off-duty days and brought them in.

Cutting Jeremy's hair was harder than I had thought it would be. He couldn't sit up or even hold his head straight on his own. I lifted his head off the pillow with one hand and clumsily drove the heavy clippers across the surface of his scalp with the other hand, nicking him in one or two places. When I was finished, Jeremy's entire head was covered with an eighth of an inch of dark-gray stubble.

I stood back and looked at Jeremy before handing him the mirror. Above the loose, faded, thin cotton gown, his head looked too large for his wasting body. Through the stubble of hair, four long incisions showed plainly where the drains had once entered his brain. The two more recent incisions were still sutured with a black cross-stitching of surgical thread. Too raw to be called scars, these bright red gashes lent the only color to a black-and-white portrait. Jeremy's skin was blue-white without a trace of its former golden undertones. His lips were a darker slash of gray. The right half of his face was stiff and frozen, his mouth immobile, his right eye pulled upward and outward by his rigid facial muscles. His once-beautiful eyes still dominated his face, pained whirlpools sunk deep in bruised-black sockets. Jeremy's eyes were old, older than he was, older than anyone's who had not seen his own death close at hand. One sees the same look in photographs of people who have felt great cruelties. "I have suffered much," Jeremy's eyes said, "and I will suffer more, and still, I go on."

"Jeremy, dear, you know that you've been very sick. I don't want you to be surprised. You look different from how you used to look, okay? When you get better, you'll look like yourself again."

But still he said, "Mom, I want to see," and I gave the mirror to him.

Jeremy stared at his image for a long time. His lips quivered and tears ran down his face. "Mom, I look so awful," he said finally. "I didn't know I had scars. The scars look so bad." His lips pressed together hard and formed an upside-down *U*. He gave one deep sob, and then he put the mirror down and was quiet.

"Sweetie, you don't look awful; you just look sick. Soon you'll get better, your hair will grow out and cover the scars, and you'll look just like you did before, sweetie. Please don't be sad."

Jeremy looked up at me with a steady gaze and nodded once or twice but did not speak, then turned his face away and closed his eyes.

The mirror hadn't lied. I had. I knew that it was a lie even as I said the words, and Jeremy probably knew it too. No matter how much rehabilitation he underwent, Jeremy would not look the same. He would not *be* the same. The damage had been too great. From now on, for the rest of his life, he would always be a broken bird, too injured to fly freely.

Consolations

ANNELISE TEETERED between childhood and womanhood that fall. In October, the middle school sponsored a dance for the sixth, seventh, and eighth graders—what we had called a sock hop when I was her age. When she diffidently asked whether she could go, I responded, "Yes, dear, of course," and then thought no more about it.

This was a colossal failure on my part. If I had taken the time to think back to my own first junior high dance, I would have vividly remembered my terrified anticipation leading up to the event. *What should I wear? Who will I dance with? HOW will I dance?* But I had been largely oblivious to Lisie's changing social needs. I didn't want Annelise's and David's lives to be defined by their brother's illness. But in spite of these good intentions, my focus had contracted, and I saw life outside the hospital only through peripheral vision. A lot escaped me.

On the evening of the party, I realized for the first time with horror and abundant self-flagellation that Annelise had no special ensemble to wear. She had never asked for much in the way of material things—none of our kids did—and she hadn't brought it up. I hadn't recognized the importance of the occasion. *You are a BAD MOTHER! How could you not buy her a new dress? Oh, my poor little girl.*

When Annelise emerged from her room, I was stunned. She had pulled together a stylish combination: a long black skirt that had once been mine, an amethyst tank top, and a short cardigan with the sleeves pushed up. The only new item was a pair of black platform sandals that we had recently bought on sale. She had accessorized with a mismatched choker and bracelets that somehow looked just right together, applied a touch of lipstick, and swept her masses of tawny gold hair up into a contemporary disheveled twist. She descended the stairs with slow and careful grace on the unaccustomed high heels. "Hi, Mommy," she said, slightly shy. "I'm ready to go."

I suddenly did not recognize my little girl. This lovely woman-child would walk down many stairways toward me in the years ahead, in a new dress or a prom dress or someday in a wedding dress, but she would never look more beautiful to me than that day, the day on which I discovered how beautiful she was.

———

One evening that October, David and I were lying on the master bed. I had just finished reading from our current chapter book, as we did every night, and turned off the bedside lamp. I was thinking about Jeremy and another painful morning, less than twelve hours away. David was looking out of the big window next to the bed, stargazing. The night sky was exceptionally clear. It burned with a thousand points of cold white fire, a snapshot from billions of years in earth's past. David was enthralled with astronomy but didn't yet have complete command of the vocabulary. "Mom!" he exclaimed, "Look at all the consolations!" So I did, and they were beautiful. My heart lightened, and floated out the window into the night. I held David's small soft hand and stroked his fair hair back from his forehead. We were quiet together, as we looked up and out into the dark, at a skyful of consolations.

Air Lift

I have found life so beautiful.

—Helen Keller

SHORTLY AFTER JEREMY WAS MOVED into the rehab ward, while my parents were with him, I made a trip to the second floor of the hospital to check out the gym where he would soon begin daily therapy. It was a long, open, untidy space crammed with weights and pulleys; exercise machines; short boards, long boards, slant boards; large colorful plastic balls; low, thickly padded tables; bins and shelves filled with small pieces of colored plastic; empty wheelchairs, crutches, braces; and posters of handicapped athletes racing bikes, climbing mountains, and playing basketball. Eight to ten children were being stretched, pulled, wheeled, measured, fitted, and comforted. It was a lot to take in after the relative quiet of Jeremy's room, and I retreated quickly.

Just down the hall I noticed a side corridor with an overhead sign marked "Garden." The short passageway ended in concrete steps leading down into the out-of-doors. And there, indeed, was what used to be a garden.

This space had evidently served as the hospital's

grand main entrance decades ago. Old black-and-white photographs posted along the passageway showed a semi-circular drive sweeping up to a gracefully proportioned entry, flanked on either side by broad bands of lawn and sheltering trees, and overlooked by a handsome two-story *U*-shaped building, with tall bay windows, ground-floor French doors, porticos, and cornices. This, the hospital's oldest wing, was now used largely for storage and administrative offices. As I stepped outside and looked up, I recognized traces of the building's former beauty, not quite obscured by renovations that had chopped once generous rooms into small cubicles, replaced mullioned windows with plate glass, and grafted squat steel-framed extensions onto the building's exterior. I share Kris's love of old buildings, and even now I found it in myself to wonder how such mutilation could have been inflicted in the name of serving progress.

Over the years the hospital had expanded in the opposite direction, and this former entry courtyard had been cut off from the street. An elevated freeway no more than one hundred yards away blocked access on one side, and an elevated train track ran to meet it on the other. Remaining in the middle were a few hardy trees, oaks and a magnolia, perhaps even the same trees that had grown to maturity along with the hospital. A narrow edging of grass had managed to stay green in this inhospitable environment, and a number of straggling bushes and small flowering plants kept it company. The space was dominated by a large expanse of old asphalt, broken and buckled in places.

I wondered briefly why so much of this courtyard had been paved over. Surely a bit more grass, a few more shrubs would have filled the space more pleasantly? But the asphalt was low maintenance, and the hospital probably did not have the budget to employ a large gardening staff.

I found a seat on one of several concrete benches set in the grass border, turned my face up to the sky, and just sat quietly, with eyes closed. After weeks of living in completely artificial surroundings, here was a small connection to the natural world.

I was never so happy as in the out-of-doors. Contact with wildness had nourished our family life and kept us emotionally healthy. On weekends we searched out the surprisingly large swathes of undeveloped land that still existed in the Bay Area's beaches and wooded hills. Carrying our children until they were old enough to keep up, we walked, we splashed and swam, we searched for agate stones and let the sand run through our hands. We always returned from these expeditions with a clear sense of what was essential and what was merely busyness, of the importance of keeping a firm and constant grip on the physical world that gave us life.

In the courtyard, the drone of traffic faded from hearing. For the first time in weeks I felt the sun like a warm hand on my skin. Random lyrics from an old song floated to the surface: *And the sun pours down like honey, on our lady of the harbor* . . . I took a deep breath. Fresh air, soothing my throat and lungs, so different from the cold dry air forced through the hospital's ventilation system, which cut through mucous membranes like a knife.

Sunlight, fresh air, the smell of new-cut grass, one or two determined bees, a reverie. I sat for a long time.

Then an immense roar erupted directly overhead, though nothing was in view. The sound beat against me in great waves. Something was slicing through the air. A long minute later, a small, bright-red, extremely low-flying helicopter emerged from behind the building and, before the idea of its existence had fully registered, approached my courtyard for a landing. The mystery of the asphalt was solved. This hospital was a regional trauma center. Sick and injured children from all over Northern California were transported here for treatment, some by air. I was sitting at the edge of a helipad.

The helicopter landed quickly. The door popped open and three men lifted out a gurney. They unfolded its scissored legs, and its wheels made contact with the ground. Strapped tightly to it was a small motionless form, cocooned in blankets, with a knitted cap covering its head. One of the attendants pushed the gurney across the bumpy asphalt at a brisk pace, aiming for the hospital entrance just behind me. Alongside trotted a second attendant, holding an oxygen mask over the small invisible face. On the other side, a third attendant held an IV bag high in the air.

Moving in concert, they swiftly, efficiently, rolled the gurney up the concrete ramp and through the doorway. The interior of the hallway was dark, and my sun-dazzled eyes could not see them once they had entered, but I knew the way to the ICU very well, and I could imagine their progress.

As quickly as it had arrived, the helicopter left again, lifting straight up in a gravity-defying leap, then angling to the side as it arced over the freeway and away. I was left behind, with a new comprehension of the little courtyard. A threshold, a peaceful place that said to those within, "look, the world is with you still," and to those that enter, "come in, come in."

My brief moment on this tiny broken shore had ended. The natural world beckoned, but my life still lay in a small dark room cut off from everything that held meaning, except for the one most important thing.

From: Fiala, Marie Lawson
Sent: October 3, 1998 11:03 P.M.
To: Jeremy Network
Subject: Looking Backward/Update No. 17

Tonight closes the first four weeks of our new life. I am amazed anew by the difference between Jeremy's condition as recently as six days ago and the boy who lies in the bed before me, asleep. It is more than just his ability to speak. The last of his tubes came out this week. (I counted that, at the start, Jeremy's body was breached by nine separate lines—two in his brain, a feeding tube, a ventilator, arterial lines in his arm and groin, IVs in each foot, and a catheter.) He can eat small bites of real food. His vision shows tiny improvement. The swelling in his right leg recedes. I can now sit next to his sleeping form for an hour at a time without wondering whether he will die in the next moment. God willing, the AVM will lie dormant and we will regain our son.

We are not the same people we were four weeks ago. Jeremy and our family have been profoundly changed. Living with the moment-to-moment possibility of loss imparts a moment-to-moment awareness of what one has, and of the presence of the divine in one's daily life. Based on what I read in my torrent of incoming mail, the reverberations of this catastrophic injury have touched many of you as well. I am reminded of a line from Alfred, Lord Tennyson, which I may not have quite right (being without my Norton Anthology): "Our echoes roll from soul to soul/and grow forever and forever. . . ."

I have puzzled over this strange juxtaposition of unbearable pain and unbearable beauty. Just tonight I found an explanation in a story from an elegant and eloquent book given to us by friends, Kitchen Table Wisdom. The author, a physician and therapist, tells of treating a young athlete after he had lost his leg to cancer. Filled with anger and bitterness, at his first therapy session he was asked to draw an image of himself. He drew an outline of a vase; running through the center of it he drew a deep crack, going over and over the crack with a black crayon. After time and healing he began to reach out to counsel and minister to other young patients. In his final therapy session he was shown the drawing of the vase. Remarking that "it's really not finished," he took a yellow crayon and drew lines radiating from the crack in the vase to the very edges of the paper. Thick yellow lines. Smiling, he put his finger on the crack and said softly, "This is where the light comes through."

Water Magic (1)

T HE REHAB WARD BATHROOMS caught my eye
early on. Unlike the ICU, rehab had several
large rooms specially configured for bathing or showering
disabled patients. I longed for the benison of water. I longed
to wheel Jeremy into one of these rooms and let warm water
pour over him in a cleansing stream. I longed to lay him
in the deepest tub I could find until every part of him but
his face was underwater, floating, suspended, freed from
gravity. I longed to hold him in my arms and walk into
the very center of a river and let the current carry away
the accumulated pain layered over us like dirty clothes. I
wanted to wash away the sweat and blood and tears, to
hold Jeremy reborn—pink and clean and full of hope.

"Can I give Jeremy a shower," I began to ask the
doctors, and "When can Jeremy have a shower?" and "Is it
time yet?"

"Not yet," the doctors answered. "His incisions are too
raw; it is not wise to move him more than necessary." "Not
yet," they said, and then again, "Not yet," and finally, after
a month in the hospital, "Yes, he is strong enough. Yes."

Jeremy seemed as excited as I was about this prospect.
"Really? I can have a shower? That's great!" I imagined that,
unbathed for so long, his skin felt full of crumbs and itches,
as the Rhinoceros felt in the *Just So Stories*.

After dinner, one of the nurses, Eduardo, wheeled the
shower gurney into Jeremy's room and parked it next to

the bed. The gurney had a white PVC tubing framework, over which was stretched bright-blue plastic mesh, through which water could drain. Together Eduardo and I edged Jeremy sideways from the bed onto the gurney. I heaped towels and blankets next to his feet, along with a bottle of shampoo and a round green cake of lemon-scented soap, and we were off.

The shower was a large square room, completely tiled in white, with a drain in the floor and a handheld shower head attached to a hose suspended from the wall. I turned it on experimentally. The water dribbled out in a parsimonious stream. This would not provide the warm-water extravaganza I had imagined. The hose was barely long enough to reach the full length of the gurney. I would have to wash Jeremy one small part at a time. Still, this was a distinct improvement over the basin-and-washcloth method that we had been using for weeks.

I began with Jeremy's face and, most satisfying of all, his hair. Finally I could wash his remaining hair properly. It was harder than I had expected. I held the shower head in one hand and used the other hand to lift and move Jeremy's head as well as to lather and scrub. Since Jeremy was lying on his back and couldn't roll by himself, large areas were inaccessible to the spray. Ah, well. He was quiet as I narrated. "I'm going to turn your head to one side, sweetie, and wash the hair on that side. I've got to be careful, can't get your stitches and incisions wet. Let's rinse. Good. Now the same thing on the other side." The waste water ran light tan, and then clear, down the drain.

I moved on to Jeremy's upper body. Again the one-handed lathering was awkward. *How can I move Jeremy while I'm holding the soap and the sprayer? How do I manage the washcloth? What do I do with the soap while I rinse?* I found clumsy solutions. The important thing was to get him clean, and quickly.

The shower room was unheated, and the anemic spray

did not generate enough steam to warm it. "Mommy, I'm cold," Jeremy said. He began to shiver.

As I finished washing each part of his body I draped it with towels and blankets, then moved on to the next area. Jeremy's teeth chattered audibly. "Mom, I'm freezing."

When I was done I had a cold, wet, dripping boy covered with cold, wet, dripping towels on a cold, wet, dripping gurney. My own clothes were soaked as well. I fetched more towels, dried off Jeremy and the gurney, and wrung out my tee-shirt. Soggy discarded linens were piled high. Jeremy's back, which I couldn't reach, was still wet. "Mom, please, I'm so cold."

I pulled the heavy gurney to the door, propped the door open with one foot, pushed and pulled the gurney through the doorway, and wheeled Jeremy down the hall and into his room. Eduardo returned, rolled Jeremy onto his side so that I could dry his back, then helped slide him into bed. I dressed him in a clean hospital gown and covered him with several blankets. Finally finished, he was finally warm. The shower had taken forty-five minutes, a mountain of towels, all my energy.

This had not been the full-submersion baptism I had imagined, but it had been lovely. Jeremy's skin was cool and smooth and soft. He smelled sweet, like a newly washed baby. He glowed with the possibility of health. The water had worked its magic.

From: Fiala, Marie Lawson
Sent: October 5, 1998 11:45 P.M.
To: Jeremy Network
Subject: Travels with Jeremy/Update No. 21

As I sit next to Jeremy's bed, the light from the computer screen illuminates the outlines of a large photograph on the wall. The room is too dark to make out the picture itself—Jeremy cannot sleep with any lights on—but I know the scene so well that I can fill in every detail. It is a small beach on Maui where we have vacationed every year since Jeremy was born, where I have stood perhaps a thousand times. I can close my eyes and walk every footstep from our front door to the water's edge. Jeremy has stood there every year to be photographed against the lucent water and sand, foam curling around his feet, squinting into the sun, each year more visibly humoring his mother. For some reason, the thought that he might never stand there again, that there might be no more photographs, early on became the locus of my pain.

Now we dare to breathe again. Each day Jeremy makes small progress. His right arm and leg occasionally surprise us with new movements. His thrombosed leg looks close to normal in size. His lungs are nearly clear. His speech and thought continue to return, although he often has trouble finding the right word and instead selects an analogue that means something slightly different, like saying he would like another "coat" of blankets rather than another "layer." This is common with brain-injured patients—the brain goes to the right storage location for the concept but then clicks on the wrong word.

Each day brings new pleasures. Today a lying-down shower on a waterproof gurney. Jeremy and I both love the water. He looks forward to his next shower. I hope for one more time on our beach.

Relativity

I LOVE WALKING. A steady pace, arms swinging in synchrony with legs, breath keeping time, the solid reassuring contact of feet to ground, all elements moving together in a perfect rhythm that speaks to me of what it means to be human on this planet. Time slows down and space expands when I walk. A minute lasts a long time measured in steps. A mile is a long space measured in minutes. When I walk, I feel the shortness of my stride and the shortness of my life next to the earth's immensities of age and distance. Walking illuminates my just and proper role as one tiny inhabitant on a sphere whose surfaces my feet could not cover in a lifetime.

On the day that Jeremy entered the hospital, when I saw him in a coma and learned that he was paralyzed, I prayed only for a future in which he and I would walk together again. And if not that, I prayed for a future in which I would push him in a wheelchair and we would talk.

Ten days after Jeremy's Greenfield filter had been installed, the doctors decided he was stable enough to ride in a wheelchair for the first time.

After breakfast, Jeremy's two physical therapists joined Kris and me in his room to begin. Mary, the older, more experienced therapist, had dark-brown wavy hair and serious brown eyes and a quiet smile. She was petite but strong, strong enough to manipulate Jeremy's limbs and body better than I could. Shelley was younger and taller. Her auburn hair floated in lighter-than-air curls around her heart-shaped face, and her windchime laughter made even the most painful therapies easier for Jeremy to bear. He liked them both, although he could not tell them apart or remember their names from his morning therapy sessions to his afternoon appointments.

"You're going to have an outing. We're going to get you up in a wheelchair," said Mary.

"Thank you!" Jeremy exclaimed. "I'm so happy."

First, a wheelchair had to be found. I had imagined something high-tech, sleek and low with wide wheels, perhaps painted a bright metallic shade. I learned immediately that style, color, and accessories don't matter. Most importantly, the chair had to be the right size so that Jeremy's back and neck were fully supported, so that his feet didn't drag on the floor, so that armrests and legrests could be attached at the right places and angles. Jeremy was tall, and most of the pediatric chairs were too small for him. Eventually the therapists found an old and heavily used veteran, with a battered steel framework, a brown plastic seat, and large old-fashioned tires. Compared to two-wheeled analogs, this chair was no racing bike, or even a mountain bike. It was closer to the heavy old Schwinn I had learned to ride as a child.

The chair was a close fit, but not close enough. Using ingenuity and found materials, Mary and Shelley customized it further. Kris took great interest in this process, and helped where he could. They wrapped pieces of cardboard with toweling and strapped them with duct tape to make cushions to raise the seat and bring the back forward. A sheet of Formica was cut down to make a tray, which they attached to the chair with a C-clamp to support Jeremy's right arm. More cardboard, gauze, and tape made a cushioned splint to protect Jeremy's forearm from abrasion. Pieces of webbing served as a seatbelt. The emerging contraption looked like a Gypsy caravan.

When the chair was finally retrofitted, Mary and Shelley began the long, careful transfer process with help from Kris and me. *Transfer* means moving a patient from one piece of hospital equipment to another: gurney to bed, bed to chair, chair to walker. Each transfer protocol is closely choreographed. Nothing is improvised. First, we wrapped Jeremy's legs firmly from toes to torso in Ace bandages, three rolls for each leg, to force the blood back up the veins and keep it from pooling. Over the bandages went non-skid socks to keep his feet from slipping out from under him. We inched Jeremy up from supine to seated and swung his legs over the side of the bed.

Jeremy had had a few practice sessions so that his blood pressure no longer free-fell when he sat up. Still, he was faint and dizzy and unable to hold a sitting position without help. While Kris and I kept him upright, Shelley moved the wheelchair next to the bed and locked the brakes. Standing on either side of Jeremy, Mary and Shelley crossed arms under his shoulders and behind his back and lifted. For an instant, Jeremy was standing, although not supporting his own weight. The therapists pivoted and lowered him into the wheelchair. Kris and I would perform this same maneuver many times in the future, and discover that it requires more skill and strength than we suspected as observers on this first day.

Once seated, Jeremy slumped heavily forward. Only the seatbelt and our hands on his shoulders kept him from pitching onto the floor. Mary attached two clanky metal appliances to the front of the chair to lift his legs off the ground, shifting his center of gravity backward. The Formica tray was clamped on and Jeremy's limp right arm laid on top of the tray, cushioned by the padded splint.

I wanted to propel Jeremy on his first outing, and Kris, graceful as always, ceded me that privilege. With Kris walking next to us, I wheeled Jeremy out of the room. My only comparable experience was pushing a stroller, but the wheelchair was far heavier and less maneuverable.

As we walked down the hall to the elevators that would take us to the rehab gym, a few hospital visitors passed by and I faintly registered the Look directed at us for the first time. The Look is what most healthy people give someone who is in a wheelchair. They don't look directly at the wheelchair passenger, or smile, or nod. Instead, their eyes slide surreptitiously over the wheelchair occupant and then quickly away without acknowledgment. The Look says, "What is wrong with him?" The Look says, "He is different than I am." The Look says, "He makes me uncomfortable."

I knew the Look well, for I had used it myself when we had first moved onto the rehab ward.

I would see the Look often from now on, every time I took Jeremy out in a wheelchair. The fleeting overview, the eyes skittering away to the side, the studied partial averting of the head, the determined "I'm not noticing anything" expression on the face. This first time, though, the Look was outweighed by the pleasure of moving through the world with Jeremy again. We were walking. No, we were flying.

The peach-painted walls and white doorways slid past the edges of vision. I looked down. Jeremy's head flopped loosely from side to side and forward. I could see his bluish scalp between the individual hairs. The tiny spatters of dark color on the light linoleum floor blurred beneath the wheels, our pace transforming them into narrow strings of pigment, like letters on a printing press moving by too fast to read. The wheels made a tiny repeated sound with each revolution, swish-swish-swish-swish-swish. I was mesmerized by the flowing lines on the floor and the sound. Step, step, step. Swish-swish-swish-swish-swish.

When I finally looked up, the illusion of speed evaporated, and we were only halfway down a long hallway, walking at a measured pace.

We reached the bank of patients' elevators. One stopped, and the few people who were already on board moved to the back and corners to make room. The elevator descended slowly. We all studied the lighted panel over the door. I felt the other passengers glancing over at Jeremy, then away. The Look again. Kris protectively shifted closer to Jeremy. I knew that he had seen it, too.

Seeing us, a particularly compassionate stranger might think, "Poor boy, I wonder what happened to him." Or even "His poor parents, how hard this must be for them."

But I felt only elation, fizzing in my chest like champagne. *Look!* I wanted to say. *This is my son, and he can sit up, and we are out for our first walk. It has been so long since we walked together. Isn't it wonderful?*

When the elevator stopped, we got off and walked the short distance to the rehab gym, which was as noisy and active as it had been during my earlier reconnaissance. I pushed Jeremy down the long central aisle and back. He received a few curious glances, but the patients, staff, and parents here all lived in a world in which a wheelchair was just an everyday appliance, and no one's look spoke of aversion.

This first visit was brief. It was a shock to see how weak, gray, and gaunt Jeremy looked against the backdrop of the colorful rehab workspace. The expedition had drained his small store of strength. I watched him crumple beneath the weight of the gym's colors, sound, and movement. He slumped heavily to one side, his head resting against the back of the wheelchair seat. The purple-black shadows around his eyes stood in sharp relief against his parchment skin. It was time to leave.

Back in Jeremy's room, the transfer process was reversed. Mary and Shelley moved him from the wheelchair to the edge of the bed, then swung his legs up onto the mattress. We tenderly laid him down, as I had laid him in his crib as a baby, with my hand cradling his helpless head.

Jeremy gratefully accepted gravity's embrace and sank onto his pillows. His eyes closed, and he was instantly asleep.

From: Fiala, Marie Lawson
Sent: October 7, 1998 11:37 P.M.
To: Jeremy Network
Subject: Our Whole Child/Update No. 19

We met with Jeremy's rehab team yesterday to plan his treatment program. Jeremy will be working daily with Dr. Joe, physical therapists, an occupational therapist, and a speech therapist. It's not clear how long his recovery will take.

Jeremy, for his part, seems to be living entirely, and joyfully, in the present moment. He does not ask what lies ahead. Instead, he is profoundly grateful for being alive and awake. The smallest things make him happy: a cold drink, being able to wear his new school tee-shirt, a warm washcloth for his face, and especially visitors. Several friends dropped by tonight, making Jeremy, as he said, "glow from the inside." He is working hard at rehab; much of what is required of him is painful, but he never complains, never gets angry, never holds back. When I told him that I would be writing this message and asked him if he wanted to say anything, he responded, "Tell them that I'm doing great, I'm just doing great." And he meant it.

Among the many beautiful cards we have received is a brilliant photograph of Comet Hale-Bopp, taken last year. It has fascinated Jeremy since before he was able to speak; he pointed it out on his hospital wall and had me take it down to show him. For me, it has become an image of his undiminished spirit streaking across the night sky.

A Place to Call Home

Try to bear lightly what needs must be.

—Plato

M Y YOUNGEST SISTER, who lives in Seattle, had come for her second visit since Jeremy's hemorrhage. We were not close, this sister and I. She had been twelve years old when I fled our family home to go to college in California, leaving her behind, feeling abandoned. Our lives had veered apart on very different trajectories. We saw each other infrequently. Now we had experienced eerily similar tragedies. Three years earlier, her own nine-year-old son had been gravely injured, his skull fractured in a brutal car accident. That calamity and its aftermath had nearly destroyed her as well.

A month ago, when my sister first heard of Jeremy's hemorrhage, she had boarded the next plane for San Francisco. However distant we had grown, we were still bound by blood and our common grief. And on the first morning after Jeremy's collapse, she set out to cure me of any illusions I might have had about his condition. "You have to face the fact," she lectured from across the kitchen table, "that everything you've known is over. Jeremy's brain has been scrambled like an egg.

It can't be put back together again. Jeremy will never be the same; your life will never be the same."

I sat silent, shocked. *What on earth is she saying?* I had just come home from the hospital, where I had been up all night waiting for Jeremy to come out of surgery and then sitting beside him in the ICU. All I was prepared to face that morning was the fact that he was still alive. I felt as if she had stabbed me without provocation. Time proved her to be right, but I wished that she had wielded the sharp blade of truth more gently.

On this second visit, she joined me in the hospital cafeteria for coffee while Jeremy worked with his therapists. The cafeteria was one of the more pleasant spaces in the hospital. One side was mostly plate glass that admitted daylight, along with a view of the freeway. The walls were decorated with large framed photographs of children receiving medical treatment. They looked exceptionally happy, and I wondered every time I saw them whether the photographer had posed models in hospital-like settings. None of the live children I encountered bubbled with smiles and laughter, or seemed delighted to be here. I had seen only small sad faces, weighted with disappointment, deadened with resignation, aged by pain. The pictures were a jarring contrast to the living pictures just a few feet away from this room, the ones I took home with me at night.

My sister and I made our way through the food service line, served ourselves coffee out of tall stainless steel urns, and found spoons and milk and sugar at the condiments counter. I was grateful for her company, although wary of ambush. Still, I did not see it coming until we were seated at a corner table and she had studied the plastic tabletop for a few moments. Then she looked up with a "this is for your own good expression" that I recognized and distrusted. "Marie, what are you going to do about your house?" she asked abruptly. I didn't understand her question.

"What do you mean?"

"Well, Jeremy will be coming home in a wheelchair, maybe permanently," she responded. "Your house isn't wheelchair-accessible. Think about the hill, all those steps. You don't even have space for a bedroom or bath on the main floor. You can't go on without thinking about how you will bring Jeremy home. How will he live?"

"I . . . I hadn't thought about it," I stammered.

"Well, you'd *better* think about it," she said. "The *rest* of the family certainly has been." She sat back in her chair and stirred her coffee.

Again, I was caught off-guard, and this idea staggered me. Now that Jeremy had defied medical predictions by regaining his speech and some movement, I was thinking of his recovery as a linear process. He had been working with physical therapists for hours every day. I had assumed that he would simply continue to make progress over time. It had not occurred to me before this moment, as I sat looking into my sister's complicated blue gaze over the rim of a coffee cup, that Jeremy might not reach the ultimate goal, that he might not walk again. She was right. We had to think about how to bring him home.

Over the next few days I asked the doctors new questions: "How far will Jeremy's recovery take him? What should we expect as far as our housing needs after he is discharged?"

The answers were indefinite: "Jeremy may be ready to leave the hospital in two more months. Brain injuries are unpredictable; it's impossible to say how much progress he will have made by then. Most likely, he will go home in a wheelchair."

Even at age thirteen, Jeremy weighed more than I did. Carrying him up and down stairs was physically impossible for me and hard even for Kris, who was tall and strong. Jeremy could not live in our old home unless he was able to walk out of the hospital on his own, and I needed to stop believing in that future.

"What do other families do in similar circumstances?" I asked the hospital social worker, hoping for an answer that had eluded me.

"Some people move in with other family members," she answered. "A few can afford to buy a second home while renting out the first one, until the long-term picture becomes more clear. And some people sell their home and buy a new house that is handicapped-accessible."

Our choices quickly contracted to a single point. We had no family who could take us in, and we were not wealthy enough to own two houses. I loved our peaceful tree house. We had invested years of heart and labor to make it beautiful. Now none of that mattered. "We'll have to sell the house," I said.

"And start looking right away for a new one, with level-in access," Kris agreed. "That's going to be hard to find in our hilly neighborhood."

"You're right. They didn't build ranch style houses in the 1920s and 30s."

During the next few days, Kris went into high gear: finding a realtor, looking at listings, and narrowing down the choices. A week after our decision we were standing on the sidewalk outside a low white bungalow that would formally go on the market two days later. The house matched what we needed: the same neighborhood, a flat lot, a paved level entry from the street, and a bedroom and a bathroom on the ground floor. The realtor had been able to arrange an early viewing. The East Bay real estate market was hot, and if we wanted this house we would have to pull together an offer in less than a week.

Although the house was only a few blocks from our current home, it was shaped by a different era and purpose, having been built in the late 1940s to provide affordable housing for veterans returning from the Second World War. The workmanship was solid but unimaginative. The boxy rooms were cramped and small. The walls were flat white planes without cabinetry or trim. When this small development had been laid out, no one had bothered to plant trees, and few homeowners had thought to do so since. Without the softening grace of leaves and boughs and shade, the rooflines and utility poles were etched in sharp relief against the empty sky, and the sidewalks ran like bleak rivers of concrete at the edges of an asphalt sea. Whatever warmth or welcome found here would depend entirely on what we could bring to it.

One of the comfortable aspects of my marriage to Kris was that we almost always came to the identical decision, whether choosing a vacation destination, a school, or a movie to rent on a Friday evening. This was no different. "It's not pretty, but it has everything we need," Kris said after our first tour.

"I think we should make an offer. At least we can stay in our neighborhood."

"I'll get a contractor out to look at it right away."

In the next forty-eight hours, whichever one of us was not in the hospital filled out paperwork, arranged inspections, and made back-to-back phone calls. But as soon as we started looking into financing, we realized we had a seemingly insurmountable problem. We had enough total equity in our home to make the down payment on the new house but not enough to take out a sufficient bridge loan, which meant that we would have to complete the sale of our old house before we could close escrow on the new one. That was impossible; the seller of the new house wanted a quick closing, and our house hadn't even been listed yet. *Does this mean we can't buy any house? How will Jeremy come home?*

Desperate, we asked a close relative, who had inherited money, for help. Could he and his wife loan us the amount we needed for the down payment for sixty days until we could sell our current home? Kris called me at the hospital to report the answer.

"They're not gonna do it," he said.

"What will we do?" I asked, feeling like I was suffocating.

"We'll make it work somehow. If I have to carry Jeremy up and down the stairs, I'll carry him." Kris was able to muster a weak chuckle. "Good thing you married a boatman."

Not knowing where else to turn, I called the chairman of my law firm and explained the situation. "Just tell me how much you need," he said before I could finish my question. "Whatever it is, we'll have a check to you tomorrow."

Living in extreme circumstances teaches you many things about other people. I will never forget my colleagues' unquestioning generosity.

Our realtor called us at the hospital late in the evening after the offer had gone in. Kris picked up the phone in Jeremy's room. "Mmm-hmm, mmm-hmm, I see," he said, his face giving nothing away. Jeremy didn't know about the potential move yet. He would be terribly grieved to learn that we were going to leave our home, but within hours he would forget and reexperience the loss each time we told him. It was better to wait until the move was closer.

Later, in the hall, Kris reported that four other offers had been made and that the sellers would decide the next day. As I returned to my chair at Jeremy's bedside and slipped my hand around his, I didn't know what outcome to hope for. "Yes" meant losing our old house. "No" meant further anxiety. Surprisingly, I felt no pain, only an empty waiting. I nudged at the idea of moving, like a tongue on a loose tooth. Nothing. *Maybe I've been immunized against further sadness, have reached absolute zero, the state where all emotion ceases. Maybe there's nothing left to be taken away.*

Twenty-four hours later the realtor called to congratulate us. Our offer had been accepted. I felt dim relief. One more logistical hurdle standing between hospital and homecoming had been cleared.

I stayed with Jeremy the night after the realtor's call and came home the following afternoon. I had driven the route so many times that the map was etched on my brain: out of the parking structure, three miles east on a busy avenue, and a right turn uphill into our quieter neighborhood. Here, the winding streets discouraged traffic. The older houses were clad in weathered cedar or stuccoed in shades of gray, beige, or white. They were built with deep sheltering eaves and capacious porches that invited slow conversation on warm evenings. The yards were small and steep but lovingly kept. Neatly trimmed rectangles of bright green lawn bordered the walkways. Everywhere flowers rioted and bloomed. Vines sent exploratory tendrils up posts, over trellises, and alongside window frames. I took a deep breath through the open car window. The dry sterile hospital room where Jeremy was stranded seemed very far away.

Finally, another right turn onto our curved narrow street on the very crest of the hill. I rounded the last bend, registered our own brown shingles with dark-green trim ahead, pulled up to the curb, turned off the ignition, and stepped out of the car. As I started toward the house, I saw the large "For Sale" sign. It had been driven deep, down through the impatiens and soft loam of our flowerbed. I stopped, dropped to my knees on the sidewalk, and doubled over, clutching my duffle bag to my chest.

I was wrong. I was not too frozen to feel.

From: Fiala, Marie Lawson
Sent: October 16 1998 2:33 P.M.
To: Jeremy Network
Subject: Hard Work/Update No. 23

On Tuesday we made an offer on a new house, which has been accepted. In our neighborhood, on a flat lot, mostly built on one level with a ground-floor bedroom and bath for Jeremy, not a style or vintage that would have attracted us under different circumstances. But a house we can love because Jeremy can live in it with us. A few people have asked me, "But what if by some miracle Jeremy walks out of the hospital, and you have sold your lovely home? How will you feel then?" And I tell them that if that happens, I will feel very, very happy.

This stage of Jeremy's recovery feels very much like wading through deep, fine sand with a blindfold on. The going is hard, we don't make much forward progress, and we don't know how far the plateau extends. We may enter a further period of rapid improvement tomorrow, next week, or not at all.

As Jeremy slowly grows stronger he spends more time in his wheelchair. His right arm and leg show small improvements. He can curl his fingers weakly around one of mine, his slight movement just past the threshold of perceptibility; he can raise and lower his toes across a range of a quarter- to a half-inch. Jeremy's speech and thought are still confused. He struggles to find and force out the words that say what he means. His eyes work independently of each other, which means that he sees two separate images of everything. This is probably the single biggest obstacle to returning to a life that includes reading and writing. I don't think I could stand it, but Jeremy bears it uncomplainingly.

Jeremy has two rigorous rehab sessions every day, plus traveling to the cafeteria for dinner and, sometimes, for lunch as well. What for most people is an unthinking slide out of bed in the morning is hard work for us, more than an hour of wiggling and tugging into clothes, moving the few inches from bed to wheelchair, and attaching the various appliances that keep Jeremy comfortable and serve the functions previously performed by his muscles. Then repeating the entire sequence in reverse when he comes back. I am so far beyond the borders of any tiredness I knew before. I move through these routines almost mindlessly, occasionally lifting my head to survey a landscape that has changed little in the past week.

Next week we make contact again with UCSF to start preparations for the gamma knife therapy that, we hope, eventually will protect Jeremy from the threat of a rebleed. Only after he is through the radiation therapy can I slowly, over many months, stop holding my breath and start believing in the possibility of a normal lifespan for our son.

Water Magic (2)

I pray not because it changes God,
but because God changes me.

—C. S. Lewis

ANY OF THE PEOPLE who participated in the first prayer vigil were exhilarated by the outcome, perhaps feeling that they had touched the hem of something unknowable or even holy. The e-mails kept coming, with the same request: let's hold a second vigil. We finally said yes. My acquiescence masked a tangled skein of feelings: fear, anxiety, and a slender strand of hope.

The prospect of another communal prayer vigil was terrifying. Jeremy's Internet congregation had elevated hopes after the dramatic aftermath of the first vigil. For many, this was their first experience with prayer in years. Or ever. I was queasy at the possibility that my family's private struggle might become the public occasion for their disappointment.

And more, this matter of relinquishing control and giving myself over to God was always hard for me. With every new medical catastrophe, my mind fought to take charge. And, indeed, there were many times that Kris's and my intellect, education, and force of will made a difference in Jeremy's care—in the matter of replacing his drains, for instance. But ultimately, neither I, nor Kris, nor the doctors had saved Jeremy's life, nor could we heal him. *Thy will be done.*

And even more, praying for Jeremy's recovery breached the limit that up to now I had set on my relationship with God. *Don't test your faith.* The Bible tells us to ask God for what we need. We don't know whether, or how, God will answer. It takes devotion, or desperation, to accept the possibility of disappointment yet try. It's like being on an airplane with the oxygen mask stowed in the overhead compartment and the life vest in the pocket underneath the seat. It is good to know they are there. And even better never to have to find out if they work.

———

As a Catholic girl taught by nuns before Vatican II, I early on acquired a literal conception of prayer. I believed in the magical powers of words. Uttered by the right person with the right intentions, words could transform a communion wafer into the actual Body and Blood of Christ. Surely lesser miracles also could be accomplished by means of prayer. If a prayer went unanswered, it was because it did not agree with God's plan, or because the supplicant was undeserving.

So I prayed for things that were missing in my somber young life. Childish things: dresses that weren't handed down; shiny black patent Mary Janes like the other girls at school wore, instead of scuffed brown-and-white saddle shoes; a pet kitten to hold and love. These things did not materialize. My prayers, it seemed, went unheard. This did not surprise me, for I was invisible in my home, and I thought I was invisible to God as well.

Still, I kept the habit of prayer through adolescence and into adulthood. I was happier as an adult than I had been as a child, and I no longer felt unworthy to hold an an ongoing conversation with God. Prayer became like talking to someone just around the corner in the next room. Someone unseen, but listening. I confessed my failings, which were frequent. I was quick to anger and spoke too bluntly. *I'm sorry, Lord, for my temper and brusqueness.* I had scant patience for those who did not take responsibility for fixing their problems. *Forgive my intolerance.* I loved my children with all my being, but I had to constantly pull myself back from directing the course of their lives. *Teach me forbearance.* I prayed to praise the Maker for what He had made. I would look out my office window in the late afternoon, as the sun declined in the sky, painting the horizon pearl and mauve and violet. Below and far away, the Bay gleamed like a mirror in the fading light, cupped by distant shadowed headlands. *Thank you, Lord, for this your marvelous creation.* I prayed for intercession, for the friend diagnosed with breast cancer before her fortieth birthday, a law-firm partner whose son had died three days after he was born, the colleague facing quadruple bypass surgery. *Show them your mercy, oh Lord.*

I was less comfortable with prayers of supplication. I mostly asked for intangible things.

> *Lord, help me find courage.*
> *Guide my feet to the right path.*
> *Give me wisdom to make good choices.*

I did not always hear an answer clearly, and sometimes not at all. But sometimes, days or weeks or months later, I would realize that my prayer *had* been answered, the right path chosen, the right choice made, even if in ways I could not have imagined at the moment of prayer.

I found the courage to leave my beginnings behind, and build a sturdy new life. I took the path to the river. I chose motherhood. Now I wanted the most important thing imaginable, the only thing that mattered, but my doubt was as strong as my desire.

———

The second vigil was again scheduled for a Sunday evening at eight o'clock. I returned home from the hospital late that afternoon, tired beyond telling. I was a bubble, an emptiness separated from surrounding space only by a thin stretch of skin. As I floated through dinner preparation and our evening meal, I considered foregoing the prayer session altogether. Annelise and David didn't know what was planned. My parents would shoo me and the children upstairs after dinner while they cleaned up, to give us private time, and they would never ask what we had done. What if we just read a story and I tucked them in? Tomorrow morning would bring what would come, whether I spun hope into prayerfulness this evening or not.

Eight o'clock ticked nearer, and I still hadn't decided what to do. After dinner, retreating to the master bedroom weighed me down even more. Kris and I were sorting our possessions in preparation for moving. Because the new house was much smaller than this one, we had been setting aside things we could live without, to give to charity or throw away. The bedroom was chaotic: open cardboard boxes, half-emptied closets and drawers, heaps of shoes and clothing, and tangled wire hangers. The out-of-place objects screamed at me, a cacophony of shrill voices demanding to be set to rights. I was tormented by the disorder but too tired to clean up. I could think of only one thing: the prayer vigil. What to do about the prayer vigil?

At ten minutes before the hour, I found a decision. I would pray because it was all I could do at this moment to help Jeremy.

I trotted quickly back downstairs, pulled a prayer book from the living room shelves, then excavated boxes in the dining room for candles: a squat, fat, cranberry-colored candle; two lumpy hand-dipped beeswax tapers, souvenirs of a long-ago visit to a Shaker farm; and one bayberry candle, used as a dinner table decoration. Then back upstairs to circle them on top of my dresser around the violet healing candle I had just brought home from the hospital, a friend's gift to Jeremy. One for each family member.

"Lisie! David! Can you come in here? Help me light these candles, and we'll say some prayers for Jeremy."

We piled onto the bed, the only uncluttered surface left in the room. I opened the prayer book and began to read, hoping to find faith in the empty space beneath my skin.

———

Northern Idaho, where I lived during my teenage years, is a geographic extension of the arid high prairie lands that sweep eastward from the Washington Cascades until they crest and break against the mountains of western Montana. In the Idaho Panhandle's isolated farmsteads, water was an imperative unknown to city dwellers. There were no municipal water systems, no aqueducts and pipelines from distant reservoirs. Water came from deep beneath one's feet, supplied by wells drilled down to the great aquifer that underlay the region. But even that vast underground sea was not impervious to the demands of civilization; and during the years I lived there, the water table was steadily drained in the service of irrigation lines, thirsty livestock, kitchens and bathrooms, and even the occasional swimming pool, as incongruous in that rough setting as a sapphire in broken concrete.

When a well ran dry, as it did more than once on our small parcel, life stood still. The open taps were silent. There was no water for brushing teeth, bathing, or cooking, for washing hands, dishes, or clothes, for watering sun-baked vegetable gardens or hayfields, for thirsty farm animals or humans to drink. Every cup of water needed to sustain the life of the household and farmyard was hauled in on the back of a pickup truck. Sometimes the well returned to life with the next heavy rainfall. But sometimes it did not, and then a new well had to be dug, deeper than the old one, deep enough to reach the black waters seeping quietly through the porous substrate, far beneath the soil.

By the time the well digger came, the need was great and hope was a small, shriveled thing beneath the torrid sun. Potential sites were scouted. The well digger walked to each in turn, looked at the ground, examined the foliage, and seemed to listen for the sound of water far below. Sometimes a dowser was asked to help, a local man who, it was said, could divine water with a rod. He held a fresh-cut forked willow branch, the two short ends in his hands, the longer third arm pulling down toward the ground, answering the call of water from below. I had held the divining rod myself, unbelieving, and felt it turn and twist in my hands, felt it point to the pull of water like a compass needle drawn to the north. By these means a new well site was chosen, and drilling began.

Drilling was slow and dirty and noisy. Foot after foot the drill drove down, through roots and soil and then mostly through stone. The air was filled with dust, and those who worked or watched were soon begrimed, white eyes staring out of coal-rimmed sockets, dirty bandanas tied over noses and mouths. The drill whined on and on, ten feet, fifteen, twenty, producing only noise and dust. Slowly it gained twenty-five feet, thirty, thirty-five. Noise reverberated through the bones. The drill bit broke and was replaced. In the temporary lull, the watchers were tense and quiet. The well digger charged by the depth of the bore. What if no water came? Forty feet, forty-five, fifty. Every foot ate money. The drilling continued. Water must be found. Fifty-five feet, fifty-eight, sixty. The prospect of failure darkened the air. Still the drilling went on. Eighty-one feet, eighty-two. At eighty-three feet, the drill found water, unseen, but there all along.

———

I chose simple prayers that Annelise and David could read

with me. We began with the Lord's Prayer, which they both knew. Then a prayer for a sick child—"Heavenly Father, grant that your child, Jeremy Day, may be restored to that perfect health which it is yours alone to give"—followed by the Twenty-Third Psalm. The children took up the prayer book solemnly, with respect for its maroon-leather gold-stamped cover; gilt-edged, voile-thin pages; and satin marker ribbons. They read aloud in turn.

Annelise was a strong reader. Her long tawny hair veiled her bowed head, falling almost onto the pages on her lap, as she carefully pronounced each syllable: "He maketh me to lie down in green Pastures; he leadeth me beside the still waters." When her turn was over she placed the book on David's lap.

David did not have full command of reading yet. He frowned fiercely at the small print, his words falling in disjointed cadences in his high, light voice. He forgot to breathe until his air ran out, then punctuated mid-sentence with a loud gasp: "Sur-e-ly go-od-ness and mer-mer-cy sha-all fol-low me all the da-ays of my life. . . ." I held Lisie's hand and stroked David's hair absently.

When it was my turn again, I paged through the Psalms for a favorite verse and started reading: "My soul has a desire and longing for the courts of the Lord." As I continued, the text captured and pulled me in deeper. "The sparrow has found her a house / and the swallow a nest where she may lay her young; / by the side of your altars." I was drawn to the meaning beneath the words, like the witching willow to water. "Happy are they who dwell in your house! / they will always be praising you." Comfort seeped in a cool stream through the broken, dusty spaces of my heart. "Those who go through the desolate valley will find it a place of springs, / for the early rains have covered it with pools of water." By then, I was crying. Annelise and David held onto my hands tightly as I read the last few lines through jagged sobs. "For one day in your courts is better than a thousand in my own room. For the Lord is both sun and shield;/he will give grace and glory."

Amen.

From: Fiala, Marie Lawson
Sent: October 19, 1998 12:38 A.M.
To: Jeremy Network
Subject: A Place of Springs/Update No. 24

Just before 9:00 last night the phone rang. It was Kris from the hospital. He and Jeremy had prayed together; then he muscled Jeremy into the wheelchair one more time so that he could remake the bed. As he worked he heard Jeremy's voice behind him, "Daddy, look at me!" Turning he saw Jeremy standing, unsupported, in front of his wheelchair. He stood for a full fifteen seconds. Before Kris called me, Jeremy was able to stand up another three or four times without holding on to anything, keeping his balance, supporting his weight on both legs. He even took the first step (a small shuffle, actually) to what might someday become walking.

Kris asked Jeremy what had happened. He said simply, "A feeling just came over me, and I did it."

The rehab team's reaction to hearing that Jeremy had stood up was an amusing mixture of amazement and horror. One of the rehab docs told Jeremy, "No unauthorized standing!"

Kathleen Norris, who writes about faith with a poet's sensibilities, says in her book Amazing Grace that life is like a circle, with God at the center and our lives as lines drawn from the circumference toward the middle. The closer the lines crowd in toward God, the closer we also move toward each other, and the closer the lines are to one another, the closer we become to God. I feel intimately connected to people I have known for years without really knowing, and to people I have never met. Our gratitude to all who have prayed for Jeremy's recovery is boundless. We receive this gift with the deepest humility, knowing that we can never thank you adequately for what you have given us.

Deconstruction

It does not matter how slowly you go
so long as you do not stop.

—Confucius

LIVING WITH JEREMY forced me to deconstruct every activity of daily living. A normal life is compounded of countless small movements that merge so fluidly into one another that they usually go unnoticed. As with a movie, we don't see the tens of thousands of individual frames, only the resulting sweep of action. The individual frames we can take for granted. But Jeremy's days unfolded frame by frame.

7:00 A.M. The custodian awakened us by banging into the room, emptying wastebaskets, collecting soiled linens from the hamper, and pushing dust from one corner of the floor to another with a wide fluffy dry mop. A nurse's aide followed. She flung aside the curtain that cordoned off our side of the room, slapped a breakfast tray onto the bedside table, and announced in a loud, insistent voice, "Good *morning*. Time to get *up*."

No one cared about privacy here. No one cared, either, about how tired Jeremy and I were or that we had been awakened throughout the night by the crying toddler in the next bed. We lived by a Procrustean schedule, fitting our waking and sleeping to administrative timetables that had nothing to do with our needs.

I pushed aside the tangled sheet and blankets and sat up wearily on the edge of the window seat with my face in my hands, trying to pull myself to wakefulness without the help of coffee.

7:15 A.M. I walked over to Jeremy's bedside, bent down and kissed his forehead, and rubbed his short bristle of hair. "Hi, sweetie. How're you doing this morning?"

Jeremy was even more tired than I was, but responded cheerfully in a groggy voice: "Hi, Mom. I love you. I'm okay. I need to go to the bathroom."

I brought his wheelchair from its corner, positioned it next to the bed, and locked the brakes. Then I lowered the bedrail, bent forward, put my arms around Jeremy, and helped him sit up. With practiced motions, I transferred him from the edge of the bed to the wheelchair and pushed him into the small adjoining bathroom. Moving the chair back and forth repeatedly, I maneuvered it until it was parallel to the toilet. Once again, I wrapped my arms around Jeremy's chest and pulled him briefly to a standing position. He clung to the steel grab bar bolted to the wall with his left hand while I untied and lowered his pajama bottoms, all the while looking away to spare his sensibilities. Then I helped him onto the toilet seat.

All the weeks in the hospital, Jeremy had been unable to attend to his excretory functions without help, first catheterized, then wearing a diaper, and then using a urinal and bedpan. The mechanics of helping him had not bothered me, but to Jeremy the loss of privacy had been a constant low-grade mortification. I couldn't leave him alone in the bathroom. He was too unsteady to balance on the toilet without falling. I gave him the small bit of personal space that was possible by looking up at the ceiling while he urinated. Then I hoisted him to standing once again, pulled up the pajamas, and reseated him in the wheelchair. Back and forth, back and forth, until the wheelchair was facing the small bathroom sink. "Jeremy, while we're here, let's wash up, okay?"

"Sure, Mom."

The occupational therapists had said that Jeremy must perform as many of these daily functions as possible by himself. I turned on warm water and wet two of the paper washcloths that were all the hospital provided, squeezed out the excess water, then laid them over the edge of the sink. "Go ahead, honey, wash your face."

Jeremy picked up each washcloth in turn with his left hand, tried repeatedly to shake it open one-handed, and ran it over his face. He reached across the sink for the small towel hanging from a ring on the wall, and dabbed himself dry.

Next, toothbrushing. Unscrewing the toothpaste cap was a formidable task. Jeremy placed the tube between his chest and right arm with his left hand, then leaned forward against the edge of the sink to keep his right arm from falling away. He used his left hand to turn the cap. The tube fell to the floor because he couldn't apply enough pressure with his right arm to hold it. I picked it up and handed it to him, and he started over. When he had the cap off he laid his toothbrush, bristles up, on the rim of the sink and squeezed toothpaste onto it one-handed. Then the reverse right arm–chest–left hand procedure replaced the cap on the tube.

After ten minutes, he was ready to begin brushing his teeth. Jeremy had trouble coordinating his hand movements with the position of the toothbrush. He moved the brush up and down jerkily. Foam dribbled out of his mouth, down his chin, and onto the hospital nightgown. I handed him a paper cup of water, and he tried to rinse and spit. Here the paralysis really caused problems. Jeremy couldn't swish the water around with his cheeks and tongue. He poured the water into his mouth and let it run out again through gravity flow, some into the sink and some onto his chin, where it cascaded down onto his chest and lap. Then another round of washcloths, to wipe off toothpaste and spittle, and he was finished.

"Hey, today I did that all by myself, Mom!" Jeremy was in a buoyant mood. His helplessness grated at him; he fiercely wanted to recapture his physical independence.

"Yes, sweetie, you did great."

Time elapsed since I had gotten him out of bed: about forty minutes.

8:00 A.M. Now he was sitting in bed with the mattress back raised and a breakfast tray holding a cup of apple juice, a bowl of congealed Cream of Wheat, and a few watery curds of scrambled egg on his lap. I unwrapped a straw and put it into the juice, then placed a towel across Jeremy's chest and under his chin. Learning to feed himself was also prescribed therapy. He gripped a spoon in his left fist and raised it shakily. Pieces of egg fell off and caromed down his front.

"I'm sorry, Mom, I'm sorry," he apologized after each wayward bite.

"It's okay, son. Don't worry. You're doing fine."

Another spoonful of cold egg wavered its way to his mouth, which opened long before his hand could pilot the spoon inside. Jeremy chewed with awkward deliberateness. Chewing is a complicated unconscious act. Tongue and teeth need to act in synchrony to stir, moisten, and masticate the food, then push it to the back of the mouth. The muscles on the right half of his face, including cheek and lips and tongue, still had little movement. He had to pause and consciously move his throat to contract and swallow.

One small spoonful at a time, Jeremy finished what was on his tray. It took him thirty minutes, and a third of the food ended up on the towel. I brought in another wet paper washcloth, which he used to clean off his face.

9:15 A.M. It was time for the first of Jeremy's two daily appointments with Nancy, his occupational therapist. Nancy was in her mid-twenties, tall with broad shoulders and strong hands. In overalls, with her thick black hair in a fat plait down her back, she looked like a farm girl. She had a rounded freckled face and dark-brown eyes behind oval glasses. Nancy's work centered on teaching daily living skills. Today she was going to help Jeremy learn to get dressed.

Following her instructions, I had brought in clothes: boxer shorts, a large tee-shirt, sweatpants, white cotton crew socks, and a new pair of duckfooted size thirteen skateboarding shoes that I hoped would fit over the brace that would cover Jeremy's right foot. Nancy decided that the window seat was the best place for him to work because it was wide and low enough for Jeremy to sit without support.

I stacked the clothes next to him on the plastic cushion. "Let's start with the tee-shirt," Nancy said. Jeremy picked up the folded garment with one hand and tried to shake it open. It unfolded but remained two-dimensional, the front and back stuck together. He shook again, and again, with no results. My hands itched to reach out, to take the tee-shirt away from him and pop it over his head. I held back the impulse.

Since the shaking strategy wasn't working, Jeremy laid the tee-shirt flat on his lap, picked up his right arm with his left hand and tried to push it between the two layers of fabric. He worked slowly and steadily. "Okay, okay," he said to himself. "I know I can get it."

At first he succeeded only in pushing the tee-shirt onto the floor. I picked it up and handed it back, and he kept on trying. He had been at it now for almost twenty minutes. Frustration rose and tightened in my chest.

Nancy, sitting in a chair facing Jeremy, offered suggestions and encouragement in a low quiet voice. "See if you can work your right hand inside the shirt. There you go. Now pull the bottom edge with your left. Can you work your right hand through the sleeve? You're close, you're close . . . there, you've got it! Now keep pulling, keep pulling. Pull the sleeve over your right hand and arm. There, you're getting it. Good job, Jeremy, good job!"

At last, Jeremy worked his right arm through the sleeve. The shirt still lay on his lap. He lifted his right arm up into the air with his left hand and tried to keep it there while pulling the tee-shirt down over his head.

"Mom, I need help!" he said.

He had become hopelessly entangled. His right arm had fallen away, trapping his head and shoulders in a tight band of fabric. He couldn't find the neck opening.

I was gripping the arms of my chair to keep from reaching out to help him, holding tightly to the wood and to the impatience that was screaming in my head. I breathed slowly and deeply several times. This was about helping Jeremy, I reminded myself, by letting him struggle and learn.

Nancy finally relented and helped pull the tee-shirt the rest of the way over Jeremy's head. He worked his left arm up under the tee-shirt and out through the sleeve and pulled the bottom edge of the shirt down all around him with one hand, then leaned against the window behind him and sat for a few moments with his eyes closed, tired. Thirty minutes had gone by.

10:00 A.M. Before he could don pants, Jeremy had to put on a compression stocking, socks and his leg brace. The compression stocking was made of heavy elastic and covered his right leg all the way to his hip. The blood clot had damaged the valves inside the veins in this leg. In a healthy person, the valves act as tiny elevators to move blood up out of the leg and back to the heart. The compression stocking replaced that function by putting pressure on the veins from the outside to push the blood uphill.

The particular brand he wore now was a "T.E.D. Hose." Jeremy, who hadn't captured the name quite right, called it his "Ted Hoe."

The stocking was so tight that even I had trouble getting it on him. Nancy was pitiless, however. After turning the stocking inside out, she handed it to him and said, "Start by working it over your toes." Jeremy couldn't lift or move his right leg, so he bent double at the waist—while I kept both hands on his shoulders to keep him from toppling over—and began pulling the stocking onto his toes and foot with tiny movements of his fingers, gradually turning it right side out. At first it popped off repeatedly. Eventually, he worked it up high enough, to his instep, so that it stayed on. After that it was a matter of pulling it up higher bit by little bit. Over and over Jeremy grabbed a tiny fold of fabric, stretched and pulled it with his fingers, then shifted to another part of the stocking: top, bottom, side, and side. The higher it got, the harder the going. At mid-calf he couldn't go any further.

"Can someone help me with my Ted Hoe, please?"

I looked over at Nancy for permission; she nodded yes. Even holding on to the stocking with both hands, it took a lot of strength for me to pull the stubborn elastic over Jeremy's knee and high up onto his thigh. I could not imagine how he would ever be able to do this on his own.

Socks were next. The cotton crew socks were a much looser weave than the compression stocking, but getting them onto his feet was still a problem. He held the ribbed edging in one hand and tried to pull it over his toes. The movement was similar to trying to capture an agile fish by scooping it out of the water with a small strainer. Time and again he missed the opening, and the sock slid ineffectually over the top of his foot. Jeremy tried again and again.

"I know I can get this, just a few more tries."

By now my internal tension was almost beyond control. My hands darted forward of their own volition to help him. I pulled them back. I was far more frustrated than my son.

Nancy had seen it all before. "I know it's hard," she soothed. "He's got to learn to do this for himself. He won't always have you there to help."

I tried to imagine daily life after leaving the hospital. At this rate, it would take Jeremy at least an hour to dress himself every morning. How would he ever be able to get ready for school? The weekday morning pace had already been frenetic before this had happened. I made a hot breakfast, packed three lunches, fed the cats, filled water bottles, hustled David through the bathroom and into his clothes, searched for backpacks, homework, missing shoes. If I were helping Jeremy wash up and dress, how would I get three children out the door on time?

While I played these uncomfortable scenarios over in my imagination, Jeremy persisted. Finally both feet were wearing socks. They were crooked but serviceable.

Because we were running out of time, Nancy let me help Jeremy on with the leg brace. It was custom-molded out of plastic to fit his right foot and leg, from toes to knee. It kept his ankle at a right angle, and provided additional support for his calf muscles. Without it, his right ankle would have straightened and his foot hyperextended permanently, and Jeremy wouldn't have been able to walk on the sole of his foot.

Once his foot was firmly seated in the brace, it was fastened with webbing straps that threaded through D-rings and closed with Velcro. Someday soon, Jeremy would have to learn how to manage this one-handed as well. For today, I did it for him. This small helping act provided a welcome release for the frustrated energy that had built up inside me.

The sweatpants were easy in comparison to what had gone before. It didn't matter so much that his right leg was immobile. The pants were loose enough to slide easily over it. Again, I thought about school and the world outside the hospital. Jeremy had lived in jeans or shorts. Both now seemed out of the question. He would not be able to put on trousers made of thick, unyielding denim. In any event, the leg brace was too bulky to fit under jeans and too unsightly to be bared by shorts. I would have to buy more sweatpants.

Finally, shoes. Again, Nancy let me put them on. Thankfully, the right shoe fit over the leg brace. As I tied the laces, I was mindful of the many small coordinated finger movements required. Jeremy had learned to tie his own shoes in kindergarten. In high school, he would need help.

10:45 A.M. Jeremy was dressed. Nancy moved him into the wheelchair, buckled the seatbelt, and took him down to the rehab gym for physical therapy.

"Bye, Mom, see you soon," he said cheerily as they left the room.

Three and a half hours had gone by since we had started the morning washup. I was still wearing the clothes I had slept in and felt dirty, exhausted, and despairing. My poor son required as much care now as an infant. And because of his age and sensibilities, these were not tasks that could be handed off to a babysitter. How would I work, how would we live?

I started to consider seriously the possibility that one of us, probably Kris, would have to give up his job to stay home and care for Jeremy. I wasn't physically strong enough to help him through a day by myself. The weight of these worries threatened to paralyze me. I summoned up a survival skill that I had learned before I can remember. I went to the room in my head where the things I couldn't do anything about were stored. I imagined pulling open a heavy planked door, gathering up the bundle of worrisome thoughts, and placing it in a box on a shelf, then closing the door and pushing home a heavy steel deadbolt. Now the room where I lived was freed of clutter.

No sense planning for an unknown future. What I knew right now was that I had forty-five minutes to take a shower, dry my hair, dress, straighten up Jeremy's room, and make both our beds. I would have to hurry.

11:45 A.M. Jeremy returned to his room gray with fatigue. He had spent an hour ascending and descending a flight of stairs, seated, pushing himself up or down to the next step using his left arm and left leg. It is a cliché that disabled people are capable of remarkable accomplishments even with severe physical limitations. What is not obvious from the outside are the hours of heartbreakingly hard work, practice, and failures that make those achievements possible.

4:30 P.M. Jeremy had fed himself lunch (mashed potatoes, Jell-O, fruit yogurt), had another physical therapy session in the rehab gym, received a few visiting schoolmates, and taken a short nap, which was interrupted by doctors' rounds. There was time for a shower before the dinner tray arrived.

Even though it was laborious, I tried to give Jeremy a shower once a day. He loved the uncomplicated pleasures of warm water, lemony soap, and feeling all-over clean. I helped him undress, wrapped him in two blankets, and transferred him back into the wheelchair for the seventh or eighth time that day. He held soap and towels on his lap as we rolled down the hall.

Jeremy had progressed to seated showers. This bathing room had a normal bathtub with a handheld shower attachment on a wall-mounted bracket and four or five grab bars bolted into the tiled walls at various heights. Nancy had shown us the technique during several training sessions. I fitted a special seat sideways across the tub at its mid-point. Jeremy could not sit down inside the tub. He wouldn't be able to get up on his own, and it would be difficult and dangerous to try to pull him out of the tub, wet and slippery. The tub seat allowed him to stay more or less on the same level as the wheelchair, so that I could move him in and out with a series of lateral transfers.

"One, two, three, go." I transferred Jeremy from chair to tub's edge. "One, two three, go." I rotated him and swung his legs inside the tub while he held on to a grab bar. "One, two, three, go." I transferred Jeremy from the edge of the tub onto the seat, while he moved his grip to a different grab bar.

Then warm water and soap. Jeremy lathered those parts that he could reach with his good arm. He couldn't wash his feet, legs, left arm, or back. These I lathered for him with one hand, holding the shower head on him with the other. All the while he clung tightly to keep from falling off the seat.

When we were done, I dried him off quickly, repeated the three-stage transfer process, and wrapped him in blankets when he was back in the wheelchair. He sat patiently, shivering, as I mopped up the water that had cascaded onto the floor and piled wet towels into the laundry hamper.

Back in Jeremy's room I dressed him in a clean gown and pajama bottoms, and transferred him back into bed. My muscles were shaking. Jeremy was tired too. He lay quietly, eyes closed, still shivering. I piled on more blankets, and leaned over and hugged him until he warmed up. He made a small mound beneath the covers. My right arm slipped easily over his ribs and tucked beneath his back. I laid my right cheek against his chest. Through the bedding, I felt his sporadic shudders.

5:30 P.M. The dinner tray arrived, with soup, pureed chicken, juice, and ice cream. Jeremy fed himself again. The soup made a terrible mess. Then one more transfer to the wheelchair for a final trip to the bathroom.

The morning routine was repeated: Jeremy used the toilet, washed his face, and brushed his teeth. These simple actions took even longer as weariness dragged at both of us. Jeremy worked doggedly until he was done. His head drooped and he leaned heavily on me as I moved him back into bed for the last time.

7:00 P.M. Before Jeremy slept, I popped a movie into the VCR, and we watched a little bit of *Rain Man* together. His eyelashes fluttered against his cheeks. I turned off the TV, and we said our prayers. "Our Father, who art in heaven, hallowed be thy name . . ." I prayed for every part of Jeremy's body that was injured. "Lord, we ask your grace and healing for the blood clot and the AVM in Jeremy's brain, and for his eyes, so that he may see straight again, and for movement to come back to his right arm and hand and right leg and foot, and for his chest, where the filter is, and for the whole length of the blood clot in his vena cava and right leg and foot."

I turned Jeremy onto his left side, arranged pillows under his right arm and leg and against his chest and back to keep him from rolling, straightened out his twisted nightgown, and gave him sips of water through a straw.

"'Night, Mommy, I love you," he said thickly. "Thank you for helping me. I'm sorry I'm so much trouble."

"Good night, Jeremy dear. You aren't any trouble. I love you so much. It makes me happy to help you. God bless and keep you all night long . . ."

I rested my forehead on the edge of the mattress and dozed off briefly, waking with a start thirty minutes later, cold and stiff.

8:30 P.M. I stood next to Jeremy's bed and watched him before I turned off the lights. Despite the pillows, he had turned from his left side partly onto his back, his neck reaching far to the right, toward me. He slept with the depth of an infant or the truly exhausted, breathing slowly and evenly through slightly parted lips. With his face in repose, the paralysis was barely noticeable, his skin a smooth, faint rose beneath the sooty fringe of lashes. He looked very young. I turned him back to his side and readjusted the pillows.

We would be interrupted many times in the night by nurses taking vital signs, hallway noise, a monitor alarm sounding, Jeremy needing to turn over or use the urinal, other children crying. For now, the room was peaceful.

Even in the middle of this terrible new life, I felt proud of Jeremy's determination. He never questioned the fairness of his fortunes or the wisdom of going on. He simply persevered until the task was done. In his quiet strength lay his salvation, and ours.

From: Fiala, Marie Lawson
Sent: October 24, 1998 7:35 P.M.
To: Jeremy Network
Subject: The End of Our Day/Update No. 26

Day ends. Jeremy sleeps connected to a monitor that measures his heartbeat and blood oxygen levels, our early warning system should he hemorrhage again. The sensor, taped to one finger, shines with a red light. When Jeremy sleeps in the dark room with his hands clasped on the center of his chest, the red light glows through the blanket. It looks like the prayer card pictures of the Sacred Heart the nuns handed out when I was little. I lie on the narrow window seat, watching the digital readout that tells me that Jeremy breathes, his heart beats. No stars are visible in the city-lit night sky but a gap in the blinds frames a steady bright light, an unknown planet roughly 45 degrees above the horizon. Jeremy breathes and I watch the sky. For now it is enough.

All Hallow's Eve

TWO MONTHS HAD GONE BY without my noticing that the seasons were changing. It was Halloween. Our kids had always been wildly excited about this holiday. Annelise, our performance artist, was thrilled about dressing in costume, while the boys relished the prospect of delving into their evening haul of trick-or-treat candy without parental limitations, for once. Normally they decided what they wanted to be for Halloween weeks in advance, and Kris and I helped them plan and put together costumes.

I felt sick when I realized that Halloween was the next day and that we were completely unprepared. Somehow the holiday had gotten lost among the myriad details of caring for Jeremy and finding a way to bring him home.

"Hey, guys, I just realized Halloween is coming up. I'm sorry, but I haven't done anything about costumes yet," I said at home that evening.

"Don't worry, Mommy, I've figured out my costume," said Annelise. Her middle school no longer held a Halloween parade, but the students were allowed to change into costumes in the afternoon. Annelise had thought it through by herself and had decided what she wanted to be for this one day. She had assembled a witch's outfit from the big costume box we kept in the basement—a long black dress, pointed hat, and a straw broom. On Halloween, she sprayed her long hair black and covered her face and hands with green paint. Years later, when Annelise and I saw the Broadway production of *Wicked*, I recognized her vision in the green-skinned Elpheba, the eponymous Wicked Witch of the West. It had been Annelise's idea first.

It was too late to go out and buy something for little David to wear. He excavated the costume box and came up with a rubber Tyrannosaurus Rex mask that completely covered his head and a black cape that he wore over a black turtleneck and jeans. "What are you, sweetie?" I asked.

"I dunno," he said. "Something scary."

The next day, before going to the hospital, I drove to David's school for the Halloween parade, an excited procession of small children inhabiting, for a moment, a world populated entirely by their imaginations. Their voices rose in a babble of ebullient shrieks and laughter. Among the glittery swirl of ninjas, ghosts, aliens, and the omnipresent fairy-princess-ballerinas, David trudged along solemnly in his T-Rex and black cape get-up. The mask limited his range of vision, and he couldn't see more than one or two steps ahead of himself.

"Hey, David, what kinda costume is that?" other kids asked him, not entirely kindly. "What are you supposed to be?"

"I dunno," he answered stoically. "I dunno."

Please, be kind to him, I thought. *Can't you see how hurt he is?* I couldn't say it. Eight-year-old boys are not always kind, and David would have been even worse off with his peers if his mother had intervened. I gave David's shoulder an encouraging squeeze and kept smiling on the outside. "The parade is starting, dear," I said. "I'll see you later. We'll have fun trick-or-treating tonight."

"Sure, Mom," David said gravely. Then he turned and marched away.

By the time I got to the hospital, the nurses had pulled together a costume for Jeremy from somewhere. Maybe they kept their own costume box. He was sitting in his decorated wheelchair wearing a gold cardboard crown studded with bright plastic jewels, a velvet cape trimmed with fake white fur, a pillow stuffed inside his tee-shirt to create a big belly, and a lopsided smile.

"Mom! Look at my costume! We're going trick-or-treating!"

He sounded not much older than David.

The rehab and oncology kids, including Jeremy, proceeded at a sober pace along the halls of the hospital, stopping to trick-or-treat at the nurses' stations and administrative offices. Many were in wheelchairs; others were accompanied by IV stands or oxygen tanks on carts. The costumes were far less elaborate than those at David's school—a scary mask on a boy whose legs no longer moved, a pair of angel wings on a little girl whose right side and right eye were permanently frozen. We rolled alongside a young boy about Jeremy's age, a cancer patient whose baseball cap concealed his bare head, or so I thought until I looked down at lavender sneakers tied with silver laces and belatedly realized—a young girl. Something about the anticipation on all those young, damaged faces, those children who still wanted to believe in something magical, shredded the defenses I had been maintaining all day. My eyes welled with tears. I blotted them on the hem of my shirt.

Jeremy and Darren, another young teenager from rehab, made their way to the front of the parade and then decided to race down the long straight hallway. Their speed was limited by how quickly they could propel their wheelchairs by hand. Off they went down the corridor, their costumes flapping, laughing hysterically and spinning their wheels for all they were worth. Darren, who had paralyzed legs but two good hands, quickly moved out in front. Jeremy, who had only one hand to spin his wheels, lost the race but not his smile. He was alive, and it was Halloween. It took no more than that to make him happy.

A Sigh of the Weary

Hard times, come again no more.

—Stephen Foster

NORMALLY A SATURDAY FEELS light and airy. The burdens of the work week are temporarily pushed aside to reveal wide vistas of time before Monday morning crunches down with steel jaws again. Once Saturday was a time to cook long slow meals, hike along one of Berkeley's wild creeks, take the kids to a movie, and maybe stop for ice cream afterward. But a Saturday in the hospital was oppressive with the prospect of too much empty time. Hospital weekends were long and lonely, with no therapy appointments to break up the day, minimal doctors' rounds, and few visitors. People didn't come to the hospital on weekends. They were too busy cooking meals, hiking, watching movies, and going for ice cream. On my Saturday shifts at the hospital, it was just me and Jeremy, shuttling between bed and wheelchair, trying to find ways to fill up the slow and dusty hours.

So I was elated when the doctors said that Jeremy could go home for a visit one Saturday afternoon, his first since he had entered the hospital. We had applied for this furlough more than a week before but hadn't been sure when it would be approved. It would be a dress rehearsal of sorts, to identify problem areas at home that Jeremy's therapists could help us work on before he was discharged, and it would also give Jeremy a chance to say good-bye to the house where he had grown up. We would be moving soon.

Kris drove our old maroon VW van to the hospital and pulled into the parking lot, where I waited with Jeremy in his wheelchair. The van door slid open and Annelise and David spilled out. "Hi, Jeremy, hi, Jeremy, you get to come home!" They danced around him on the pavement, too excited to stand still.

Together Kris and I executed a wheelchair-to-car transfer. The first stage, from the wheelchair to the floor of the van at the open side door, went exactly as the physical therapists had taught us—cross arms behind his back, stand, pivot, sit—but transferring Jeremy from the floor to the high middle seat had not been choreographed. Kris ended up bodily lifting him by his armpits and dragging him into position. We pulled out into the street.

Instead of being ecstatic at finally leaving the hospital and riding in the car, Jeremy was terrified. His perspective had contracted, and now the outside world seemed too large, too loud, too bright, and frightening. Even at slow speeds, the car moved too fast for him. He closed his eyes and clutched the armrest tightly with his left hand. Kris slowed down and tried to avoid sudden stops and accelerations, but Jeremy didn't let go of the armrest until we reached our destination.

I had been nursing a fantasy of a happy family outing and a welcome change from hospital food. "Jeremy, would you like to go to out for lunch?" I asked, mentioning a favorite neighborhood Chinese restaurant.

"Okay," he said. "If you want to."

Hope quickly parted from reality as we navigated from car to restaurant. It had started raining. Kris and I struggled to pull the heavy wheelchair out of the back of the car and unfold it. Annelise held an umbrella over us, but by the time we got Jeremy out of the car and seated, all three of us and the chair were soaked.

Our familiar neighborhood suddenly looked entirely different. A small bump where a tree root pushed up the sidewalk became a major obstacle; we had to stop, turn, and back the wheelchair over it. The restaurant tables were too close together to maneuver the chair between them. When Jeremy needed to relieve himself, there was no easy wheelchair access to the restrooms, and we had to move two restaurant tables and chairs to clear a path. We attracted unwelcome attention. Jeremy looked odd: his hair didn't yet cover his bright red scars; the right side of his face drooped; he wore a black patch over his left eye; his right arm hung loosely; he wore a thick elastic stocking and a bulky orthotic device on his right leg. People stared at him. A few made audible remarks, as if being in a wheelchair somehow had rendered Jeremy deaf as well: "I wonder what happened to *him?*"

Jeremy didn't seem to notice. I hoped he didn't. I, tiger mother, noticed everything, and returned stares fiercely.

We finished our meal quickly and drove home. I was eager to get Jeremy into a place that was quiet and safe from intrusive eyes. Kris muscled Jeremy out of the car and carried him in his arms down the outside steps and into the house, where they collapsed together onto the family room sofa. Jeremy lay back tiredly, looking at the treetops outside the windows. "I'm happy to be home," he said.

Both of our cats immediately found him and curled into warm brown curves in the hollows next to his sides, purring. For a while he dozed, smiling.

The difficulties of navigating in these surroundings confirmed our decision to move into a more accessible house. But my heart said, *Oh, it feels good, so very good, to be home just one more time.*

The afternoon waned and our visit was drawing to an end. Kris carried Jeremy upstairs to the bedroom he shared with David, with the rest of us trailing behind them. It was a cheerful room, with two twin beds covered in green and blue plaid quilts and matching pillows, and shelves covered with books, puzzles, Transformers, Legos, and an extensive hat collection. Kris laid Jeremy on his bed.

By now Kris and I had told Jeremy several times that we would be moving to a new house, and he had forgotten several times. Kris told him again: "Son, do you remember that we told you we're buying a new house? Living here would just be too hard. We can't carry you in and out of the house and upstairs to your room every day. You're growing up; you're getting too big, even for your old man."

Jeremy's eyes widened and his face fell. A sob broke from his chest, and another, and another.

"We're sorry, Jeremy, we're so sorry. I wish it could be different," I said.

"I know . . . I know," he answered.

He turned to face the wall and cried—for this pain and loss, for all the pain and all the loss of the past two months. Kris, sitting on the edge of the bed, stroked his hair. Annelise and David repeated, "It's okay, Jeremy. It'll be okay." They could not console him. Finally, he fell asleep again. I sat on the floor next to the bed, resting my head on the edge of the mattress, and closed my eyes.

I was so tired, so tired.

I had been looking ahead to Jeremy's discharge as an ending, but with this preview of life at home, I saw that it would also be a beginning of something new and hard. We would have all the same responsibilities as we did in the hospital—Jeremy's bathing, feeding, transport, rehab exercises—but with less help and no medical support. My mood had declined with the sun outside. *How on earth would we do it all?* I wanted to huddle into a tight ball and wrap my arms tightly over my head to shut out the sight of our future.

"Sweetie?" Kris's voice. "It's getting close to five o'clock. We have to get him back. Here, let me help you up."

He pulled me to my feet, and I leaned against him. We stood for a moment together, looking down at the peaceful face of our sleeping son.

The Measurement of Distance

T
HE QUESTION I WAS ASKED most often during the months of Jeremy's hospitalization was "How do you do it? How do you keep going?" If there is an answer, it lies in how one measures distance. Any hill, measured in inches, can be surmounted. Any day, measured in moments, can be survived.

———

During the slow hot summers in Idaho I worked with my family in the fields, driving a tractor or baling hay. Anyone who has spent summers haying does not forget the feel of it. Alfalfa hay is bound with two strands of steel wire into fifty-pound rectangular bales. Two or three times a summer, depending on the number of hay cuttings the weather allowed, the haying crew walked up and down forty or fifty acres of field. The bales were neatly lined up in rows, perhaps fifteen feet apart, just as they were dropped from the rear end of the baler up ahead. Alongside, a tractor pulled a flatbed trailer. Every fifteen feet the process was this: bend, slide gloved hands under the wires securing the bale, lift the bale to the top of one bent knee, then boost with the knee and with the backs of both forearms, straighten up and half throw, half push the bale onto the trailer, where another crew member grabs the baling wires, boosts once again, and stacks the bale on top of and next to the bales that came before. The stack had to be regular and tight or else the entire five-bale-high load might unbalance and topple off the side of the trailer.

Alfalfa hay has thick stiff stalks that harden when dry. The severed edges of the plants that pattern the surfaces of a bale are wickedly coarse and sharp enough to cut through long-sleeved shirts and jeans into the soft flesh of forearms and thighs. The temperature in the fields was in the eighties or nineties, a dry, torpid heat. Each lift and boost and toss of a bale released a cloud of hay dust—pollen and crumbled leaves and desiccated blossoms—that settled in hair and eyes and crept under clothing and stuck to the bitter sweat running down neck, chest, and back.

A day spent haying was a long day. Work began early and continued until evening. A fifty-acre field was covered with thousands of bales. You walked, stooped, lifted, boosted, tossed, pushed, walked again. Clean and jerk, clean and jerk. Again, and again, and again. Long rows of misery stretched endlessly ahead, and after three or four hours without stopping you had achieved only a modest reduction in the number of bales dotting the field. After five or six hours your legs trembled and your hands ached from the pressure of the wires cutting through the gloves. After eight or nine hours your lungs burned with each breath of dust-thickened air, your legs were blocks of stone, your shoulder joints were on fire, the raw skin on the top of your thighs and undersides of your forearms stung cruelly. You didn't stop until the crew boss called quits.

There was only one way to reach the end of a haying day. One step at a time. One step at a time.

From: Fiala, Marie Lawson
Sent: November 9, 1998 1:28 P.M.
To: Jeremy Network
Subject: Countdown To Reentry/Update No. 30

I told Jeremy this afternoon about his upcoming gamma knife radiation treatment. It was time; Jeremy's doctors recently had alluded to the procedure in front of him, and he is too smart not to hear the clues. We go to UCSF on November 19 and 20 for the surgery. The procedure sounds horrific. After an initial angiogram, which is invasive in its own right, the surgeons will bolt a rigid steel framework into Jeremy's skull. The framework will support an encircling array of more than one hundred radiation beams focused at the center of Jeremy's brain. Delivery of the radiation itself will take several hours.

Jeremy took the news philosophically. He believed me when I told him that he has nothing to fear from this process. I wish someone could give me that same assurance. Terror about the gamma knife radiation grips me like cold steel. One of the risks is that the radiation may permanently worsen Jeremy's right-side paralysis by damaging critical nerve pathways. Those words meant something different when I first heard them almost two months ago. Now, Jeremy has so much to lose. Still, we have to gamble with Jeremy's mobility to secure his life. While I dread what lies ahead, I am also impatient for the date to arrive. All the recovery that has taken place so far is meaningless if Jeremy bleeds again.

If all goes well, we hope to have our son home before

Thanksgiving. Jeremy still won't have use of his right arm, only limited use of his right leg, and significant visual impairment. Yet he is alive, awake, can speak and hear us, can give love, and receive ours in return. That is all I ever wanted, and I am content with it. For the rest we can only move forward, step by small step. Our ultimate destination is unknown, but isn't that true for all of us?

When it all becomes too much for me, I find comfort in the thousands of years of pain, doubt, wisdom accumulated in the Psalms:

> I do not occupy myself with great matters,
> or with things that are too hard for me.
> But I still my soul and make it quiet,
> like a child upon its mother's breast;
> my soul is quieted within me.

From: Fiala, Marie Lawson
Sent: November 13, 1998 12:34 A.M.
To: Jeremy Network
Subject: Jeremy's Surprise/Update No. 31

Today Kris and I were sitting in Jeremy's room waiting for the sound of his wheelchair tires swishing on their way back from physical therapy. We can usually hear him coming from some way down the hall. Suddenly his voice sounded in the doorway: "I Ii, Mom and Dad!" I was confused. There had been no sound, yet there was Jeremy, leaning on a cane, his proud therapist beaming over his shoulder. He had started walking in the rehab gym downstairs, had walked to the elevators, gone up two floors, and walked to his room.

Yesterday Jeremy could stand, take a few shaky assisted steps from bed to wheelchair, but nothing like this. Some combination of nerve, muscle, mind that had silently been knitting together had suddenly crossed a threshold and allowed him to walk. He walks slowly and haltingly—it probably took him twenty minutes to walk a fairly short distance—and the trip exhausted him, but he did it on his own. Kris and I were teary and joyful. Jeremy was glowingly happy. He asked me to put on the "Hallelujah Chorus" from Handel's Messiah, one of his favorite pieces of music: "The Kingdom of this world, is become, the Kingdom of our Lord . . ." We played it loudly. The rehab nurses remarked that we must be getting ready for Christmas. I think Christmas has arrived, early.

Partings

THE DAYS LEADING UP to Jeremy's discharge from Children's Hospital were a cyclone of activity. Kris and I were going through a lengthy and complicated close on the sale of our old home to a difficult buyer. The house was torn up and half packed; we had just closed on our new house and were meeting with a contractor and architect to plan modifications to Jeremy's bedroom and bathroom. The phone rang incessantly, and I was scouring the *Yellow Pages* and making repeated trips to medical supply houses to buy or rent the equipment and supplies that Jeremy would need to live at home—a wheelchair, an electrostimulation apparatus, compression stockings, grab bars, a walker, a cane, a shower seat, and more.

Kris and I had dozens of short, dense conversations daily:

"The architect needs to know the turning radius for the wheelchair."

"Can you ask my mom and dad if they can stay with Jeremy while we go to the title company offices to sign papers?"

"We'll need to widen the doorway to his room."

"Let's rent a storage locker for the stuff that won't fit in the new house."

My head felt like it was going to explode, but at least I wasn't thinking too much about leaving our tall, gabled, brown-shingled house set among the trees for the homely square white box at the bottom of the hill.

The last week at the hospital was just as ragged. I spent hours arranging Jeremy's discharge from Children's Hospital and admission to UCSF, planning his post-discharge rehab therapy schedule, and, critically, obtaining preapproval for the gamma knife surgery from our insurance carrier.

We had learned with horror four days before Jeremy's discharge that Luci, the gamma knife coordinator at UCSF, had not even contacted our insurance company about the procedure, which would cost well into six figures, let alone obtained the necessary preapproval to go ahead. This was supposed to have been done a month earlier. Without authorization the hospital would not proceed, and Jeremy would drop off the gamma knife schedule until the next opening, months later.

I made a cascade of increasingly insistent phone calls to Luci, whose burbling disembodied voice I was beginning to detest. Each time she acquiesced in whatever I was asking: "Gosh, I don't know what happened. [Laugh] I'll get those forms over to Blue Shield right away. What was your son's name again?" Then she did nothing.

The day before Jeremy's discharge Luci still had not put one piece of paper into the carrier's hands. I finally bypassed her altogether and called our insurer directly to find out what they needed, then found, photocopied, and faxed over the necessary medical records and drafted a letter for Dr. Joe's signature justifying Jeremy's need to receive the treatment. The people at Blue Shield were efficient, helpful, and compassionate. They went out of their way to push the paperwork through quickly. Finally at 4:00 P.M. on the last day, the carrier gave an oral authorization and I gave a huge sigh of relief.

We had a quiet moment the next-to-last night. Father Bruce came by one last time. He had been to the hospital regularly despite the demands of his busy parish, bringing us peace in a time of sorrow. And usually coffee as well. I was always happy to see his smiling bronzed face above the stark white collar and black shirtfront.

We talked about the gamma knife and about the many changes facing our family. To help us mark this important transition, Bruce had come prepared to celebrate the Eucharist with us, just as he had on that awful day three months earlier. He laid out his supplies on the tiny bedside table. Together we spoke the familiar words of the service.

"The Lord be with you."

"And with thy spirit."

"Let us pray . . ."

Afterward, Jeremy started crying. "What's wrong, dear?" I asked. "Are you worried about the operation?"

"No," he said, wiping his face with his good hand. "I'm crying because I'm so happy to see Father Bruce and take communion. It makes me feel all shiny and clean, like taking a shower inside."

"Good-bye, Jeremy," Bruce said, resting a hand on his head in benediction. "It's been a great privilege visiting with you. I'll see you in church."

———

On Jeremy's last evening in the hospital, the staff threw him a party in the rehab gym, with a decorated cake and sodas and funny hats and a big sign reading "Good-bye and good luck, Jeremy!" All of his doctors and therapists were there, as were other hospital employees who had become our friends and most of the other rehab and burn unit patients.

I took away images I'll never forget. Dr. Joe with his big laugh, wearing a perpetually askew tie, this one decorated with dinosaurs, taking photographs with a Polaroid camera. Imari, Jeremy's former roommate, sixteen months old and recovering from cancer of the spine. She had left-side paralysis and the world's most beautiful smile. Melissa, who had come in with third-degree burns over her head, neck, and most of her body. I had found it hard to look at her at first, but now she was just a little girl who loved chocolate cake, although she had no fingers to hold her plate. Marcellus, Jeremy's last roommate, who lived two blocks from the hospital and had been a patient off and on for fifteen years with cancer that had paralyzed his legs and destroyed his hearing. Graylin, our friend the custodian, who had formed a special attachment to Jeremy and often stopped by his room to chat after finishing his shift in the evening. At that moment these people seemed more real and connected to us than did anyone outside the hospital because they knew what we had lived through better than anyone else could.

Many of these children had been in the hospital when Jeremy was admitted, and would still be there when he was gone. Their good-byes were shaded with wistfulness. *When would they go home?* I wondered. *And what would home be like when they got there?*

Dr. Joe said, "Come on, let's get a picture of the three of you." Kris and I stood behind Jeremy's wheelchair, each of us resting a hand on his shoulder, and Dr. Joe pressed the shutter release. He handed us the photograph. Our images gradually emerged from the milky-green paper. Jeremy, with a spoonful of cake in his left hand, smiled a huge crooked smile. Kris and I smiled, too, but our smiles were a thin veneer over layers of exhaustion and fear.

After the good-bye party, we packed up. We left Jeremy's room cleaner than it had been when we moved in, peeling the bits of masking-tape residue off the walls, piling dirty linens into a hamper, throwing away paper cups and straws and tissues, and neatly arranging unused hospital supplies in the standard-issue pink plastic basin. Then we carried everything that belonged to us—television, tape player, toiletries, books, blankets, pictures, cards, clothing, stuffed animals—four floors down and outdoors into the parking lot, and loaded up our van. Last of all we brought out Jeremy in his wheelchair, wrapped in blankets against the November damp and chill, and drove home.

Moving out of the hospital was just part of a much

larger leaving behind. The world I had created for myself out of material things, at home and at the hospital, was now jumbled together in cardboard boxes, without regard for chronology or categories. It was a strange feeling to be so completely stripped of everything that had identified me. I was a ghost ship, anchor cut away, ensign lowered, and name scraped off the hull, slipping away from my old life silently, into an uncertain future.

From: Fiala, Marie Lawson
Sent: November 18, 1998 11:27 P.M.
To: Jeremy Network
Subject: Leave-taking/Update No. 33

Jeremy has touched many people at Children's Hospital. The ICU nurses from our early weeks, the janitorial staff, even the security guards from the lobby come up to see him regularly. As I wheel him around the hospital, he is greeted by people I don't even know. Many of the hospital employees live in the heart of war-torn West Oakland. Our paths would never have crossed had we not taken such an abrupt detour, but Jeremy has made strong connections with the people who work to support his medical care. Pain is a great leveler, and love, faith, and compassion are common denominators understood by all.

Thank you for your prayers; thank you for your messages and letters; thank you for the acts of generosity too numerous to name. They enfold us like a warm blanket. We're unable to give back for now, but know that our gratitude is yours forever.

Sailing Into the Storm

The North Wind made the Vikings.

—Scandinavian folk saying

B EFORE FIRST LIGHT on Thursday morning, one
week before Thanksgiving, Kris, Jeremy, and I
drove westward, chasing the night. The Bay Bridge was
illuminated by lamps that overarched the roadway, but on
either side the air and the waters of the Bay merged into a
single blackness. Ahead, the lights of San Francisco marked
the streets in the pre-dawn gloom. Behind its darkened
windows a million souls still slept, or stirred and wakened,
turned toward welcoming arms beside them, tied on running shoes, filled the coffee pot, showered and shaved, let
the dog out, started their days. None of them knew that we
drifted silently by in our steel bubble, that we climbed the
empty streets, up hillsides, higher and yet higher. None of
them knew our reasons or our pain.

We were bringing Jeremy to the UCSF medical center
for gamma knife surgery. This was unlike the other treatment
decisions Kris and I had made during the past three months.
When Jeremy's skull was opened twice, when the drains
were inserted and then removed from his brain, when the

Greenfield filter was installed in his chest, we had been making the only decisions possible in medical emergencies. This was different. We would allow the doctors to take our boy, who once again could speak and stand and even walk a little, and deliver massive doses of radiation to his brain. We hoped that in two or three years this procedure would destroy the AVM that had nearly taken his life.

There were few other choices, to be sure. We could have found a neurosurgeon willing to operate—there were neurosurgeons who would have tried to excise the AVM in spite of its location at the very center of Jeremy's brain—and brought him home permanently in a wheelchair, and most likely blind as well. We could have opted for embolization with Super Glue and immediately closed off the AVM, but risked the same grim side-effects. Or we could have done nothing, let Jeremy slowly recover as much function as he could, and waited for another hemorrhage. These were not courses we could take. Instead we turned and steered deliberately into harm's way in the hope that somewhere, past the radiation storm, lay a sunny port where we could anchor, and rest.

The gamma knife is a modern marvel. It was invented by Dr. Lars Leksell in 1968 in Sweden. It is misnamed. It is not a knife at all but a complex apparatus consisting of 201 cobalt-60 radiation beams that would be pointed simultaneously at one small section of the AVM after another. The machine acts like a surgeon's scalpel, or knife, in that the computer-controlled beams can conform the radiation to the target's shape with great precision. The high-energy gamma rays damage the abnormal tangle of blood vessels in the brains of AVM patients and form scar tissue. Once the scarred vessel walls thicken, they clog up and become sealed off. Blood can no longer pass through them. It takes two to three years for the irradiated tissue to atrophy and wither away, safeguarding the patient against a further hemorrhage. At the time of Jeremy's surgery, fewer than fifty gamma knife units had been deployed world-wide, and UCSF's unit was less than a decade old. Had Jeremy been born ten years earlier, he would have had no treatment options except traditional surgery.

However, because of the location of Jeremy's AVM, the risks were significantly greater than usual. Most AVMs are much closer to the surface of the brain than Jeremy's was. Nerve tissue higher in the brain is, in a sense, more "disposable"; portions can be excised without affecting function. With a lesion deep in the thalamic region of the brain, as Jeremy's was, there was no redundancy. The gamma knife's margin of error was a millimeter from the intended target, give or take. Even a millimeter would make a big difference in the outcome when operating on the thalamus, which was only fifteen millimeters long.

Thank you for giving him this chance, Lord. I pray that it goes well.

UCSF had told us to arrive by 6:00 A.M., and we were there on time. The medical center is a cluster of tall floodlit buildings on the crest of a hill in the center of the city, towering over the neighboring Victorian homes and modest apartment houses. The hospital complex abuts on an undeveloped eucalyptus grove, and the damp air was filled with a pungent cough-drop smell. Kris pulled up close to the hospital entrance. We unloaded Jeremy's wheelchair from the trunk of the car, then helped Jeremy out of the car. I quickly pushed him indoors to escape the chill.

Even at this early hour, the admissions office was crowded with patients and their families, waiting for their paperwork to be processed and to meet with a clerk. When I gave Jeremy's name to the receptionist, she turned the pages of the patient manifest in front of her, frowned, and looked through it again. "Just have a seat," she instructed. "We'll call you when we're ready."

I had spent enough time in hospitals by now to recognize trouble when I heard it. "Is there a problem?" I asked, trying to seem calm.

"No problem," she answered brusquely. "Just sit down and we'll call you. Next, please."

I turned to Jeremy with a bright smile and pushed his wheelchair into the small waiting room. Painfully lit by fluorescent bulbs, it was filled with rumpled people who had awakened too early. There were only a few empty seats in a far corner. I threaded my way through chairs, tables, bags, legs, and other obstacles. The legs remained outstretched as we attempted to pass, blocking our progress. I was already gathering together a bad mood, a volatile mix of sleep deprivation, impatience with bureaucracy, and anger at the vapid stares directed toward Jeremy. I imagined recklessly driving the heavy wheelchair full speed ahead, crushing feet, pushing aside handbags, and knocking over tables piled with outdated magazines. *This is a hospital, for heaven's sake! Doesn't whoever set up this overcrowded room know that people come here in wheelchairs?* Instead I kept the false smile firmly fixed. "*Excuse* me. Can we get past? *Thank* you."

Kris, returned from parking the car, found us barricaded in our corner. His hair was still damp from his shower, and he looked exceptionally handsome in a blue chambray shirt that matched his eyes. I told him about the receptionist incident. "I'm sure it'll be fine," he soothed. "I'll go check what's going on." Kris is much better at handling people pleasantly under adverse circumstances than I am. He waited patiently in line, smiled genuinely at the woman behind the desk, and held a short conversation. He returned and sat down.

"You're not going to believe this," he said, frowning. "Luci didn't tell them that Jeremy was checking into the hospital today. They don't have an admission order for him." Luci was the gamma knife coordinator who had already botched the insurance approval. Now, this. I was boiling with frustration. Kris explained that the admitting office needed to verify Jeremy's status with the neurosurgery department and then would attempt to find him a bed. But it was 7:00

A.M., and Luci—the point of contact in neurosurgery—was not at her desk yet.

Jeremy handled the wait, as he handled all else, bravely. He couldn't read—his double vision interfered, and he couldn't remember the beginning of a paragraph by the time he reached the end of it—but he had brought along *The Dark Is Rising*, the book we were currently reading to him. Kris picked it up and read aloud: "The snow flurried against the window, with a sound like fingers brushing the pane. Again Will heard the wind moaning in the roof, louder than before; it was rising into a real storm." I slumped forward in my seat, holding Jeremy's backpack protectively in my lap, anxiety percolating through my veins. Jeremy had been discharged from Children's Hospital just last night. He was still an invalid; he needed to keep his thrombosed leg horizontal to avoid swelling. He needed to get into bed.

To calm myself, I practiced the breathing exercises I had learned in preparation for Jeremy's birth. In with the good air, out with the bad, in with the good air, out with the bad. Kris read steadily on: "Will tossed uneasily. It was growing worse every minute. As if some huge weight were pushing at his mind, threatening, trying to take him over . . ."

At eight, Luci still was not in her office. Jeremy, Kris, and I played Greed, tossing the dice, counting points, adding up our scores. It was hard to concentrate. I strained to listen every time the phone rang at the reception desk. Maybe it would be Luci. No, not yet. After half an hour, Jeremy was tired. "I'm sorry, Mom and Dad. Do you mind if we stop playing?" I stood behind him and rubbed his shoulders.

At nine, still no Luci. Jeremy had been sitting in his wheelchair for three hours. The wheelchair was designed only for transportation, not prolonged sitting. The hard seat hurt his buttocks. There was nothing against which to lean his drooping head.

At 9:45, Luci had been in, but was away from her desk.

Jeremy wanted to practice walking. With Kris's support, he got shakily to his feet, leaning on his cane. They slowly walked with old-man steps into the hall and out the front door, then to one end of the short U-shaped entry drive. Jeremy took one tentative slow-motion step after another. His right knee didn't bend; his foot didn't flex. With every other step he swung his right leg forward from the hip, heavy and inanimate as a stump. Kris walked close by, arms held out, ready to catch him if he toppled. They covered fifty feet in fifteen minutes, reached the end of the crescent drive, and turned around. Ten minutes later, they had made it halfway back to the entryway. I was worried at their extended absence, and went out to look for them. We inched our way back to the waiting room together.

At 10:30, I went to a pay phone in the hall and left an angry message on Luci's voice mail. At eleven, the telephone rang at the reception desk. I heard the words "Jeremy Lawson" at our end of the conversation. Five hours after we had arrived, Luci finally made contact.

Now, there was a further problem. Because he hadn't been on the admit list, the hospital had no room reserved for Jeremy. They couldn't find a bed for him. "We're doing our best," said the admitting clerk, who by now felt sorry for us.

Noon. Still we waited. Six hours was longer than Jeremy had been out of bed since before his hemorrhage. He was faltering, too tired to play games, alarmingly pale. He ached from the long hours in the unpadded, low-backed wheelchair. We were all hungry. There was no food here, and we couldn't leave to find a cafeteria in case they should call us while we were gone. Jeremy didn't complain. He only asked from time to time, "Mom, will it be much longer?" Or, "How much longer, do you think?"

"Not much longer, Jeremy," I answered, "not much longer. Then you can lie down." *Please, please,* I thought endlessly, *just find us a room, find Jeremy a bed, please, please,*

please. Kris picked up the book and resumed the story: "This night will be bad. And tomorrow will be beyond imagining."

At 1:30, the admitting clerk called us to the desk to say that Jeremy had an appointment to see Dr. Walker, an interventional radiologist, one of the team leaders for the gamma knife surgery. We had been sitting in the waiting room for seven and a half hours, almost the length of a work day. Jeremy looked small and shrunken, his face tight with pain and exhaustion. A maelstrom whirled in my head: fear over Jeremy's condition, rage at Luci and at the hospital, fatigue. It was a relief to move toward a destination, even if it was only an examining room in the basement of this building.

When we reached it, Kris and I helped Jeremy stand. He leaned on us heavily as we boosted him up onto the examining table so that he could lie down. Even that hard paper-covered surface, too short and too narrow for his frame, was a gift. Jeremy was shivering. Kris and I piled our jackets over him, then sat and waited, each with a hand resting on Jeremy's body.

Mercifully, a nurse quickly entered to check Jeremy's vital signs and obtain some preliminary information. "So, how are you today?" she asked briskly, as she wrapped the blood pressure cuff around Jeremy's arm. "You're here for the gamma knife, right? What is your son being treated for?"

It was time for me to launch into the story I had told so often, describing Jeremy's condition with all the appropriate medical terminology, a story designed to reassure medical personnel that *this* patient had competent, rational parents who could be entrusted with information, parents who would not lose their composure or become hysterical if the news was not good. I took a deep breath, but no words came. Instead, I felt tears welling to the surface. I tried desperately to hold them back. *This nurse isn't responsible for hospital admissions; this isn't her problem; stop it, stop it, stop it!* No use. I bowed my head. Tears overflowed and fell onto my lap. My grip slipped further; sobs burst through my self-restraint. In seconds I was wracked with weeping, unable to answer even the simplest questions.

As I wiped my face repeatedly on my sleeves and took deep shuddering breaths, Kris sketched out our morning in a few words. The nurse was silent for long moments after he finished. I braced myself, expecting to hear, "I'm sorry about your problems, but we really need to complete this form. The doctor will be here in a minute." Instead, she said gently, "Excuse me. I'll be right back."

We waited. I kept crying, drowning in the hopeless misery of the morning and of the days that had gone before. Kris stroked my hair silently. Jeremy tried to reassure me. "It's all right, Mom," he said. "Don't be sad, Mommy. It'll be okay. Don't worry about me, I'm fine, really."

I clung to Jeremy's hand, crying harder, undone.

The door opened and the nurse reentered, carrying something. "I've talked to the Dr. Walker," she said. "He's arranging to find you a room right now. We'll have Jeremy in bed as soon as the doctor finishes meeting with you. And here, I've brought you some juice."

———

It was eleven that night in the pediatric oncology ward, where a room for Jeremy had been found. Seeing him back in a hospital brought sweet relief. Here, if Jeremy bled, if his heart stopped, his lungs failed, help was only steps away. The world outside seemed a terribly tenuous place. There was no ease in the open spaces, where if a child fell to the ground, and his heartbeat and breath stopped, he was dead in the amount of time it took strangers to decide to call for help. No longer at peace in the old dispensation, I could not imagine how to live there again.

By contrast with Children's Hospital, UCSF was wealthy.

Jeremy had a quiet, private room. No hallway noise seeped in through the set of double airlock doors that insulated young immune-compromised cancer patients from microscopic dangers. He had his own television, VCR, and a built-in Nintendo console (which he was unable to play). Shelves of videotapes were free for viewing. The closet across the hall was stacked with freshly laundered linens: warm blankets, sturdy nightclothes, real fabric washcloths. The abundance was astonishing. The hospital cafeteria stocked an array of hot and cold dishes, row upon row of desserts, salads, roasted meats, fresh fruits, juices, cereals, sandwiches, casseroles. The choices were overwhelming. At dinner time, I wandered from counter to counter, my tray bare except for a bottle of water, unsure what to select. Jeremy was allowed to order almost anything he wanted at mealtimes. Pizza? No problem. An ice-cream sundae? Absolutely.

We were unaccustomed to these amenities, and to the constant attention from Jeremy's nurse, whose patient caseload was smaller than at Children's. I felt a sudden fierce protective surge for the overworked staff making do, and doing so much, at the little hospital across the Bay. Dr. Joe supervised inpatient and outpatient rehabilitation for dozens of seriously disabled children, often with noncompliant families who missed appointments or failed to follow his instructions. I saw him talking with these parents in the rehab gym. He never lost his patience, or his smile. Mary and Shelley, Jeremy's physical therapists, were forced to jury-rig equipment using duct tape, foam, and cardboard but invested the project with creativity and good humor. Nancy, our occupational therapist, never showed frustration with the small, repetitive tasks that her patients tried, failed at, and repeated over many rehab sessions. We owed them so much.

It was late, and Kris had gone home for the night. He would return early in the morning for Jeremy's surgery. Jeremy slept. Because this was a normal ward, not the ICU, I was allowed to stay in his room overnight, but I was awake, waiting for a preoperative visit with the neurosurgeon who would head the gamma knife team tomorrow. Finally he arrived.

Dr. McPherson had curly dark graying hair, a military mustache, a sober demeanor, and intelligent, intensely blue eyes behind his glasses. He must have been exhausted—it was nearly midnight, and his surgery schedule had begun at least as early as our day—but he was completely focused, with no hint of impatience or fatigue. He woke Jeremy and tested his reflexes, vision, and sensory and motor responses, then suggested, "Let's step down the hall and talk privately." I looked apprehensively at Jeremy. He was badly disoriented, especially in this new setting. Despite our explanations, he was not sure where he was, or why. Mine was the only face he recognized here. I was afraid to leave him alone, but Dr. McPherson was waiting. "Sweetie, I have to go talk to the doctor. I'll be back, I'll be back," I reassured Jeremy before I walked out the door.

In the small meeting room on the ward, Dr. McPherson meticulously explained what would happen tomorrow. The procedure was long, and complicated. Jeremy would be taken to surgery at six in the morning, placed under general anesthesia and intubated, his breathing once again supplied by a ventilator. A metal stereotactic frame would be bolted to his skull with steel pins screwed into the bone. The frame allowed the radiation sources to be focused precisely at the tiny target area in his brain.

Next, a neuroradiologist would take an angiogram. A flexible narrow catheter would be inserted into the femoral artery in Jeremy's groin, and threaded up through his abdomen and chest, through the heart and into his neck, as close as possible to his brain. Dye would be injected into the catheter, and X-ray images taken, providing a high-resolution picture of the AVM and the blood vessels that fed it. The results of the angiography would be fed into a computer to construct a 3-D map of the AVM. Like a pointillist picture, the AVM would be painted in with successive shots of radiation, each of which lasted from five to ten minutes. The computer plotted how many shots of radiation were needed to fill it in and where they should be placed. The object was to obtain complete coverage of the AVM while spilling over as little as possible onto the healthy surrounding tissue. When it was over, Jeremy would be brought out of the anesthesia, stabilized overnight in the hospital, and, if all was well, return home the following day. To wait.

Dr. McPherson's briefing took an hour. Throughout it my anxiety climbed. I *knew* that Jeremy was awake, and afraid. His agitation flowed down the hall and jolted me like an electric current. When I finally returned to his room, he was wild-eyed. "Mom, where *were* you? Where did you *go?*"

"I was meeting with the doctor, remember, Jeremy? About your surgery tomorrow. We were just down the hall. Remember, I told you I would be talking to the doctor for a while?"

Of course he doesn't remember. It's not his fault.

"But you were gone so *long*, Mom. Where *were* you so long?" Jeremy's voice shook. He gripped my forearm hard with his left hand. I could feel him trembling.

"You're okay, dear, you're okay. I'm back now. Don't worry, I won't leave you again."

Just as I had finally calmed Jeremy and he had relaxed into sleep, a nurse and a lab technician came in, wheeling a cart. It was one in the morning, but they needed to take vital signs and draw several vials of blood. As always, finding a good blood vessel was hard, and the technician made several failed attempts before a vein in Jeremy's forearm yielded up four test tubes of dark red fluid.

Sleep-deprived and tired beyond bearing, Jeremy had lost his emotional resilience. Each needle stick pushed him closer to breaking. When the nurse announced that she also needed to start an IV line, Jeremy gave a low despairing wail: "No, *please*, not another IV." His body shook like a loose window sash in a gale. Waves of tears sprang up and over his bottom lashes, and slid down his cheeks.

I lowered the rail on the near side of the bed, climbed up, and slid down next to Jeremy on the narrow mattress, holding him. He shivered against me.

The IV went badly. After the technician and the nurse each had made two unsuccessful attempts to find a vein, they gave up and summoned a resident. It was not the resident's lucky night either. He tried to find a vein in Jeremy's feet, turning each foot this way and that in the light, hoping to find a prominent blood vessel to make this miserable task easier, pressing down on the faint blue tracings that he found, eventually settling on one after another, aiming the needle carefully and piercing the skin, only to fail. I held Jeremy tightly to give him my warmth. He oscillated in my arms, crying even harder, but silently, with each new puncture.

The resident finally laid down the needle, swabbed the blood from Jeremy's skin, and applied three more Band-Aids. "I'm going upstairs to find the medical ward resident," he said glumly. "Maybe someone new will have better luck."

I held Jeremy tighter, squeezed my eyes closed, and prayed with all my might. *Dear Lord, have mercy on this your child, spare him from further pain, strengthen and guide his caregivers' hands. Watch with those who weep this night . . .*

The new resident was quick and efficient. He expertly assessed both of Jeremy's arms, settled on a vein on the back of Jeremy's left hand, and drove the needle home with one swift thrust, mirrored by Jeremy's convulsive recoil.

"It's over, dear, it's all over, Jeremy," I said. Violent shudders racked his thin frame. The nurse and technician packed up their cart and left, turning off the lights in their wake. I held him tenderly, a small broken animal. We fell to sleep together.

————

It seemed that no sooner had my eyes closed than a knocking pulled me from the trough of sleep. It was 5:30 A.M. Jeremy and I had been asleep three and a half hours, and the orderlies had come to take him to surgery. I blearily followed the gurney around corners, into the elevator, and down unfamiliar hallways to the pre-op waiting area. This large room was curtained into perhaps twenty cubicles, each enclosing a patient waiting for surgery.

Jeremy was near panic, breathing rapidly, eyes wide and dilated. "Ssshh, ssshh, ssshh, Jeremy, ssshh, ssshh, ssshh." I sat close to the gurney, stroking his hair and singing to him softly. "*Dona nobis pacem*" . . . grant us peace. Jeremy held tightly to me with his good left hand, patched with adhesive tape and trailing the IV line, his eyes fixed on mine.

When I ended the song, the elderly gentleman in the next cubicle, who was with a patient I assumed was his wife, poked his head around the curtain. "That was nice," he said. "Please, keep singing." So I did.

Kris was suddenly there, having driven in after a night at home with Annelise and David. Somehow he had found us in this obscure location. We said the Lord's Prayer together, one more time: "Our Father, who art in heaven . . ." Jeremy was wheeled away to the operating room. Kris and I began the painful task of waiting. It was only six in the morning, and Jeremy would be in surgery for at least ten hours, perhaps more.

Kris found a seat in a waiting room and read. I tried sitting down, but the mounting pressure of fear quickly drove me to my feet. I drifted aimlessly through the hospital corridors. After the tumult and tension of the past few days, it was strange to be suddenly becalmed in the horse latitudes, sails slack, waiting for wind. Down the hall, a drink at the water fountain, through another waiting area, around a corner, back to my starting point. My feet fell into a regular rhythm. The circuit became a walking meditation. Down the hall, pause for a drink, through the second waiting area, turn, back to Kris. Ghosts rose from the deep. Jeremy lying on the kitchen floor; doctors rushing into the hospital trauma room; waiting outside the surgery center while Jeremy's drains were implanted; red crystal drops falling into a plastic bag; riding across the darkened Bay in an ambulance; light flashing off a glittering Greenfield filter. My feet continued their course. Down the hall, a drink, the second waiting area, turn, back. Ghosts continued to rise. Jeremy's hand tied to his bed frame; Jeremy's lips silently pleading for water; Jeremy's eyes searching out Comet Hale-Bopp on the ICU wall; the top of Jeremy's bald bobbly head as I pushed him in a wheelchair through the hospital halls. I walked, letting the images drift through me. The minutes and hours drifted past with them.

At midday, Kris and I were still moored in the waiting room. We had taken one quick nervous break for a cup of coffee and a sandwich, then resumed our stations.

Dr. Walker, the radiologist who had been our angel of repose the previous day, suddenly appeared. He was in his mid-fifties, with carefully combed and parted blond hair, sparkling blue eyes, and ruddy cheeks. He radiated calm and kindness. "We're done with the mapping procedure," he said. "It will take at least an hour to program the computer to direct the gamma knife. You can see Jeremy briefly. I'll send someone out to get you."

Fifteen minutes later, a nurse dressed in surgical scrubs strode briskly into the waiting area, calling "Lawson? Lawson?" Jeremy was being moved from the operating room to the radiotherapy department, where he would wait, anesthetized, while the computer was programmed. "We need to hurry," he said. "Your son will only be in transit for a few minutes." He walked away quickly, Kris matching him stride for stride while I trotted to keep up. Down the hall, turn, another turn, another hall, more turns. I was completely disoriented.

Then ahead, a cluster of people and a gurney waited at an elevator bank. Could this be . . . Jeremy? The still form on the gurney was draped with lines and surrounded by equipment. I stopped, suddenly afraid to go any closer, then pushed myself forward.

It was Jeremy . . . barely recognizable. My stomach twisted and my knees turned to jelly as I caught sight of the two steel bolts drilled into his forehead and the heavy metal framework that had been bolted into his skull. Strips of tape criss-crossed his closed eyes. Little of his face was visible between the stereotactic apparatus and the ventilator mouthpiece. Jeremy had been "bagged." The tracheal tube had been temporarily disconnected from a mechanical ventilator while he was being moved; the doctor standing beside him pushed rhythmically on a football-sized bladder to pump air into his lungs. The familiar thicket of IV line, monitor leads, catheter tube, and arterial lines, from which he had been freed weeks ago, draped his body once again.

A buzzing blackness laced with flashes of light fell across my eyes. *Ah,* a faraway voice observed, *this is what it feels like to faint.* I took slow deep breaths and told myself sternly, *Stay upright. You can't lose these moments.*

Kris and I both stepped to the gurney and bent over Jeremy, whispering quick quiet prayers: "Watch over your child, oh Lord, in this time of pain and danger, gather him in your arms and keep him safe, restore him to us whole and wakeful at day's end . . ." The elevator doors opened. The surgical team pushed the gurney onto the elevator, eyes intently watching monitor displays.

"Someone will find you in the waiting room when it's over," the doctor offered over his shoulder. "Should be, oh, another four or five hours, at least. Just stay in the neurosurgery area." The elevators doors whispered shut on his last word.

Kris and I were left alone. We reached out simultaneously and clasped hands, silently turned and searched for a sign to guide us back to our place of vigil.

From: Fiala, Marie Lawson
Sent: November 20, 1998 12:15 A.M.
To: Jeremy Network
Subject: All Is Well/Update No. 35

It is late and I am tired, but we are through it. The gamma knife finished tonight at 5:00 P.M., eleven hours after we started. We were at Jeremy's bedside as he awakened from the anesthesia. His first slurred words were "Mommy, Daddy, is the procedure over?" When we assured him that it was, he gave a hoarse "Yay!" Jeremy was groggy, and ached from the many holes made in his body today, but at peace.

Before Jeremy woke up, our neurosurgeon took us into the computer room and explained in detail the enhanced images of Jeremy's brain. We learned something new. As of this morning Jeremy's AVM was smaller than at the time of his last angiogram in September. It was previously three cubic centimeters in volume; today, before the gamma knife, it measured approximately one cubic centimeter. His brain has quietly been healing the AVM all the while that we have been noticing the obvious recovery of speech and motor function. The consequences are important. Less brain tissue was irradiated today than expected, and the predicted success rate of eradicating an AVM that small is higher.

Kris and I asked Dr. McPherson how he explained the reduction in the size of the AVM. He offered that unexplained healing occurs from time to time. It is, he said, as if the hemorrhage calls the body's attention to the abnormality, which the body then attempts to heal along with the injury from the bleed.

Jeremy's body has shown an awesome power for recovery, far beyond what was predicted for him by his doctors. The power of prayer to facilitate healing is now well documented, and I have no doubt that the enormous outpouring of prayer offered on Jeremy's behalf energized and marshaled his body's own resources in that endeavor. It should not be surprising that the AVM, too, was affected.

I know that to some people the vague medical explanation "healing happens" will be more palatable than the possibility of the divine at work. I am reminded of reading a Hindu myth in Kitchen Table Wisdom; it recounts that the gods decide to reward an impoverished beggar by dropping a bag of gold in his path. The poor man, who had spent his life traveling the dusty roads barefoot, his feet torn by rocks and thorns, trips over the bag, curses it for a stone, and walks on. Many bags of gold have dropped in our path during the past months. To some they may look like stones. To me, they look like riches.

Coming Home

AND THEN WE BROUGHT our son home.

The second day after the gamma knife procedure, Kris picked up Jeremy and me at UCSF and drove us to Berkeley, to our good old house, which we would be leaving within the week. Jeremy was terribly weak from the high dose of radiation. He could not sit upright for more than a few minutes. In the car, he slumped heavily against his seatbelt. "Hang in there, son," Kris said.

"Don't worry, Dad," said Jeremy. "I'll make it."

Kris pulled up in front of the house and tenderly carried Jeremy from the car, down the outside steps, through the kitchen and dining room, and upstairs to his bedroom and then laid him in bed like a baby. "There you go," he said, smoothing Jeremy's stubbly hair. "You're home."

"Thanks, Dad, I'm sorry I'm so much trouble," Jeremy mumbled, and was instantly asleep.

I plugged in a new baby monitor next to his bed. The receiver sat on my nightstand, another small red light to tell me all night long that he still breathed. I tucked in Annelise and David, bestowed kisses and blessings, and shook out extra blankets over their beds.

Before I slept I came into Jeremy's room several times. I bent over his bed, listened, stroked his forehead, and held my hand to his nose and mouth to feel his warm moist breaths against my palm. David slept in the same room. Annelise dreamed just down the hall.

Kris and I turned to each other in the same bed for the first time in three months.

In the middle of the night it felt as if we all, even the house itself, were breathing with just one breath.

From: Fiala, Marie Lawson
Sent: November 22, 1998 11:47 P.M.
To: Jeremy Network
Subject: Homecoming/Update No. 37

We are at home together . . .

The upcoming Thanksgiving holidays will provide a focal point for looking back over the ground we've traveled. A friend asked me recently why I haven't been angry at what has happened to us. Anger has been an irrelevant emotion. We are small ships afloat on a vast ocean. It is in the nature of the ocean to have storms as well as sunlit green expanses. Life is made of both pain and joy. We have no special dispensation to be exempt from the former while hoping for the latter. I try with God's help to bear the burdens with grace and to live the joys fully. This particular pain has not been more than I can bear. Jeremy is alive. It is that, above all else, for which I am thankful.

Five Hundred Miles

COMING HOME was sweetly peaceful. Being home was different from what I had imagined. Seeing Jeremy in the house where he had grown up as a normal boy cast his new disabilities in stark relief. The difference struck like a hammer on his first morning back. After I got Annelise and David onto the school bus, I went upstairs to the boys' green and blue bedroom to help Jeremy wash up and dress. "G'morning, Mom," he slurred.

He slowly and painfully pulled himself to his feet, and I helped him shuffle down the hall to the new plastic chair we had set up in front of the sink in the kids' bathroom. In the hospital he had looked robust, especially compared to his early days there and many of the other children who were in worse shape. Now the large mirror over the vanity revealed a terribly injured child superimposed over the image of the sunny boy who had run up and down the stairs and swum and played tennis all summer. I couldn't believe how . . . damaged he looked.

Daily living was grueling because our old home was not wheelchair-accessible or equipped with grab bars and the other devices Jeremy needed to move around safely. We had to constantly improvise instead of relying on the routines developed in the hospital. "Jeremy, the sides of the kids' bathtub are too high to get in safely, and there's nothing to hold onto. How about if I wheel you into the master bathroom, and you sit on the floor of the shower stall? We can use the handheld shower head to wash you off."

He required constant care—bathing, dressing, putting on elastic hose, attaching his leg brace, rotating his eye patches, elevating his right leg, preparing and cutting up his food. When he was awake I read aloud, played games, practiced his therapies, and did small drills to exercise his mind.

"Sweetheart, would you like to sort these blocks into different bowls by size and color?" Or, "I'll hold up a playing card, and you tell me the number that's on it." It felt like being at home with a very young toddler.

We were also in the middle of a packing maelstrom. The moving van was scheduled to come in three days. For someone like me, with my passion for order, the house was a nightmare of half-filled boxes, opened drawers, and drifts of packing paper. I stumbled from task to task all day, unable to finish any one thing. I was lucky to get in a shower by dinner.

On our second evening at home, I walked slowly down the stairs to the main floor after getting the children settled in bed and sat down hard on one of the bottom steps, just above the entryway, utterly defeated. Our life was not going to normalize. How could it have been otherwise? As my sister had said three months earlier, Jeremy's brain had been scrambled like an egg. It would never be the same. Yet hope is a hardy seed that takes root in the most inhospitable soils. I had somehow beguiled myself into believing that, after a period of transition, we would return to our former life. To Before. Instead, we now lived permanently in After.

I thought back on my meeting, just before Jeremy had been discharged from Children's Hospital, with the therapist who had been evaluating his academic abilities. I had been so narrowly focused on Jeremy's physical health all these months that I hadn't taken in the full implications of his brain injury until she went over his test results.

"You must stop thinking of Jeremy as just a normal child in a wheelchair," she said. "He has significant cognitive deficits. He can read, but has virtually no recall of what he's just read five minutes later. He can't sequence properly, which means that he can't put the steps needed to organize information—such as solving a math problem or outlining a paper—in the right order. Those problems will cut across every area of schoolwork. Jeremy will need special education, probably for a long time, with teachers who are trained to help him compensate for his areas of weakness."

There was no roadmap to a solution, or even help in finding our way. Earlier, when I had thought ahead to Jeremy's eventual discharge from the hospital, I had had a vague expectation that "someone" would help us access what we needed: intensive long-term rehabilitation, care for Jeremy while we were at work, equipment, tutoring, special education materials and support. It hadn't worked out that way. There was no "someone."

To take care of Jeremy, we would have to make dozens of phone calls, research treatment options, track down scattered resources, apply for such publicly funded help as was available, and calculate what else, if anything, we could pay for. Even for Kris and me, with two good jobs and a sturdy health plan, the past three months had squeezed us hard financially. We owed hundreds of thousands of dollars in medical costs that our insurance hadn't fully covered. And although my law firm colleagues had been supremely patient so far, I would have to go back to work soon.

How am I going to find the time to do all this, and my job as well? How will we pay off all those bills? How can we possibly rebuild a life that works?

Too, I badly missed the familiar rhythms of life in Children's Hospital, which had provided a structure for dealing with Jeremy's illness. That structure was suddenly gone, with nothing to take its place. I felt something like withdrawal, as if Kris, Jeremy, and I had been marooned on a desert island for months and then suddenly rescued and returned to the real world. I was lost without the peculiar intimacy fostered by isolation and by jointly facing down death. In some ways I actually missed our little island and the undiluted relationship with Jeremy that was possible there.

Sitting on the stairway, with my face in my hands, my mood was dark and tattered. My world seemed stripped of everything that had once mattered. I didn't know how to live with a crippled child who might never be able to fully care for himself, go to college, find someone to love and marry and bear him children. The signposts by which I had once measured out a future were gone.

I tried to pray, but all that came into my mind were the words of the old folk tune: *Lord, I'm one, Lord, I'm two, Lord, I'm three, Lord, I'm four, Lord, I'm five hundred miles away from home.*

Prayer is a powerful tool, but it doesn't inoculate one against depression and despair. I felt myself sinking.

God, I could really use some help here.

No one answered. I sat and thought about how we had come here, and how far we had come. Jeremy's collapse in the kitchen. The ICU. Jeremy's coma, and his paralysis when he awakened. The terrible days after the blood clot was found. The candle vigil. The prayers of the last three months whispered through my mind.

Jeremy, stay with me, breathe . . . breathe . . . breathe . . .

Please don't let me be the one left behind . . .

I would give the world and all in it to push Jeremy in a wheelchair and be able to talk to him.

Let the clot hold, let the clot hold, oh, please, let the clot hold.

Oh God, the strength of the weak and the comfort of sufferers: Mercifully accept our prayers, and grant to your servant Jeremy the help of your power, that his sickness may be turned into health, and our sorrow into joy . . .

They had all been granted. Every one. Jeremy lived. He was still his own dear self. We were at home, together. It was all I had ever wanted, and that knowledge brought me to the surface like a raft beneath my feet.

I stood up. We still had a long, long way to go. Best get started.

One Year After

Illuminations

W E HAD A NEW FAMILY MEMBER; Rosie, a Portuguese water dog. She had been born three days after Jeremy's bleed and was now one year old. Nearly grown, she was knee-high, with waving black hair, a long feathered tail, cocked ears with soft ends that flopped forward, and an intelligent amber gaze. Her face, with a short muzzle and wide forehead, looked more primate-like than canine, especially when she tilted her head to the side and wrinkled her brow to listen to what someone was saying.

Last spring and summer we had taken her to parks and along trails we had never visited before. Jeremy was always willing to push himself to take a short hike. His gait was awkward, lurching from side to side. He wore a thick compression stocking on his right leg to prevent fluid from building up in the aftermath of his blood clot, and over that he wore his toe-to-knee leg brace. He could not run, trot, skip, or jump. His right arm hung heavily, permanently bent at the elbow. When his muscles spasmed, as they did when he was under stress or trying to hurry, it contracted and curled up even more. He had little fine-motor control of his right-hand fingers, and his thumb was drawn tightly inward across the palm, depriving him of an opposable grasp. He could not hold a pencil, open a jar, button a button, or tie a shoelace with that hand. But he could walk, slowly.

On a Saturday in September, we took the kids and Rosie

to Wildcat Canyon, a regional park stretching northward from Berkeley along the spine of the East Bay hills. The canyon at the center of the park drains Wildcat Creek, one of the region's natural waterways.

The trail we chose ambled parallel to the stream for a ways, winding around gently domed hills covered with aromatic grasses and through overhanging groves of oak and bay. Annelise and Rosie ran ahead. Jeremy followed, laughing with David, a much shorter replica of his tall brother, two bright heads gleaming in the sun. Kris and I brought up the rear, delighting in our family and the golden hills and malachite trees silhouetted against the brilliant late-summer sky.

We paused in a creekside clearing with easy access to the stream. Annelise, David, and Rosie went down the bank and were knee-deep in water in a twinkling. With Kris trailing behind, they splashed their way downstream through still pools and shallow water flowing rapidly over glinting gravel. They stopped fifty yards away in a larger pool where the creek widens and bends. Annelise and David took turns throwing deadwood for Rosie to retrieve, which she did with the mindless joy of a dog born to water, while Kris stood laughing at their game. The heavy mid-afternoon sun filtered through the green canopy overhead, outlining the leaves above, the man, the tall girl, the small boy, and the wet dog with golden borders, like a medieval prayer book.

Jeremy had decided not to chance the slope and slippery stones. The two of us sat at the top of the bank, watching the antics below. A wide shaft of sun illuminated his face. I turned my camera on him and snapped a photo in mid-laugh, freezing his slanted eyes and crinkled nose and upturned open mouth in my memory forever. At the moment the camera shutter closed, he was happy, and so was I. It did not matter that I had done my very best and that it was not enough. It did not matter that I could not keep Jeremy safe, that I could not keep any of us safe. All that was true and mattered between us endured, between the darkened spaces left by loss. In the light of the westering sun, we shone brightly, a constellation, a family.

From: Fiala, Marie Lawson
Sent: September 12, 1999 12:50 A.M.
To: Jeremy Network
Subject: Peace Be with You/Update No. 47

Last Sunday marked one year since Jeremy fell out of our safe comfortable life, taking all of us with him. I have in front of me the photograph we took during Jeremy's coma: his head is heavily bandaged; tubes run from his brain, mouth, and nose, and lines snake from monitors and IV bags to his chest and arms. His oldest teddy bear snuggles close, sharing his sleep. His face looks ethereal, as if he were already halfway into another world.

The contrast with the young man who started high school this month could not be greater. Jeremy is vital, joyously alive, happy to be where he is. Yes, he confronts many daily challenges besides those that beset most ninth graders. How to carry all of his books with one arm. How to zip his jacket. How to open the yogurt container in his lunchbox. He is physically still frail, and easily tired. His injury has left him with impaired memory so that learning nations and capitals, names and dates, vocabulary words, the stuff of ninth-grade English and World Civ classes, is difficult. He works doggedly late into the evenings to keep up and continues to show gradual improvement. Thursday evening he looked up at 10:00 P.M. from reading and answering questions about politics in Afghanistan and said, "Mom, this is fun!" It may not always be fun, but at the moment Jeremy experiences the pleasure of having an almost-normal life to the fullest.

I have spent much time thinking about what the year has

brought us. There has been great pain, much of it still there below the surface like a dark roiling sea. That reservoir may not drain for years. At the same time I have been privileged to receive gifts I could not have imagined.

Jeremy, who came as close as possible to the point of death and back again, returned to us a fundamentally altered person. In many cultures over many ages a near-death experience has marked a rite of passage, a rebirth into wisdom. Jeremy came back to us wise. The refiner's fire burned away all the excess baggage that burdens so many of our lifetimes, leaving his soul as clear as mountain water. I feel the difference daily. Jeremy believes that he visited with God while his body slept in the hospital. Who can say that he did not?

Kris and I have been given the gift of Jeremy's life a second time, after knowing that we might lose it. Every day in our life as a family since has been precious as a result. The reality of death has given new meaning to our lives. Only now can I appreciate the moment-to-moment miracles I formerly took for granted.

There is more power in the love of humans for one another and in their joining through concerted prayer than in all that science has yet devised. I felt your love and healing energy flow through us and to our son throughout the many crises we weathered. At times, during the candle prayer vigils, the force of the current was as physically overwhelming as being carried by a river. Many of you who shared in these ceremonies felt it too. I recently spoke to a friend whom we had not seen in years about her experience of the first candle prayer vigil. She was living in Italy at the time and had heard about Jeremy through the e-mail network. On that Sunday she visited the small Catholic church in her town to pray for him. A choir of children's voices suddenly rang out high and pure: "Hosanna!" Our friend walked around the church, lighting candles for Jeremy, tears running down her face. She said it was one of the most powerful experiences she had ever felt. She cried as she recounted it, almost a year later. Two days later she read that Jeremy had spoken, and translated the message into Italian for all her friends and neighbors. The power of prayer and hope and wonder knows no boundaries.

The strongest, clearest knowledge of all that this year has brought is the hardest to articulate. From the earliest days in the hospital I was in the presence of something much greater than ourselves. God did not leave us comfortless. God's love was as real as the doctors and nurses and machines that sustained Jeremy's life.

I will never be able to thank you, our families and friends, who cared for our home and Annelise and David, who supplied us with nourishment and shelter, who helped us in ways too numerous to count, who gave us gifts of stories and poems and other instruments of healing. I will never be able to thank you and the many other unknown people who were moved to pray on Jeremy's behalf. You have been tightly woven into the tapestry of our lives; you will be with us forever. If I can offer one small gift in return, I share with you the discovery that the universe is a place of great glory and mystery as well as great danger, that the light is stronger than the darkness, and that love really does conquer all in its own fashion in the end.

I wish you God's peace, always.

Rowing to Mars

A T YEAR'S END we took Jeremy back to UCSF for an MRI scan that would tell us how much progress had been made in reducing the size of his AVM. After the gamma knife surgery a year ago, the walls of the defective blood vessels should have steadily thickened, constricting the AVM's blood supply. Eventually the vessels would become dry shadows tracing a circulatory pathway that no longer existed, no more able to carry blood than the Martian canals could bring water to the parched red sands.

When the gamma knife procedure is successful, the radiation takes two to three years to complete this work. Dr. McPherson, the neurosurgeon, did not expect that Jeremy's AVM would have dried up completely after one year, but he hoped to see a considerably reduced blood flow through it. He had warned us, though, that in a small but significant number of cases—between 10 and 20 percent—the radiation took no effect and would have to be repeated, restarting the clock for those unlucky patients.

Over the past twelve months I had increasingly discounted the possibility of failure. In fact, although I didn't admit this even to Kris, I harbored a secret conviction that this first check-up would reveal that the AVM was completely gone, or nearly so. After all, Jeremy's recovery had exceeded medical projections by staggering margins. Kris and I had continued praying, as had our congregation at Father Bruce's church. We had also worked harder than we ever had before to propel Jeremy back into a normal life.

Both Kris and I had returned to our jobs shortly after Jeremy came home from the hospital, but taking care of Jeremy became a second full-time job for both of us. We labored in turn over schoolwork. As the hospital therapist had predicted, information sequencing and lack of memory were huge impediments to his learning. Jeremy wrote beautiful sentences, but was unable to organize them into paragraphs and papers without help. Either Kris or I sat next to him at the desk in his new bedroom every afternoon and evening and helped him build frameworks for his thoughts, as he picked out letters on the computer keyboard with his left hand. "What's the first thing you want to say, Jeremy? And what idea belongs next?" We did memorization drills; helped him relearn multiplication, long division, fractions, and algebra; scheduled testing and assessments; and arranged home instruction in the areas in which Jeremy had cognitive deficits. We took daily walks to build his stamina, drove him back and forth to the hospital twice weekly for rehab, and put him through a rigorous home therapy program. And over it all, like a thick dark blanket, lay the knowledge that the time bomb in his head was still ticking, ticking away and that some day, any day, next year, next month, that night, it might detonate again.

My old nemesis, control, was back and in charge. I convinced myself that all this effort would be rewarded. *Haven't we done everything we could possibly have done? After everything we've suffered, don't we deserve a happy ending?*

The MRI scan was taken in mid-December, and the follow-up appointment, when Dr. McPherson would go over the films to explain the findings, was scheduled for the first week of January. I couldn't wait that long. Just before Christmas, I called the neurosurgery department and asked the nurse practitioner to track down Jeremy's results. She called me back that afternoon at my office and read me the radiologist's report: "[C]ompact nidus high flow arteriovenous malformation supplied entirely by the anterior choroidal artery. . . . Lateral view confirms the deep nature of this malformation . . ." The findings were almost identical to the scan taken just before the gamma knife surgery. Jeremy's AVM was unchanged.

I hung up the phone with shaking hands and called Kris. By the time he picked up on the third ring, I was crying so hard that all I could produce were quavering breaths. "What's wrong?" he asked, with an immediate edge of fear in his voice. "Is it Jeremy? Has something happened to Jeremy?"

"No, no," I managed to get out. "It's not that." Between sobs, I told him what I had just learned. "Jeremy's . . . AVM . . . is . . . still . . . there . . . no . . . change." Kris broke down, too, and for many minutes the telephone line between us carried only the sounds of our weeping.

We talked late that night, after the children were asleep, to decide what to say to Jeremy. All along we had told him as much about his medical condition as he was able to understand. This time, though, we found reasons for delay.

"It's almost Christmas. Jeremy's looking forward to the holiday and the break. It seems cruel to spoil his vacation," I reasoned.

"Right, and if we tell him now, he'll have to wait three more weeks before we see Dr. McPherson. There won't be anyone to answer his questions," Kris corroborated.

"Let's wait, and tell him just before the appointment," I said, with huge relief.

But the relief didn't last long. I carried this secret like a boulder on my back through the holidays. Every morning of the past year, I had told myself that Jeremy was a bit safer that day than the day before. Every evening, I had been grateful that he was one day closer to recovery. It had been an illusion. *Tick, tick, tick, tick.* Jeremy was no closer to safety than he had been a year ago. It felt like I had been rowing our small scull against a strong current with all my strength, head bent and shoulders hunched over the oars, and had looked up a long time later to discover that I was still at the starting line, with the entire race yet to run.

In January, Kris and I drove Jeremy to the UCSF complex in San Francisco again. The neurosurgical department was situated on the top floor of a building on the very crest of the hill, facing north, with an unobstructed view from eastern to western horizon. The waiting room had huge expanses of glass that afforded patients a multimillion-dollar view of the Golden Gate Bridge, the forested swath of Golden Gate Park, San Francisco Bay, and the Pacific Ocean merging into clouds on the horizon.

Much had changed in Jeremy. He had grown three inches in the past year. The strong planes of his face had emerged, and his voice had deepened. On the surface he looked almost normal, with his hair grown out and blond again, covering his scars. His color was good and his eyes sparkled. While a closer look revealed the asymmetry in his face—his eyes looked at different places in space, his smile only lifted one corner of his mouth—he was worlds away from the huddled gray form we had strapped into a wheelchair the year before.

As we waited for our appointment, I told Jeremy gently and somewhat vaguely about the MRI results: "Sweetheart, I did talk to the neurosurgery nurse about the MRI test . . . She said they didn't see much change on the scan . . . but you know, we won't *really* know for certain until Dr. McPherson looks at the pictures and gives us his opinion."

I was stunned at the force of Jeremy's reaction. He was furious that I hadn't told him sooner. "Mom, don't you remember, when I was in the hospital you *promised* you would always tell me the truth about my condition," he said. This was true, although I was surprised that he remembered, as he had forgotten almost everything else from that time. "How *could* you not tell me?" he demanded. "How *could* you?"

"I'm sorry," I apologized weakly. "I didn't want to spoil your Christmas. I didn't want you to worry about questions that you couldn't ask for three weeks." My explanations didn't placate him, and I stopped protesting. Besides, he was right. I should have told him.

Who were you really protecting? Him? Or yourself?

I walked over to the north wall of the reception area and rested my forehead against the dreaming window, looking down. Just a quarter-mile from here, at the foot of the hill, was the jewel-box apartment where I had stroked my cat and drunk my coffee before Kristor's advent into my life. Tendrils of ocean fog curled around treetops and over rooftops, moving inexorably eastward, erasing everything in their wake. In contrast to the pale gauze landscape below, the Berkeley hills were realms of gold across the Bay. What a fey and lovely city this was, and how far away the intervening years had taken me.

"Jeremy Lawson?" The nurse called us into a small examining room. On one wall, two long sheets of film were clipped to a light box. They showed repeated black-and-white images of the interior of Jeremy's brain. While we waited for Dr. McPherson, I walked over to study them, thinking I might be able to identify the AVM. I wanted to take the measure of my enemy. The films showed an organic circuit board: metallic white filaments curling over a shadowy dark background. I knew that the fluorescent white strands were blood vessels, but they all looked equally twisted and knotted to my eyes, and I couldn't pick out the cluster that had caused Jeremy so much harm.

Jeremy had been sitting on the edge of the examining table with his head bowed, staring at his shoes. I realized that he was crying silently. I crossed the room and put my arm around his shoulder. Kris hugged him from the other side. Jeremy gave one or two sobs. "This whole year has been wasted," he whispered.

"I know, Jeremy, I know," I said. We rocked back and forth in silence for a few moments. "It hasn't really been wasted. When I think about where you were a year ago . . . oh, Jeremy, you've come so far."

"Yeah, but I could lose it all again in a second," he said in a low dull voice. *Yes, son, you're right.* The three of us sat silently together, Jeremy in the center, with our arms around him from either side, and waited.

Dr. McPherson entered and greeted us warmly. He looked at Jeremy with surprise. "You were a boy when I saw you last year," he said. "Now you're a young man." The examination began with the usual tests. Dr. McPherson looked into Jeremy's eyes with a light, and tapped elbows, knees, and ankles with a reflex hammer. "Touch your nose with your index finger. Follow the pencil with your eyes— up, down, left, right. Cover one eye; how many fingers am I holding up? Now? How about now?" He turned to the films and studied them. A wild hope suddenly spread its wings inside my chest. *Perhaps the nurse was wrong. Maybe we'll get our good news after all.* I almost believed that the pressure of my longing might have changed the images into what I had hoped to see.

"Well, here's the AVM," Dr. McPherson pointed out. The pictures showed a hole in Jeremy's brain tissue caused by the bleed, about the size of a quarter, with the AVM a white knot of blood vessels at one side. It looked like an image from distant space, a spiral nebula with a particularly bright star at its edge. Dr. McPherson stared at the screen, comparing the new films with those taken last year. Finally, he began to point out infinitesimal changes, too small for my uneducated eyes to register. The AVM is a faulty connection between an artery and a vein, where high-pressure arterial blood is pumped directly into the vein, without the intervening capillary system that normally steps the pressure down so the vein can handle it. The vein balloons out from the pressure, creating a swollen shunt, which eventually bursts. "I think I see some slight changes in the shunt," he said. "That might indicate the artery is narrowing."

We were so hungry for hope that we received this tidbit gladly. "That sounds like good news," Kris said. "Is that what you'd expect at this point?"

"It's within the range of results for one year after the gamma knife," Dr. McPherson responded. "The gamma knife may be working, just slowly. In any event, we can't do any more now. Jeremy will have a scan next year. We'll see what it looks like then."

"What if you don't see much improvement next year either?" I asked.

"We'll wait another year, and do another scan. We don't repeat the gamma knife until three years after the first surgery. We don't want to subject your son's brain to radiation unless it's necessary."

Since we wouldn't see Dr. McPherson for another year, Kris and I were anxious to ask the list of questions we had prepared in advance, just in case. How likely was another hemorrhage, and how bad would it be if it happened? How much should we limit Jeremy's travel? Could he go to Central America the following summer with our church youth group, which would be helping to build an orphanage in Honduras? The answers came fast and hard.

"Well," said Dr. McPherson, "all we have are probabilities. The risk of a rebleed over the past year was about 50 percent."

Fifty percent?

"The research results on the probability of a rebleed going forward are all over the map, from less than 10 to about 30 percent," he continued. "All I can tell you is that, for the patients I've treated, the rebleed rate has been at the low end of that range."

Up to 30 percent? That doesn't sound very reassuring.

"But it's good that the AVM is small, right?" I asked.

"Actually, small AVMs, like Jeremy's, can have a worse onset if they hemorrhage," Dr. McPherson responded. "A large AVM will leak slowly over several days, causing a headache, which gives the patient enough time to get to a hospital. Small ones usually rupture very quickly, so they're more dangerous."

Please, no more scary information.

As far as travel, Dr. McPherson advised us to be reasonable and not take chances, while at the same time allowing Jeremy to live as full a life as he could. He said no, firmly, to the potential trip to Honduras next summer. "If he were my son, I wouldn't let him go . . ."

Jeremy said, "I have a question." I imagined that he would want to know more about the chances of another hemorrhage. Instead, he said, completely seriously, "I've always wanted to go skydiving. Can I do that?" The three adults in the room were silent for a few breaths. I saw a smile tugging at a corner of Dr. McPherson's mouth. Finally he said, "Jeremy, I wouldn't recommend that you go skydiving, whether or not you had this AVM. I think you've had enough excitement in your life."

I was mystified. Jeremy's question seemed like a childish distraction from the purpose of this appointment, yet he was not a child, and obviously was disappointed at the doctor's answer.

Weeks later, I made the connection. That spring, one of Jeremy's writing teachers had asked him to compose a metaphor describing himself. He had written: "I am a feather fallen off a bird. Light, it drifts through clouds, searching for an unnamable something. I am like that, searching for something. Perhaps God, perhaps knowledge, perhaps the height to see things clearly. Something." Jeremy still dreamed of flight.

"Let Jeremy live as full a life as he can," Dr. McPherson advised, "but be reasonable and don't take unnecessary chances. If you travel, make sure there's a hospital nearby. I'll see you in a year."

The appointment was over. We took the elevator down in silence and pushed open the glass lobby doors onto a pearly world of damp and chill. The fog had settled heavily along the streets and sidewalks. It left tiny cold droplets on my hair and eyelashes and deadened the sound of our footfalls. Although it was still late afternoon, the street lamps were already pouring liquid yellow-violet light into the white air. We were dwarfed by the tall empty-eyed buildings of the hospital complex as we walked to our car. The prospect of a time when Jeremy's AVM would be gone and he would be out of danger seemed as distant and unattainable as a journey to the nearest planet. Yet there was nowhere else to go. I dropped my head and hunched my shoulders, and set my sights on rowing to Mars.

Solar Wind

TWO A.M. I FELL ABRUPTLY AWAKE. What woke me? Of course. The doctor's words remembered . . . *most hemorrhages happen at night.* I rose and padded down the hall, holding my breath as I opened Jeremy's bedroom door. He was sleeping normally, his long legs at an angle, his face turned toward the silvered window, a cat curled up next to his knees. His damaged right arm had fallen off the edge of the bed and hung to the floor. I gently replaced it on the mattress, pulled his blankets higher, adjusted his pillow, started to leave, then returned one more time to place a hand on his forehead. He stirred and muttered, slept again.

Back in bed I lay awake, filled with fear and self-recriminations. Most hemorrhages happened at night. Jeremy had survived one hemorrhage; he might not survive another. How could I have forgotten so easily, slipped into the comfortable complacency of uninterrupted sleep?

Space travel. A door opened and I stood in the howling void between the planets. Cold, black, airless, no up, no down. *Night where my soul might sail a million years/In nothing, not even Death, not even tears.* The wail of the solar wind filled my mind. The sound of ionized gas particles ejected from the sun, hurtling through space with no destination, out into emptiness forever. The sound of blood cells rushing through a living channel, striking and recoiling off the walls that contained them, that, I hoped, would continue to contain them. I was suspended in the current, sensing yet not feeling the bombardment pass over, around, through me.

Out in space was the loneliest place I had ever been. I willed myself back into bed, struggled to close the door that separated me from the cold abyss. Finally, soft flannel sheets and pillows and comforter again, Kris's steady breathing at my side. For a long time I lay awake, hearing the solar wind blow against the thin barrier that separated our warm room from eternity.

Two Years After

Letter from a Distant Shore

When map makers of long ago filled in the blank spaces of unexplored regions, the scholarly wrote "terra incognita" and those with a fanciful mind "here there be dragons" — but the truly hopeful among them wrote the words "more beyond."

—Unknown origin, quoted in
 Outward Bound handbook

Sing unto the Lord a new song, and his praise from the end of the earth, ye that go down to the sea, and all that is therein; the isles, and the inhabitants thereof.

—Isaiah 42:10

DRIVING SOUTH FROM THE MAUI AIRPORT to our rental unit two years after Jeremy's hemorrhage, everything was exactly the same as it had been during every visit over the past fifteen years: palm-fringed roadway, fields of pale green sugarcane spiking out of henna soil, the endless, perfect, blue curve of sea and sky above, ahead and beyond. But this time, I was jolted by an intense feeling of dislocation. The terrain was the same, but I had changed. We had been catapulted off our expected course onto a different trajectory. The life we might have lived had moved straight ahead, unpeopled, while the life that had now been given to us moved off at an angle, further and further away from where we had been. But stepping out of the plane at the Maui airport, I had been dropped back into our prior reality. Unstuck, I oscillated between the two alternate universes. The car, which knew only one road, hummed the steady music of rubber meeting hot black asphalt.

This was our first vacation since Jeremy's bleed. We had come to Maui despite lingering uncertainties about Jeremy's medical condition. He had had another CT scan in the past year, which showed no change in his AVM. We decided to come to Hawaii anyway. Two years was a long time to go without a vacation. Maui had a small general hospital, and we were betting on the fact that we would not need it while we were there.

An hour after setting down suitcases at our condo, we were on the beach. This side of the island was sparsely populated, and the mile-long arc of white-sugar sand was mostly empty. The palm-studded greenbelt descended to sand, which descended to the water, in gentle swooping curves. The water continued the unbroken line straight into the west, where its gunmetal blue met three islands, two large and one small, that defined the edge of the world.

The wavelets bubbled and tugged at my bare feet, inviting me in. *Come and play.* The salt water in my veins responded, element to element. *So good to be back.* I went deeper, past the surf line, until the sandy bottom fell away and I floated. The waves rolled in and out, in and out, endlessly breaking, receding, and reforming, rising and falling like a breath. I rose and fell with them. Before me lay nothing but ocean, constant, vast. For a moment, the fissure between life before and life after closed, and I felt whole again.

My serenity did not last long. Jeremy's difficulty in

adapting to this once-familiar world became apparent the following morning, as we packed up boogie boards, snorkels, masks, flippers, and towels for a day at the ocean. Despite his vascular surgeon's reassurance that going without his leg brace and compression stocking for short periods would not hurt him, Jeremy was terrified to do without them. Yet, so encumbered, he was too embarrassed to wear shorts. I tried to convince him to take off the brace and stocking and put on swim trunks.

"Come on, sweetie. No one here knows you. What do you care what anyone thinks?"

He flatly refused. "No, I'm not gonna do it. You don't understand."

"Please, Jeremy. You'll be miserable if you can't go in the water."

"No. Just leave me alone."

After thirty minutes of debate, I was despairing and he was in tears. I gave it up. Jeremy wore long pants to the beach, and spent the morning reading *Shogun* in the shade and watching his family playing in the water. My heart divided, I rejoiced with Annelise's and David's delighted laughter bubbling above the waves, even as part of me never left the silent, lonely figure high on shore.

Eventually, the weather succeeded with Jeremy where my entreaties failed. The second day dawned brilliantly hot, white sun blazing over blue-green-purple water. Jeremy abandoned the leg brace and long pants, and came to the beach wearing shorts, compression stocking, and Tevas. He briefly removed sandals and stocking to test the water, but felt too unsteady and afraid to walk into the waves that cascaded onto the sand. Again, he sat out the morning in the shade, seemingly immersed in his book.

On each successive day, Jeremy peeled away another layer of fear. Venturing out slowly with Kris and me next to him, he discovered that he was strong enough to stand in chest-high water. We scanned the horizon together for the next wave. A promising swell approached, but dissolved away quietly in whispers of foam. The next one built higher and higher, its glassy shoulder looming over our heads. At the last moment, we jumped, and the wave lifted us high off our feet as it passed underneath us, to a crashing meeting with the shore.

The next day, Jeremy tried boogie boarding. He hung on to the short board with one arm, and flailed his legs shoreward before an onrushing wave. David and Annelise, protective and worried, stayed close by on their own boards and made the ride with him. Annelise offered a constant stream of encouragement and advice. "Watch out, Jeremy, here comes a big one. Make sure you face the ocean, so you can see them coming. Move further out so the waves don't break on you. Look out!" When he timed it right, the water broke just behind him and carried him in a froth of spume and spray high onto the beach. Jeremy lay on the sand laughing, then struggled to his feet and staggered back into the water for another attempt.

By the fourth or fifth day, we had convinced him to go snorkeling. This had always been an important family activity. We had snorkeled all around Maui and the neighboring islands, in small coves unmarked on any map, from the deck of a catamaran, in the center of a volcanic atoll, with giant sea turtles and dolphins, through schools of fish so dense and multicolored that it was like swimming in an underwater kaleidoscope.

This time we stayed on our own beach, no less lovely than any other place we could have reached by boat or automobile. Near in, the water was intensely bright turquoise. It parted around two sides of a natural jetty, a long finger of volcanic rock that had once run liquid down the sides of Hale'akala to the sea, fought it fiercely in clouds of steam, and finally was bested. Even so, the lava advanced a full two hundred yards into the ocean before it surrendered, cooled, and hardened, to provide the habitat for a coral colony. The volcanic rock provided an accessible snorkeling ground where Jeremy would test his seaworthiness.

Putting on flippers and a snorkel mask in a rolling sea is tricky even for people who are firm of foot and can use two hands. It was beyond Jeremy's capabilities. We worked out a cooperative technique. I carried his flippers and mine under one arm, held onto him with the other arm, and we walked together past the breakpoint of the surf. I helped him pull the mask and snorkel over his head, then supported him and helped him pull on each flipper in turn. If an oversized wave caught us during this delicate balancing act, we were tumbled head over heels, to rise gasping and start again.

When Jeremy was ready he bobbed in place while I put on my gear, then we swam side by side to the reef offshore, where Kris, Annelise, and David were already adventuring. Jeremy could not swim well. The water pressure forced his right arm and hand muscles into flexion. His fist closed tightly, his arm curled in toward his body, and he could not move it. He propelled himself forward with only one arm, one strong leg, and one weak one. But the buoyant salt water and the flippers helped keep him afloat, and he slowly and awkwardly moved through the water beside me.

Once we were over the reef, it was easy to forget everything except the brightly clad fish performing a slow ballet beneath us. Sleek shapes of iridescent orange and turquoise, purple, yellow and green, black and silver, they glided and turned through the shimmering blue water, darted through salmon-pink cities of coral. We floated above them with our faces in the water, breathing through the snorkels, moving up and down with the gentle swells. It felt like flying. I reached out to touch Jeremy's shoulder and pointed to a sea snake passing sinuously below. We followed it with languid movements of our flippers until it disappeared under a rock. Jeremy soon tired and wanted to turn back, but his spirits were high.

As our time in Hawaii drew to a close, I grew unaccountably depressed. One afternoon, a week into our visit, I sat on our lanai overlooking the ocean and tried to understand my profound sorrow, so long after the original injury. Jeremy had shown himself to be brave and big-hearted. Faced with his limitations in the starkest way, he had transcended them, ventured from sand to shore to shallow water, and out into the sea. Still, for me the reminders of his losses were ever-present, and more acute than at home.

Clothes had a lot to do with it. Clothing did much to soften Jeremy's ungainly stride and obscure his irregular contours. The fact that he wore far less of it here meant that his poor twisted back, wasted right arm, and weak right leg were exposed. His physical disabilities was inescapable. Seeing him here, in this setting where he last had been graceful and strong, I was reminded forcefully that his handicaps were permanent.

I worried about his future. Jeremy would leave home in only three more years. Would he be able to take care of himself? Would the world be kind to him? Who would be there to button the buttons, open the jars, carry his packages, tie a tie, put on his flippers? Who would be his friends? Who would be his lover? No one could tell me these things.

The afternoon grew late. The ocean lay nearly still beneath the heavy sunlight, a dense quicksilver pond. The sun declined toward the horizon, striking brilliant spears off the water's placid surface. Lines from a half-remembered poem floated up from memory: "*This is the land that Sunset washes. . . . This is the Western Mystery.*" I sat for a long time, marking the sun's passage into the west. My spirits dropped with it, below the edge of the earth, and into darkness.

We took one more excursion before going home—to Lahaina, a nineteenth-century whaling village and missionary center that had become a crowded tourist attraction. The children loved the commotion and the stores selling sharks'-

tooth necklaces, gecko-printed tee-shirts, and handmade ice-cream cones. I loved the crescent harbor abrim with sailboats and the banyan tree, hundreds of years old, whose canopy overhung the entire town square and reminded me of the baobab trees that so plagued the Little Prince.

Jeremy had a different agenda. He wanted to try parasailing.

This idea had been percolating in family discussions for several days. On one of our after-dinner visits to the local ice-cream shop near our rental unit, Jeremy spotted a parasailing brochure in an outdoor kiosk amid dozens of pamphlets that advertised scuba diving, helicopter rides, deep-sea fishing trips, eco-tours, bicycling, swimming with dolphins, horseback trail rides, and other tourist activities. He was immediately captivated by the idea of hanging high in the sky beneath a parachute, pulled along by a motorboat at the end of a long tether line. "Mom, Dad! This is so cool! Can I go parasailing?"

I treated it as a joke at first. "Come on, Jeremy, you don't really want to do that, do you? Sounds pretty scary to me." But he was not easily dissuaded.

"I *really* want to go parasailing. Can't you just call them and ask how much it costs?" I ignored the request, but Kris called the parasailing operator and determined times and prices. His enthusiasm fueled by concrete information, Jeremy persisted.

"C'mon, Mom. It isn't that much money. I'll pay for it myself. Can't I go parasailing when we go to Lahaina? Dad says I can if it's all right with you."

"What!" I stared hard at Kristor, who looked slightly sheepish.

"Well, it sounds pretty harmless," Kris said. "It's okay with me if he goes, if you don't mind."

I couldn't believe it. *Am I the only sane adult in this family?* Allowing Jeremy to hang hundreds of feet in the air at the end of a string was out of the question. Impossible. I couldn't conceive of letting him go. "Look, guys, this can't possibly be safe for Jeremy. What if he lands hard in the water when he comes down? You know Dr. McPherson said he has to avoid any hard jolts." But Kris already had asked the concession operator about the risks and learned that the parasailor lands gently on the boat, not in the water, and that no sudden bumps or shocks were involved.

Jeremy kept asking and I continued saying no, but the realization that he was serious about wanting to do this and that Kris was serious about letting him go eroded my resolve. *Maybe I'm holding him back too much; maybe there's really no harm in it and I'm thinking too much of my own fears and not enough about him,* I thought one moment, and the next moment, *I can't let him do this, he's still at risk, what if something happens and he hits his head, this is crazy, what can Kris be thinking, absolutely not!* My internal debate raged to the very end of the forty-five-minute drive to Lahaina, and when we arrived, I was still at stalemate.

We headed straight to the waterfront. Jeremy was determined to pursue his quest. The parasail operator reassured us that the ride was very gentle. He had never lost a passenger. His assurances were meaningless; my fears came from a deeper place. But we were down to the decision point. Kris, Jeremy, and David, who wanted to go along for the boat ride, stood at the edge of the pier and looked at me expectantly. I couldn't blight their eager faces with a no.

Reluctantly, I nodded. "Yes, go ahead." He was almost sixteen. *I can't let my fears chain him to earth forever.*

The three menfolk went out in the boat, while Annelise and I stayed behind. Lisie was interested in browsing the waterfront shops for presents to take home to her friends. I could not bear to witness Jeremy's ascent at close range, so I went with her. The boat headed far out into the bay. Based on the operator's explanation, I knew that a parasailor wore a harness and parachute attached to a powerboat by a long cable wound around a motorized winch drum. As the boat picked up speed, the cable around the drum unwound, the wind lofted the parachute, and the sailor rose to a height of eight hundred feet above Lahaina Harbor, where he hung suspended in thin air, drifting slowly behind the tiny boat far below.

I couldn't bear to watch even from a distance. I turned my back on the water and studied the shop window before me. I imagined that Jeremy was standing on an elevated platform at the back of the boat, harness strapped around his shoulders and thighs, getting ready for the winch to release and to rise high into the air. I wondered if he was afraid. I was. *Will it always be like this*, I wondered, *this terrible fear for Jeremy's safety? Will I ever take his future for granted again?* I knew I would not. Peace of mind had been lost forever.

Moments later, I couldn't bear not to watch. I turned around, shading my eyes to scan the harbor, and was stunned at how far away Jeremy had traveled in such a short time. The boat was a tiny black streak against the lucent water. Impossibly high above it, a bright-red parachute bloomed against the azure sky. Jeremy's form, suspended beneath it, was a mere dot, almost too small to see at this distance. But I knew it was he. I watched with tears in my eyes. As he had dreamed, he was flying, graceful and free, unfettered by gravity or by his broken body.

Jeremy had found his peace, I realized. He was ready to go forward to meet the rest of his life on his own, with all the gifts and takings away that defined him now, a beautiful, perfect whole. My task was to let him go, to hold him up into the sun for as long as I could, and then to release him gently into the wind, into the care of God and the universe.

It was time to lay aside sadness.

It was time to live.

Epilogue

S UMMER TURNED TO FALL, and then winter came
again. Four months after our vacation in Maui,
Jeremy had another cerebral angiogram. This time, I waited
for the follow-up appointment to hear the results. Jeremy, Kris,
and I met with Dr. McPherson at UCSF in early January 2001.
He told us that the films showed that Jeremy's AVM had been
obliterated and that he was safe from the risk of a rebleed. We
cried, and then we laughed, and then we cried some more.

Jeremy struggled in high school, even though the
administrators and teachers at his small, independent school
were kind and supportive. His cognitive deficits affected his
performance in every academic subject. He had little stamina.
By the end of each school day he was in a mental fog, and so
exhausted that he could barely walk to his bedroom to take a
nap. Despite his handicaps, his work was evaluated against
the same benchmarks that applied to every other student
but that were much harder for him to meet. For four years
Kris and I worked alongside him, reading the same texts,
helping him structure English essays and term papers, and
laboring over math, chemistry, and physics problem sets. By
the time he finished high school, I felt as if I had completed
the curriculum a second time myself.

These were lonely years for Jeremy. He had started
high school with grave social disadvantages—obvious physical impairments, an eye patch to compensate for his double vision, a leg brace and a compression stocking, and
loose, unfashionable clothing that he could don by himself—which he never overcame, even after his condition
improved. He was unable to join in sports and had no time
for extracurricular activities because he had to spend all
his hours outside of class studying or sleeping. The other

students were not unkind but never really accepted him. He didn't complain or turn aside from what had to be done, although he often must have been unhappy.

Jeremy graduated from high school with a respectable grade-point average and was admitted to Kenyon College in Ohio, where he made a fresh start. Founded by the Episcopal Church in the mid-1800s, Kenyon is a small liberal arts college with high academic standards, small classes, an excellent faculty, and a supportive, caring community. Jeremy was well liked by his peers, had an active social life, and made close friends. The brain has a remarkable capacity for healing, and Jeremy's cognitive abilities continued to improve throughout his college years, although his short-term memory and sequencing functions were permanently impaired. He initially leaned on the disability-support services that allowed him, for example, to receive extra time on exams, but again his performance was measured by the same criteria applied to all students. He graduated *cum laude* with a degree in economics in 2008.

Although he underwent intensive rehabilitation, Jeremy's physical recovery was limited. He has persistent double vision, little use of his right hand and arm, and a pronounced limp. The blood clot permanently destroyed the valves that returned blood from his right leg, and he will forever have to wear a compression stocking and keep his foot elevated when seated to keep blood from pooling in his leg. Jeremy ignores these handicaps: he jogs, takes martial arts classes, works out at the gym, and rides a bike specially outfitted so that he can operate all the gears and brakes with his left hand. He is strong and fit.

After college, Jeremy returned to the Bay Area and found a job as a research analyst with a Silicon Valley firm. In early 2009 he moved into his own apartment. He shares his life with a keenly intelligent, warm, and beautiful young woman whom he loves, and who loves him exactly as he is. He hopes to attend business school someday.

Annelise has grown tall and slender, with a dancer's graceful carriage and a luminous smile. She graduated in 2009 from Carleton College in Minnesota, where she majored in psychology and theater arts. She now lives in Chicago, where she works two jobs, spends a lot of time riding the bus, and pursues her passions for improv comedy and the stage. She inherited her father's ethereal voice, and listening to her sing in the choir on a Sunday morning breaks my heart open all over again.

David retreated behind a wall of reserve for many years after Jeremy's hospitalization; it was not until the tenth grade that he started interacting easily with his peers and making friends. He is taller than Kris now, and strong and athletic. He graduated from high school in 2009 and matriculated at Stanford University that fall. He thinks deeply about many things, and has a particular love for history and Latin, which his teacher says he almost seems to be remembering rather than learning. He is a gifted writer.

I'm still practicing law. The firm where I had worked my entire career dissolved unexpectedly in late 2008, and the friends who meant so much to me were scattered to the winds. In my dreams I still wander its silent halls, among half-filled document boxes, opened file drawers, and drifts of paper, but the offices are empty and the people are gone. I was fortunate to find employment with a strong, respected firm, and my new partners have welcomed me warmly. Kris is the managing partner of the same investment advisory business he and his friends founded fifteen years ago, and occasionally he runs a river. I still feel a burst of joy when he walks into the house, or I see his name on my e-mail screen. We both were broken into pieces by our journey with Jeremy, and never reassembled in quite the same way. Even now, we cry easily, and too often, at the world's sufferings. And although not a day goes by that I don't thank God for our son's life, at times the sight of his poor hurt body is still like an ice pick to my heart.

With sadness and some trepidation, I face the future

without children at home. Motherhood has been the great adventure of my life. But, I tell myself, I am still a mother, and my children will still need me, even as they leave home for faraway places or just across town. They call me to share the joys and triumphs and sorrows of their lives. They call me when they are standing in the grocery store to ask what kind of detergent to buy. They call me when they ace an exam or need help editing a paper. They call me when they're in a new place and have no one to eat lunch with, or a friend hurts them, or a supervisor says something mean.

They will continue to call me when they are accepted into graduate school or hired for a new job. They will call me for advice on how to handle a problem with a co-worker or a health issue. They will call me when they need the recipe for their favorite meal. They will call me just to hear my voice because they are happy but so lonely and far away. We will not lose the connection we've had since their births, and it will sustain me until we can see each other again.

This is what matters. This is what lasts.

Berkeley, California
January 2010

Acknowledgments

I wish to thank

The Jeremy Network, the light for our path, a lamp unto our feet

Doctors Ralph Berberich, Robert Haining, Van Halbach, Jane Hunter, Steven Kowaleski, Petra Landman, Michael McDermott, Louis Messina, Richard Nagle, and William Wara, for their wisdom, skill, and compassion, and the other medical professionals at Children's Hospital of Oakland and the University of California San Francisco Medical Center who cared for our child with kindness and humanity

My mother and father, who have made of their lives a blessing

Lowell Cohn, Lisa Harper, and Jane Anne Staw, all of whom walked through catastrophe with me and helped me search the earth and even the sky for the missing parts, and find in it the shape of remembered tragedy

And my husband, Kristor Lawson, for everything that matters most

Notes

Page

15-16   Information regarding arteriovenous malformations is found at "Arteriovenous Malformations and Other Vascular Lesions of the Central Nervous System," National Institute of Neurological Disorders and Stroke, http://www.ninds.nih.gov/disorders/avms/avms.htm.

34-35   Song lyrics from Enya, "On Your Shore," *Watermark* (New York: Rhino/Warner Bros., 2005).

85   Poetry excerpted from John Ciardi, "Most Like an Arch This Marriage," *The Collected Poems of John Ciardi*, ed. Edward Cifelli (Fayetteville: University of Arkansas Press, 1997), 196.

112-13   Technical information regarding the Greenfield filter can be found at the website of Boston Scientific, the device's manufacturer, http://www.bostonscientific.com/home.bsci. The quotation is taken from "The Clot Stopper," *American Heritage* 22, no. 1 (2006), http://www.americanheritage.com/articles/magazine/it/2006/1/2006_1_34.shtml.

117   The quotation by Sir Francis Galton is from his

article, "Statistical Inquiries into the Efficacy of Prayer," *Fortnightly Review* 12 (1872): 125–35.

117 The quotation by Dr. Alexis Carrel originally appeared in *Reader's Digest* in 1941 and is quoted, among other places, in "Power in Prayer," LDS Library, http://search.ldslibrary.com/article/view/196245.

117-18 Research documenting the beneficial effects of prayer is collected, inter alia, in Larry Dossey, *Healing Words: The Power of Prayer and the Practice of Medicine* (San Francisco: HarperSanFrancisco, 1993).

118-19 The description of the 1995 and 1996 UCSF studies is based in part on "A Prayer Before Dying," *Wired* 10.12, no.2 (December 2002), http://www.wired.com/wired/archive/10.12/prayer.html.

118 The 1995 USCF AIDS pilot study is discussed at "AIDS and Alternatives," *UCSF Daybreak News* (April 28, 1997), http://www.ucsf.edu/daybreak/1997/04/428aids.htm.

118-19 The 1996 UCSF AIDS study is reported at F. Sicher et al., "A Randomized Double-Blind Study of the Effects of Distant Healing in a Population with Advanced AIDS," *Western Journal of Medicine* 169 (December 1998): 356–63.

119-20 The Columbia University IVF study is reported at K.Y. Cha et al., "Does Prayer Influence the Success of In Vitro Fertilization–Embryo Transfer?" *Journal of Reproductive Medicine* 46 (2001): 781–87.

157 Song lyrics from Leonard Cohen, "Suzanne," *Essential Leonard Cohen* (New York: Sony, 2002).

160, 241   The stories repeated in the e-mails on these pages are from Rachel Naomi Remen, *Kitchen Table Wisdom: Stories That Heal* (New York: Riverhead Books, 1996).

225-26   Development of the gamma knife device is described at "The History of Gamma Knife Surgery," Cromwell Gamma Knife Center, www.gammaknife.co.uk/internal/Overview/hist-gamma.pdf. The gamma knife radiosurgery procedure is described at the UCSF Medical Center website, http://www.ucsfhealth.org/adult/special/g/11201.html?gclid=CKT8gszTq44CFQPrYgodNQc7ZQ.

228   The readings on these pages are from Susan Cooper, *The Dark Is Rising* (New York: Aladdin Paperbacks, 1986).

268   Poetry excerpted from John Masefield, "I Could Not Sleep for Thinking of the Sky," *Sea Fever: Selected Poems of John Masefield*, ed. Philip W. Errington (Manchester, England: Carcanet Press, 2005), 103.

278   Poetry excerpted from Emily Dickinson, "This—is the land—the Sunset washes," *The Poems of Emily Dickinson* (Cambridge: Belknap Press, 1999), 297.

CAVANKERRY'S MISSION

Through publishing and programming, CavanKerry Press connects communities of writers with communities of readers. We publish poetry that reaches from the page to include the reader, by the finest new and established contemporary writers. Our programming brings our books and our poets to people where they live, cultivating new audiences and nourishing established ones.

OTHER BOOKS IN
THE LAURELBOOKS SERIES

Life with Sam, Elizabeth Hutner

Body of Diminishing Motion, Joan Seliger Sidney

To the Marrow, Robert Seder

Surviving Has Made Me Crazy, Mark Nepo

Elegy for the Floater, Teresa Carson

We Mad Climb Shaky Ladders, Pamela Spiro Wagner